Europe's  r
1

Each volume in the 'Problems in Focus' series is designed
to make available to students important new work on key
historical problems and periods that they encounter in
their courses. Each volume is devoted to a central topic or
theme, and the most important aspects of this are dealt
with by specially commissioned studies from scholars in
the relevant field. The editorial Introduction reviews the
problem or period as a whole, and each chapter provides
an assessment of the particular aspect, pointing out the
areas of development and controversy, and indicating
where conclusions can be drawn or where further work is
necessary. An annotated bibliography serves as a guide to
further reading.

PROBLEMS IN FOCUS SERIES

Europe's Balance of Power
1815–1848

EDITED BY

ALAN SKED

M

First published 1979 by
THE MACMILLAN PRESS LTD
London and Basingstoke
Associated companies in Delhi Dublin
Hong Kong Johannesburg Lagos
Melbourne New York Singapore and Tokyo

Photoset, printed and bound
In Great Britain by
REDWOOD BURN LIMITED
Trowbridge & Esher

British Library Cataloguing in Publication Data

Europe's balance of power,
   1815–1848. – (Problems in focus).
   1.   Europe – Politics and government
   –1815–1848 2.   Balance of power
   3.   Europe – Foreign relations
   I.   Sked, Alan   II.   Series
   327′. 112′094   D363
   ISBN 0–333–23086–8
   ISBN 0–333–23087–6pbk

Contents

Introduction

ALAN SKED

THE statesmen who redrew the map of Europe in 1814–15 were determined, above all else, to create a lasting balance of power. In other words, they hoped that no one power would ever again be able to dominate the Continent in the way in which France had done under the Emperor Napoleon I. Too much blood and treasure had been expended, too many thrones toppled, too many sacrifices made for the monarchs of Europe to want to contemplate his like again. The result of the Vienna Congress, therefore, was a territorial settlement which, although primarily directed against France, was also designed to prevent the potential domination of Europe by any single power. It was achieved not without difficulty – there was an ominous split between Britain, France and Austria on the one hand, and Russia and Prussia on the other, over the Saxon–Polish question – but it was achieved nonetheless. This was possible because the diplomats involved were highly realistic and (mostly) unideological men. Thus, although they paid lip-service – perhaps more than lip-service – to the notion of 'legitimacy', they also took into account not only the essential interests of the Powers but a variety of commitments entered into by the allies during the Napoleonic Wars. The 1815 Settlement as a result left no major power with a major grievance and even managed to make a few concessions to the spirit of the age. France, it was known, would receive a constitution; so too, would the 'Congress Poland' of Alexander I and the new United Netherlands.[1] Moreover, the German princes were allowed under the constitution of the German Confederation – Germany's peculiar form of unification – to grant a form of constitution themselves. Yet it is probably true to say that what liberalism and nationalism there was in 1815 was sacrificed to legitimacy and the balance of power. How then should one judge the Settlement? We shall return to this question later. However, before he reaches a conclusion, the reader should fully acquaint himself with the complex process of negotiations of which the Vienna Congress formed only the final part. He can do so by reading the account by Professor Douglas

Dakin of 'The Congress of Vienna, 1814–15 and its Antecedents' which constitutes the first essay of this book.

The Settlement, as has been mentioned, was directed primarily against France. Her boundaries were reduced by the Second Treaty of Paris to those of 1790; she had to suffer the indignity of an army of occupation; and had to agree to pay an indemnity of 700 million francs. She also lost some territory to Switzerland and Savoy. The powers, in fact, had attempted to surround her with a *cordon sanitaire*. The Kingdom of the United Netherlands (in contemporary language, Holland united with Belgium) was established to the north; the Kingdom of Savoy was enlarged to the south and the control of northern Italy was given to the Habsburgs in the form of a newly created Kingdom of Lombardy-Venetia. On France's eastern frontier the neutrality of Switzerland was guaranteed by the powers, while the Rhineland was given to Prussia, which state was also enlarged by Saxon and other German territory. Indeed, as a result of the Congress of Vienna, Prussia was placed in a potentially very powerful position. Not only would she in future have to take the lead in any war against the French: her territories were so distributed that by consolidating them economically she could bring about the economic union of Germany; to consolidate them politically she confronted the temptation of creating a united Germany. Still, all this was far in the future. In the period between 1815 and 1848 the most powerful German state appeared to be Austria who not only regained territory she had lost to Bavaria but received the presidency of the German Confederation, the spiritual successor of the Holy Roman Empire. Austria's surrender of the Austrian Netherlands, in fact, had made her a completely central European power – dominant in Italy through her possessions of Lombardy-Venetia and her treaties with the other Italian states – and dominant in Germany through her presidency of the German Confederation. Together, Austria and Prussia, it was hoped, would be strong enough to defend Germany against France or Russia. In fact the central achievement of the 1815 Settlement was that, in continental Europe, both France and Russia appeared sufficiently contained to allow a balance of power to emerge.

For a variety of reasons, however, the statesmen were unsure of their work. None of them expected peace to last for more than five or six years and the experience of the Hundred Days did nothing to increase their faith in the future. Most of them had already witnessed so many different treaties and peace settlements that the thought that one could endure with any permanence seemed something of a slim hope. Thus, apart from the territorial arrangements agreed upon at Vienna, a number of other proposals were put forward in order to safeguard the peace. All of these were aimed at guaranteeing in one way or another that the territorial arrangements would be adhered to. Most important amongst these proposals were the 'Holy Alliance' of Alexander I and the suggestion, put forward by the British Foreign Secretary, Castlereagh, of a Quadruple Alliance against France. The final outcome of the negotiations which led to the establishment of the latter, however, cannot properly be understood without a discussion of the Vienna Settlement as it affected Great Britain and Russia.

Russia, with an army of almost a million men in 1815, was militarily the most impressive power in Europe. Her defeat of Napoleon in 1812 and her march through Europe to Paris had given proof enough of that. She was economically backward but given her possession of most of Poland (Austria had been left with Galicia, Prussia with Posen), together with her unlimited reserves of cannon-fodder, this did not seem to matter. If aroused it would be very difficult for a state like Austria or Prussia to resist her. It was a source of some discomfort to the other powers in 1815, therefore, that on the throne of Russia sat Alexander I. The Tsar was intellectually fickle, apt to strike a pose and determined to capture the public imagination. Having imbibed the ideas of the enlightenment in his youth he continually expressed a desire to help the peoples of Europe. This 'liberalism' was combined with a Christian mysticism and the fusion of the two had a deeply unsettling effect on the statesmen of Europe. What on earth were the Tsar's intentions? On the one hand he demanded a constitution for the French and gave constitutions to Finland and Poland, on the other he consistently spoke of a general European guarantee against the revolution. By 1819 Metternich was exasperated with him. Having secured the passing of the Carlsbad Decrees he wrote:[2] 'It is the first time that such a group of correct, peremptory, anti-revolutionary measures have appeared. I did what I have wished to do since 1813 and I have done it because that terrible Emperor Alexander, who always spoils things, was not there'. Nonetheless, the Tsar could not be wished away. In 1818 Gentz, Metternich's closest colleague, was reflecting:[3] 'He is at the head of the one standing army really capable of action in Europe today. Nothing could resist the first assault of that army. . . . None of the obstacles that restrain and thwart the other sovereigns . . . exists for the Emperor of Russia. What he dreams of at night, he can carry out in the morning'. When in 1815 Alexander suggested that the Kings of Europe should form a Holy Alliance, the European chancelleries could not ignore his proposal. The fears which Gentz was to express three years later were already affecting their thinking.

The Holy Alliance itself was perhaps the vaguest document ever to trouble European diplomacy.[4] It bound its signatories to base their foreign policies upon the 'precepts of justice, charity and peace', to treat their fellow sovereigns as 'brothers' and to acknowledge that the Christian nation as a whole had 'no other sovereign' save 'God, Our Divine Saviour, Jesus Christ'. They were also to recommend His teachings to their peoples to bring about the 'happiness of nations'. Metternich dismissed it as a 'loud-sounding nothing', Castlereagh as a 'piece of sublime mysticism and nonsense'. In the end, however, it was signed by all the sovereigns of Europe, save the Pope (who would not associate with heretics), the Sultan of Turkey (who was not Christian) and the Prince Regent of Britain (who explained politely to the Tsar, that, much as he admired it, only Parliament could commit the nation). Metternich reworded the document slightly, and in a reactionary sense, but even in its final form he took it to mean nothing. Probably he was right. The Belgian historian, Pirenne, suggested once[5] that Alexander was really aiming to bring about a world organisation of states in which to oppose the maritime ambitions of Great Britain. But this seems extraordinarily farfetched. Alexander I at this time was exploiting his rights in Alaska and Canada (Russian territory in 1815 still extended beyond the Baring Straits) and thus antagonising that other notable maritime power, the United States. It is possible that the Tsar was thinking of undermining Great Britain's recently established links with the rebellious colonies of Spain in South America. Yet the future of these colonies was not as yet a major diplomatic issue and, in any case, any interference on the part of Russia would once again have elicited American as well as British resistance.

The final arrangements of 1815, however, were certainly the result of a compromise between Russian and British proposals. Castlereagh, who also saw a need to back up the Settlement with some sort of guarantee, had put forward the much more concrete idea of a four-power alliance against France. This alliance was to be restricted, however, to maintaining the terms of the Second Treaty of Paris only. When Alexander suggested that the powers should guarantee the whole Vienna Settlement, by a reciprocal guarantee of all their territories as well as by meeting from time to time to survey the internal affairs of all the European states, Castlereagh refused to have anything to do with the proposal. No British government, he protested, would accept such far-reaching commitments in Europe, especially if they involved a bias in favour of absolutism. Essentially he wanted to leave Britain a free hand. Thus he was to tell his Ambassador in Berlin:[6] '. . . it is not my wish to encourage, on the part of this country, an unnecessary interference in the ordinary affairs of the continent. The interposition of Great Britain will always be most authoritative in proportion as it is not compromised by being unduly mixed in the daily concerns of these states'. Metternich, too, had no desire to see the success of Alexander's plans. The Tsar had not yet lost his reputation for liberalism so that the Austrian Chancellor had no desire to see him meddling anywhere in Europe. A general guarantee would give him the means to interfere in Germany and Italy with consequences which, if they could not be foreseen, could certainly not be good for Austria. In the end, therefore, a compromise was reached. Austria, Prussia, Russia and Great Britain all signed a Quadruple Alliance on 20 November 1815 by which they undertook to ban the Bonapartes from France for ever and to take whatever measures should prove necessary in the event of any of them being menaced by the French. Thus, Castlereagh's insistence that there should be no general guarantee was met. However, by Article Six of the Treaty, the powers agreed to[7] 'renew their meetings at fixed periods, either under the immediate auspices of the sovereigns themselves, or by their respective ministers, for the purpose of consulting upon their common interests, and for consideration of the measures which at each of those periods shall be considered the most salutary for the repose and prosperity of nations and for the maintenance of the Peace of Europe'. It was this clause which gave rise to the 'Congress System', the history of which is described by Dr Roy Bridge in the second article of this book, entitled 'Allied diplomacy in Peacetime: the Failure of the Congress System, 1815–23'.

The 'Congress System' foundered principally on the issue of intervention. Did the powers have the right to intervene in the internal affairs of minor states and, if so, under what terms and conditions? Could they interfere if asked or at any time at which the peace of Europe appeared to be disturbed? Metternich, who in 1819 chose, significantly, to order German affairs not through the interference of the powers as a whole but through the medium of the German Federal Diet, and who at Aix-la-Chapelle in 1818 had once more rebuffed a proposal of Alexander I to establish a general guarantee, was quite willing to support a general declaration which gave the powers the right to intervene against revolution so long as it did not give every power a right to intervene anywhere at any time (as a general guarantee might do). Moreover, with the conversion of Alexander I to reaction (Metternich had convinced him that Europe's troubles stemmed from a general conspiracy of the revolutionary sects) not only was no risk involved, the Tsar could be positively encouraged to suppress revolutions in Eastern Europe. Thus, with the exceptions of Great Britain and France, the Powers in November 1820 adhered to the Troppau Protocol which stated that[8]

> States which have undergone a change of Government due to revolution, the results of which threaten other states, *ipso facto* cease to be members of the European Alliance, and remain excluded from it until their situation gives guarantees for legal order and stability. If owing to such alterations immediate danger threatens other states, the powers bind themselves, by peaceful means, or if need be by arms to bring back the guilty state into the bosom of the Great Alliance.

Castlereagh, of course, had already protested against such an interpretation of the purpose of the Alliance. In his famous State Paper of 5 May 1820, he had written that it[9] 'never was . . . intended as an Union for the Government of the World or for the superintendence of the internal Affairs of other States', with the result that from 1820 onwards it seemed that Great Britain would no longer be associated with any of the powers as a result of the intervention issue. The history of intervention, however, was not to be a simple one. The Eastern Powers were to quarrel over the terms of intervention in Spain (where Metternich held that French intervention might regenerate France and so upset the balance of power), while later events in Iberia forced the British themselves to reverse their stand. By 1848, therefore, all the powers, liberal or reactionary, had experience of intervening in the internal affairs of minor states in order to impose on them regimes acceptable to the powers concerned. The story is a fascinating one and told by Dr Roger Bullen in the third article of this book, entitled 'The Great Powers and the Iberian Peninsula, 1815–48'.

The Ottoman Empire had not been represented at the Congress of Vienna. The Sultan had not been invited to sign the Holy Alliance (as a Moslem he could not possibly have adhered to it in any case) and Turkey was not generally regarded as a member of the Concert of Europe. How then were the powers to react to revolution inside the Sultan's dominions? This was a question which not only split Britain and Russia but also divided Russia and Austria. Metternich regarded Turkey fondly as 'the best of our neighbours'. He was quite aware that she was in a state of decay (because, as he explained, she was Moslem rather than Christian) but as he informed his Ambassador to Russia, Prince Esterhazy,[10] 'she is scrupulously true to her word [and] we regard contact with her as equivalent to contact with a natural frontier which never claims our attention or dissipates our energies.' The Greek revolt, therefore, presented Metternich with an enormous problem. If the Russians intervened to aid the Greek rebels and caused the collapse of the Turkish Empire, the whole balance of power in Europe might well be destroyed. If the worst came to the worst the Balkans and even the Straits might fall into Russian hands. With Russian ships in the Mediterranean and troops right round her eastern frontier, Austria would then be reduced to a satellite of the Tsars. And if they had gained this position by encouraging the Greeks to revolt, where exactly would they draw the line? Which other nations would then be encouraged to revolt on behalf of Russia? Aware of the religious ties which bound the Russians and the Greeks, Metternich's only salvation was to be found in encouraging the Turks to resist while persuading the Tsar that the Greeks were no different from any other rebels. He did not really believe this himself but that did not much matter. Greece was part of Turkey, and Europe should not interfere in Turkish affairs. 'The complications which may ensue in the east defy all calculation', he wrote.[11] He did not give a damn for the Greeks:[12] 'Over there, beyond our frontiers, three or four hundred thousand individuals hanged, impaled or with their throats cut, hardly count'. Yet there was little Metternich could do, especially once Britain, Russia and France together intervened between the Sultan and his subjects. The Austrian Chancellor, Gentz mocked,[13] was reduced to looking for a '*Deus ex machina*', which, of course, he never found. Instead, there was the battle of Navarino (which Gentz likened to the Fall of the Bastille), the Treaty of Adrianople and the establishment of an independent Greece. Metternich, who had done everything possible to prevent this, at last accepted the situation only because he preferred it to the only possible alternative – a Greek protectorate under Russian influence. Was the split between Metternich and Russia over the Eastern Question, therefore, an irrevocable one? The answer, here, is no. Nicholas I, even before the revolutions of 1830, had arrived at the conclusion that the preservation of the Ottoman Empire was also in Russia's interest. After all, its destruction might lead to developments which even Russia could not control. In 1833, therefore, the Tsar agreed with Metternich at Münchengrätz not merely to confirm the Troppau principle of intervention but also to uphold the integrity of Turkey. Metternich wrote:[14] 'We acquit Russia of any aggressive views with regard to the Ottoman Empire.' The Eastern Question was still to provide Europe with many diplomatic twists and turns. Yet Nicholas adhered to his fundamental policy throughout all of them, and in 1840 it was France, not Austria or Russia, who found herself most seriously isolated as a result of Ottoman developments. The story of Russia's diplomacy between 1821 and 1841 is recounted in the light of the latest Russian literature by Professor M. S. Anderson in the fourth article in this collection entitled 'Russia and the Eastern Question, 1821–41'.

The Münchengrätz agreement of 1833 appeared in the eyes of Europe to be answered by the Quadruple Alliance of April 1834 between Britain, France, Portugal and Spain. 'It really looked as if ideological reactions to the Spanish civil war had divided Europe into two camps.'[15] But was this true? Could it not be argued that Europe, viewed more realistically, was really divided into spheres of influence with Austria controlling Italy and Germany, Russia dominating Poland and Turkey, Britain protecting Portugal and Belgium and France attempting to gain exclusive control of Spain? How much did ideology really count for in Europe in the period 1815–48?

To one man it certainly counted for a great deal indeed. When Nicholas I heard of the battle of Navarino he declared:[16] 'What will our friend Metternich say of this great triumph? He will repeat his old principles over and over again and talk of rights.' The Tsar then went on to praise the use of force. Metternich retorted:[17] 'Carnot, Danton and their like tiought and said the same. But, in spite of that, it was the boring old principles that swept them away.' Nicholas by 1833 was again agreeing with him. Alexander I of Russia had done so after 1820 and the Kings of Prussia had almost always supported such views. Thus there can be little doubt that the Eastern courts shared a common outlook during the Metternich period. Is it possible, none

the less, to talk of a Metternich system? After all, Metternich was isolated in the later twenties over the Greek Question, had quarrelled
with Alexander I over Spain and, given the diplomatic successes of
Nicholas I and Palmerston in the Near East and Belgium, never really
appeared to dominate European diplomacy at any time after 1830. In
one respect these criticisms are justified. Metternich could not take
the lead in international affairs on account of Austria's financial and
military weakness. Indeed the position of the Habsburg Monarchy
never differed very much from Gentz's description of it in 1818:[18]

> She has reduced her military resources even beyond the limits and
> proportions that prudence allows. She has neglected her army in all
> respects. . . . Her finances are recovering little by little . . . but that
> would not make it any easier for her to meet the costs of a serious
> war. She would have no liquid funds, emergency taxes would not
> pay for half a campaign, sources of credit are dried up for a long
> time to come, and nobody, from now on, can count on British subsi-
> dies. Therefore, everything combines to bind Austria to a peaceful
> system.

Gentz, however, was aware of the importance of Austria's role in central Europe. With this in mind, therefore, it is possible to argue that
because Metternich had such a clear view of how states should operate, because he could apply his principles to the administration (in
varying degrees) of Austria, Hungary, Germany and Italy and because the sovereigns of Russia and Prussia never really stopped applying the same principles in their own lands and (Greece apart) always
supported intervention against the revolution, it is justifiable to talk of
a Metternich system. This is what I have argued in the fifth essay of
this volume entitled 'The Metternich System, 1815–48'.

If it is possible, then, to see a genuine ideological camp in the combination of Austria, Prussia and Russia, to what extent can one talk of
a liberal camp composed of Britain and France? These were certainly
very different powers in the period concerned. Britain was the greatest
naval, colonial and industrial power, indeed the only truly world
power of the time. The Royal Navy afforded her a security unmatched
by any other state and her industry – although, even in 1851, agricul-
ture was still the largest single employer and landed property and
farm capital at that time still accounted for forty per cent of Britain's
total capital – was developed to such an extent that British workers

and entrepreneurs could visit the continent almost as missionaries with a new gospel to spread. In the 1820s, for example, there were 15,000 industrial workers in France and British entrepreneurs built up the metallurgical industry of Belgium. Nor was there any fear of endangering the British lead – for years to come Europe would have to buy British machines and industrial goods for want of any competition. British skills could simply not be matched and Széchenyi, for example, had to employ a British designer, Clark, to build the chain bridge over the Danube at Budapest. France, on the other hand, was a defeated power suspected by her neighbours who were bound by treaty to ally against her if she should ever attempt to upset the balance of power or, more precisely, cast off the restraints established by the Second Treaty of Paris. Militarily she may have represented a serious threat to Austria and Prussia but she simply could not hope to defeat a combination of Britain and Russia. Politically she seemed unstable to a unique degree – the White Terror, the murder of the Duc de Berri, the 1830 revolution, the disturbances of 1830–32, not to mention the many attempts on the life of Louis Philippe all serving to underline this. Worse than that, France was always regarded by Metternich and his ilk as being the home of revolution. Did not the *Cômité Directeur*, the body which planned revolutions all over Europe, sit in Paris? Did not French governments, by recommending the Charter as a form of government, export the representative and hence the revolutionary principle abroad? When Metternich received the news of the revolution of 1830 his doctor, who had to be called in, found him slumped on his desk sobbing that his life's work was at an end. Louis Philippe, of course, was to do nothing to endanger the peace of Europe – in Lamartine's phrase, France was 'bored' by his régime – but to Metternich and the Tsar, the 'King of the French' always remained a revolutionary upstart who could never be trusted. Diplomatically, therefore, France had to seek the friendship of Great Britain in order to avoid isolation. The relationship between these countries could not, on the other hand, be an equal one. France in this period was simply not an industrial power. By 1850 she possessed only half the mileage of railway track of the German states and only a quarter of that of Great Britain. As late as 1842 only forty-one of her blast furnaces were using coke. In the first half of the nineteenth century the percentage of her population living in towns of over 10,000 people only grew from 9.5 to 10.6. As a result she simply could not compete with Britain economically.

Still, could not both western powers co-operate on a basis of ideological affinity? Were not both the proud possessors of representative systems of government? Were not both – after 1830 especially – unashamedly liberal powers? Did not both fear the rising power of Russia? Yes indeed. But Palmerston would never condescend to treat the French as equals and had little sympathy for France's search for status and influence after 1815. He distrusted French ambitions and demanded that France should always follow the British lead in foreign affairs. Thus, so long as she co-operated over Belgium, Turkey or Spain, the notion of an *entente cordiale* could be supported; if and when co-operation ceased on the other hand, the putative alliance could be stopped and Palmerston could even threaten war[19] – 'the French must go out of Belgium or we have a general war, and war in a number of days', Talleyrand was told. Perhaps such language was necessary on that occasion but there can be no doubt that 'Lord Pumicestone's' hectoring manner did nothing to encourage good Anglo-French relations. In the final analysis, however, the breakdown of the *entente* was not the fault of personalities. The truth was, rather, that British and French interests clashed. Britain suspected France of wishing to establish an hegemony over the whole of northern Africa and resented an attempt by her to negotiate a customs union with the Belgians. French support of Mehemet Ali's Egypt appeared to threaten British trade in the Levant and the Arabian Gulf, while French behaviour with respect to Tahiti and Spain appeared as both deceitful and aggressive. By 1847, therefore, Guizot was reduced to looking to Vienna for support. One French historian, on the other hand, has attributed the breakdown of the Anglo-French *entente* to perfidious Albion's relentless pursuit of self-interest.[20]

By breaking with France in 1846 and forcing Louis Philippe to make advances towards the camp of the absolutist powers, England helped to bring about the revolution of February 1848. Everywhere, indeed, by stirring up national feeling and liberal agitation, she prepared to overthrow the Europe established by the 1815 treaties. But whether she tried, as Castlereagh did, to use the support of the Powers which had defeated Napoleon, or whether, as in Palmerston's day, she allied herself with the revolutionaries, her object was always to divide and weaken the Continent. After the brilliant, bloodless victories which she obtained, first on the Atlantic front and then in the mediterranean region, she went on advancing her interests throughout the world, in the face of a Europe which lacked any inner element of stability.

Flattering as this may be, however, such an interpretation smacks far too much of hindsight. For a more profound analysis of French and British policy, readers are advised to turn to the studies of Dr Bullen and Professor Bartlett which constitute the sixth and seventh articles in this collection and which are entitled 'France and Europe, 1815–48: the problems of defeat and recovery' and 'Britain and the European Balance, 1815–48'.

The final essay in the collection, written by myself, concerns 'the forces of movement'. Why were there so many revolutions in Europe in the period 1815–48? Why so many crises and disturbances? It seems to me that there is a certain mythology about the period which extends not only to the role of the secret societies but also to the role of the bourgeoisie. On the other hand there can be no doubt that the forces of liberalism and nationalism during this period were enormously strengthened by the rise of public opinion in Europe. This in turn was the result of the amazing growth in influence of the press, which at a time such as 1840 could bring Europe to the brink of war. Even over such an intrinsically minor matter as Tahiti, Aberdeen could write:[21] 'it was impossible to deny that persons of all ranks and classes had made up their minds to war.' He told the editor of *The Times*:[22] 'Had it not been for the ferment created by the press in both countries, but especially in Paris, it would have been settled much earlier.' Diplomats in the period 1815–48 had to pay more attention to their public than ever before. That Palmerston should have been accused of ushering in 'the Golden Age of the Blue Book' is surely no coincidence.

How then was peace preserved? Is one to judge the work of the Vienna Congress by saying that it preserved the peace for thirty years? Surely not. There can be little doubt that an effective balance of power was created in 1815 but other, more important factors, accounted for the lack of any major European war in the period 1815–48. All the powers were war-weary; all of them intensely frightened by the thought of revolution. Most of them were preoccupied by domestic problems and most of them were territorially satiated states. This was true of Austria and Prussia. France, on the other hand, was for long periods diplomatically isolated and could do very little to disturb the European balance. Russia, who would have been much more capable of doing so, chose not to. Partly this was due to British opposition, partly because, like Britain, Russia was occupied elsewhere; finally, it was because Russia, like all the other powers, was afraid of the unforeseen. This is the real reason why they accepted Louis Philippe so quickly. To have turned him out would have meant a war with France with consequences that no one could have imagined. The powers in any case were happiest when working in concert. The habit of co-operation had developed during the Napoleonic Wars and lasted throughout the period in question. It was not until the age of Napoleon III and Bismark that rulers deliberately tried to alter the map of Europe unilaterally. Finally, for most of the period it is probably true to say that the ideology of reaction exercised a more potent influence in the chancelleries than the ideology of movement. It is true that there were 'progressive forces' at work, but these have often been exaggerated. That they exploded in 1848 may even have been due to a series of mistakes, coincidences and accidents.

The outbreak of the 1848 revolutions, however, is a subject in itself. The aim of this volume of essays has been merely to provide the student with a comprehensive knowledge of European diplomatic history in the period 1815–48. At present no satisfactory account of the diplomacy of these years exists. For all those who would like to follow the struggle for mastery in Europe at that time, I hope this book will fill the gap. It is not a narrative account but it has been deliberately designed to convey the fruits of the latest research.

1. The Congress of Vienna, 1814–15, and its Antecedents

DOUGLAS DAKIN

THE Congress of Vienna began to assemble in September 1814, but no plenary session was held until the signing of the *Acte finale* on 9 June 1815. The Four Great Powers (Austria, Great Britain, Prussia and Russia) had decided to keep the conduct of all important business within their own hands. They nevertheless agreed, following representations by Talleyrand, the French minister, to recognise a Committee of Eight which included the representatives of France, Portugal, Spain and Sweden who, with the Four, had signed the First Peace of Paris of 30 May 1814. This committee met on numerous occasions but most of the big territorial issues were dealt with by the Four, who established committees to deal with specific problems.[1] Indeed the organisation of the Vienna Congress bears some resemblance to that of its famous successor – the Peace Conference of Paris of 1919, with a Council of Four, a Council of Ten, and various commissions to deal with particular problems.

Like the Paris Conference of 1919, the Congress of Vienna faced the task of reconstructing the European state system. Following Napoleon's defeat at Leipzig (October 1813) and the ensuing advance of the armies of the allied coalition on Paris (March 1814) the French Empire in Europe had almost completely collapsed and there were numerous questions of frontiers and status to be settled. But the peace-makers of 1814, unlike those of 1919, were untramelled for the most part by ideologies. Although Talleyrand elaborated the common-place idea of legitimacy, neither he nor the ministers of the Four Great Powers followed any rigid rules: they restored old rulers only where it suited them to do so and their territorial arrangements were designed primarily to satisfy strategic requirements, to tidy up frontiers or to provide rough justice by way of rewards, compensation or punishment. They were bound by no principle of the self-determination of peoples or ethnic groupings. Although the idea of nationalism was certainly in circulation in various forms, it was hardly likely to assert itself, being an anathema to the prevailing authorities; and for the masses, as for governments, the determination to return to the ways of peace was far more compelling than liberal and nationalist ideas. In so far as the peacemakers of 1814 had any ideological motive, it was a desire to establish some sort of balance of power. This idea was as old as the hills, but so various were its expositions that there was no consensus of opinion on what constituted a balance of power.[2] For Britain a balance of power implied a state system, a series of frontiers and stable alignments containing France within her historic frontiers. To the Austrians it meant a state system and frontiers which gave her predominance in central Europe, and security against a Russia seeking to encroach on Poland and the Ottoman Empire and to extend her dynastic influence in the German Courts. The danger of a French hegemony in Europe was for them a lesser evil and in any case they could count upon Great Britain to keep France within bounds. Similarly Great Britain looked to Austria and Prussia to check Russia, whose expansion was, in British eyes, a lesser evil than the strengthening of the French imperial base in Europe. As for Russia, her conception of a balance of power was of a quite different order: as a spasmodically expansionist power she regarded a balance of power as something to be manipulated to facilitate the fulfilment of her designs. The balance was not for her, as for Austria and Britain, a system of repose – not as Castlereagh, Metternich and Talleyrand would have termed it 'a just equilibrium'.

Like the peacemakers of 1919, those of 1814 could hardly escape completely from their war aims, from obligations contracted during the war, or from certain *faits accomplis*; and it is against this background that the peacemakers of 1814–15 must be seen if the treaties of Paris and Vienna are to be understood. At the outset of the revolutionary wars the aims of the opponents of France had been an amalgam of the traditional foreign policies and the urge to conduct a crusade against the French revolution. Both these aspects had persisted in some degree throughout the war period and, although defeat sometimes necessitated an attempt to come to terms with the French hegemony, they again loomed large in the later stages when the powers sought not only to overthrow the revolution in its Napoleonic form but to revive their historic claims. In reviving their long-cherished aims, the powers nevertheless made attempts to draw up agreed war aims and even to provide, once these aims had been achieved, means by which Europe should enjoy peace and repose. Late in 1804 the Tsar Alexander sent Novosiltov to London to propose an Anglo-Russian alliance based on certain aims which were expressed vaguely in a most idyllic form. Pitt responded in his famous State Paper of 19 January 1805[3] by attempting an essentially practical formulation of the Tsar's ideas. He proposed that a concert of powers should be established with three aims: to rescue countries subjugated by France, who should be reduced within her former limits; to provide for the security and happiness of territories recovered from France; and to form, at the restoration of peace, 'a general agreement and Guarantee for the mutual protection and security of different powers, and for re-establishing a general system of public law in Europe'. Territories recovered must, as far as possible, regain their ancient rights. Complete restoration, however, might not always be possible and should not be attempted if inconsistent with the security of the territory itself or of Europe as a whole. In this last category were Genoa, the territories forming the Napoleonic Italian Republic, the three Legations, Parma and Placentia, the Austrian Netherlands, and states on the left bank of the Rhine. These 'separate petty sovereignties would never again have any solid existence in themselves' and would serve only to weaken and impair the force which ought to be concentrated in the hands of the chief powers in order to ensure the safety and repose of Europe. In any case Austria and Prussia could not be 'brought to bear upon the common cause without the prospect of obtaining some important acquisition' in Italy and on the Rhine respectively. Such acquisition would enable Austria, in company with an enlarged Sardinia, to resist France in the south, and Prussia to reinforce an expanded Holland strengthened by a system of barrier fortresses. Should a settlement be achieved it should be placed under the special guarantee of Great Britain and Russia who had 'no separate objects of their own'.

There still remained 'one great and important question for consideration' and that was 'how far . . . the views of the allies ought to be directed towards the re-establishment of the monarchy in France and the restoration of the Bourbon family on the throne'. England and Russia were agreed that this aim was highly desirable for both France and Europe, but it ought to be 'a secondary object of the concert': only if the allies obtained 'a great and signal success' and if 'a strong and prevailing disposition for the return of the Monarch' should 'manifest itself in the interior of France' should any active or decided measures be undertaken to fulfil that aim.

Such were the war aims of Britain and, momentarily at least, of Russia. Before 1804 and in the period following the Treaty of Tilsit (1807) Russian objectives were of a quite different order and it was not until 1813–14 that the Tsar Alexander reverted to the aim of establishing a balance of power designed to contain France. His ideas, however, differed very considerably from those of the British foreign secretary, Castlereagh. Throughout the war period the Russians had pursued designs on Poland. They had benefited from the partitions of 1793 and 1795 and in 1813 they took up the idea of creating in Poland a Russian kingdom. They had also dabbled in the schemes for the 'Polonisation of Germany', the whole question of replacing the German Reich having been raised by the French occupation of the left bank of the Rhine, and by the various schemes for compensating the secular princes of that region by giving them ecclesiastical territories on the right bank. During all the protracted negotiations on this issue, the whole German balance of power was at stake, Austria and Prussia being threatened by a France operating on a grander scale than under Louis XIV, and by a Russia whose intrusion into central Europe had been 'legalised' by the Treaty of Teschen in 1779. Under these new conditions their old rivalries of the *ancien régime* had continued with a vengeance and had resulted either in their attempts to build up coalitions against France or in their endeavours to seek accommodation with her. As a consequence, Austrian and Prussian war aims, although designed for self-preservation and the establishment of a balance of power, had been rarely constant in immediate objectives.

In order to retrieve the heavy losses inflicted after her defeat at Jena in 1806, Prussia had inclined towards collaboration with Russia: many Austrians, however, had feared Russia more than France and, although ready to welcome Russian military action in so far as it curbed Napoleon, had wanted France to remain sufficiently powerful to play her traditional role in maintaining a 'just equilibrium'. Among these Austrians, Metternich was to become the most influential.[4] In 1809, when he became foreign minister, he had thought that popular risings in Germany would tip the scales against Napoleon, but by 1811, fearing that Russia would fight only a defensive war and leave Austria in the lurch, he had come to believe that it was inadvisable to encourage the Tsar and great was his alarm when the Prussian minister Hardenberg had attempted to make an alliance with Russia. Hardenberg, however, was unable to obtain satisfactory terms and on

24 February 1812 he signed on alliance with France. On 14 March
Metternich followed suit, obtaining far better terms.

Napoleon's retreat from Moscow and the Russian advance through
Poland into Germany increased Metternich's fears, which became all
the greater when Prussia, following General Yorck's defection from
Napoleon, concluded with Russia the Treaty of Kalisch (28 February
1813).[5] By this treaty Russia agreed to restore Prussia territorially,
financially and demographically to her strength before her defeat at
Jena, but not necessarily in the same territories; she guaranteed to her
East Prussia which was to be joined to Silesia by a strip of Polish territory; she promised her compensation for her losses in northern Germany, the implication being (and a verbal promise had been made)[6]
that this compensation would include Saxony. It was also implied
that Prussia would enjoy supremacy in northern Germany. Russia
was to provide 150,000 troops: Prussia was to furnish 80,000 and a
national militia. This provision showed that Tsar Alexander had decided to carry the war into central Germany; not that he intended to
fight a people's war; in the treaty there was no suggestion of creating a
united Germany, no idea even of a German constitutional federation.
The Tsar had definitely rejected the plan of his German adviser,
Stein, to encourage the people to rise against the time-serving
German princes. When, on 25 March, General Kutusov issued an
appeal to the Germans to create a new Germany he addressed himself
to both the princes and the peoples and gave no indication of the form
the new Germany should take.

Although Metternich welcomed Prussia's alignment with Russia
in so far as it would keep the Tsar committed to Europe, he had no
intention of joining them. Realising that after the Moscow campaign
both France and Russia were relatively weaker, he chose the path of
neutrality. But fearing always the possibility of a Franco-Russian
deal, he turned his attentions to Great Britain who had already
begun negotiations with Russia and Prussia.[7] What he wanted even
more than Austrian territorial gains was a negotiated balance of
power. To achieve this he would have to get Great Britain to take
part in negotiations leading to a general as distinct from a purely continental peace. But when he discovered that the British were fully determined to remove the French from Holland, Spain and the Rhine
before entering upon any peace negotiations, in despair he reverted
to a plan of using France and Russia to curb one another.

On 16 May at Wurschen, Hardenberg and the Tsar's minister

Nesselrode gave to Stadion, the Austrian envoy, the seven conditions on which they were prepared to negotiate with France:[8] these were the restoration of Austria and Prussia to the extent of their territory and population in 1805, the dissolution of the Duchy of Warsaw, the freedom of Holland, the restoration of the Bourbons in Spain, the exclusion of the French from Italy, and the independence of Germany, that is to say, the dissolution of the Confederation of the Rhine and the cession by France of the annexed North German provinces. These terms were far more drastic and less ambiguous than those Metternich had been offering, but Napoleon's victory of Bautzen (20 May) and the subsequent armistice of Pläswitz (4 June) gave him the opportunity, in negotiations at Gitsin, to reduce them. He persuaded Russia and Prussia to agree to four *sine qua non* points: the dissolution of the Duchy of Warsaw and its partition among Austria, Prussia and Russia; the aggrandisement of Prussia; the return of the Illyrian provinces to Austria; and the re-establishment of Lübeck, Hamburg and those parts of northern Germany annexed to France in 1810. At subsequent negotiations leading to the Treaty of Reichenbach of 27 June,[9] the three powers agreed that if Napoleon did not accept those four points by 20 July then Austria would fight for the seven Wurschen proposals.

Clearly Metternich was hoping that it would not come to this and that a compromise peace might still be concluded. Indeed, even when, in the famous Dresden interview,[10] Napoleon showed himself intransigent, Metternich again proffered his mediation and arranged with the French for an extension of the armistice until 10 August, and for a peace conference to open in Prague on 5 July. But the chances of peace were certainly slim. Caulaincourt, Napoleon's emissary, did not arrive in Prague until 28 July, by which time the Kallisch allies, heartened by news of Wellington's victory at Vittoria, were no longer in the mood for negotiations. Yet even at that late hour Metternich had not given up all hope. On 8 August he made, on Caulaincourt's advice, a peremptory demand that Napoleon should accept the four *sine qua non* points. To this demand, which was intended to make Napoleon see reason, he received no reply. As he waited in vain, he learned that the Russian and Prussian envoys had declared that their powers expired at midnight on 10 August. Two days later Austria declared war, Metternich and his colleagues having, during the previous months, considerably strengthened the Austrian army. Nevertheless Metternich (despite his later pronouncements that he had been fooling Napoleon to gain time) was still prepared to negotiate peace. He had come to believe, however, that Napoleon would never respond unless he was first driven back to the Rhine.[11] When on 18 August Napoleon offered a general peace he rebuffed the approach, but not without taking the occasion to force his allies to agree that the Austrian general Schwarzenberg should hold supreme command.

Although he still hoped to negotiate with France, he saw that he must first convince Napoleon that the three allies were firmly united. He therefore took steps which led to the Treaties of Teplitz of 9 September,[12] three bilateral pacts each containing public and secret clauses. Publicly the allies stated their intentions to protect one another's territories, to contribute each 60,000 troops, and to abstain from making a separate peace. The secret clauses provided for each power to contribute 150,000 men, for the restoration of Austria and Prussia to their 1805 strength, the restoration of Hanover, the dissolution of the Rheinbund (entirely independent states to obtain between the frontiers of Austria and Prussia and between the Rhine and the Alps), for the restoration to Germany of the 32nd Military District and of the German provinces under French princes, and for an amicable arrangement to be made in respect of the Duchy of Warsaw. There was no mention of Italy, Holland and Spain: nevertheless previous engagements had been reaffirmed and no great difficulty was likely to arise as the freeing of these countries from Napoleon was a British war aim. Where difficulty was likely to arise was on the question of the future of the German states. By entering the war, Metternich had accepted the aim of destroying the Rheinbund. As to what should take its place he was in substantial agreement with the Tsar who had rejected Stein's proposal to substitute for the princedoms a third, sovereign Germany. Hardenberg, too, disagreed with Stein, but he wanted a federal Germany in which Austria and Prussia should exercise control not conjointly but on a partition basis. The Teplitz Treaties left the issue uncertain: Hardenberg understood the engagements to mean that the whole of Germany should be liberated from France; Metternich, who was in the process of enlisting support among the German states, probably envisaged independence only as the exclusion of an external authority. But his task of winning support among the German states was not easy. If Austria was to be reconstructed in the 1805 level, she would need to recover from Bavaria the Inn and Hausrück district, Tyrol, Vorarlberg, Brixen, Trent, Salzburg, and Berchtesgaden. But on this issue the Tsar came to

Metternich's aid, promising compensation to Bavaria who on 8 October signed with Austria the Treaty of Ried.[13] In return for a promise of reconstruction on an adequate scale as a compact whole and for an assurance of 'full and entire' sovereignty, Bavaria agreed to withdraw from the Rheinbund, to furnish to the allies 36,000 troops, to allow the Austrian army to enter the Tyrol, and to accept the allies' war aims, together with their undertaking not to sign a separate peace.

Metternich's hopes of a negotiated peace were greatly enhanced when, during the battle of Leipzig (16–19 October), Napoleon himself made peace feelers through the Austrian General Merfeldt. Using the good offices of Baron St Aignan (Caulaincourt's brother-in-law), he sent to Napoleon the so-called Frankfurt proposals – the 'natural frontiers' for France, the absolute independence of Germany and the renunciation of every species of constitutional influence on the part of France, except for the natural and indispensable influence which every powerful state must exercise over its weaker neighbours, the restoration of the Bourbons in Spain, the existence of absolutely independent states between the Austrian and French frontiers towards Italy, and the absolute independence of Holland (its frontier and form of government to be subject to negotiation). No armistice was contemplated but, if Napoleon accepted these bases, then a peace conference would be held at a neutralised place on the right bank of the Rhine.

With the Frankfurt proposals Castlereagh, who was preparing to take a more active role in determining the fate of the continent, was far from satisfied.[14] They conflicted to some extent with his Project of Alliance of 18 September[15] which had reached his envoys to the allied Courts at the time of the battle of Leipzig. That document was clearly inspired by Pitt's State Paper of 1805 and in it Castlereagh had demanded a vigorous prosecution of the war by all the allies, the conduct of all negotiations by common consent, and the maintenance of a perpetual defensive alliance after the conclusion of peace. In seven of ten proposed secret articles he adopted substantially the Wurschen proposals of 16 May, stipulating, however, that the German provinces absorbed in the Kingdom of Wesphalia and those actually annexed to France should be restored and that a free and independent Holland should be given an adequate barrier. The other three proposed secret articles were: the restoration of Brunswick-Luneburgh; the annexation of Norway to Sweden; and the restoration of Naples (or adequate compensation) to the King of Sicily.

Castlereagh had long been highly suspicious of Metternich's negotiations. He was not in principle opposed to a negotiated peace, but he
believed that all negotiations must be conducted by a firmly united
concert of powers and that they must not be allowed to lead to a relaxation of military exertion. On learning of the Frankfurt proposals his
suspicions increased. There were indeed good grounds for his alarm.
His Project of Alliance had found support only from Prussia. Metternich, determined to get his own way in Germany, had threatened to
make a separate peace, which threat had forced the Tsar to drop
Stein's and Nesselrode's plans for consolidated districts and to adopt
the idea of separate administrations in each state, all states being
invited to make individual accession treaties with the allies.[16] In thus
vigorously upholding the rights of existing authorities Metternich was
no slave to any theory of legitimacy: he was merely out to reconstruct
a third Germany, under predominantly Austrian influence but without the old Reich, and great was his delight when, on arriving in
Frankfurt in November, he found that among the representatives of
the German princes there was not a single Bonapartist.

The French reply (16 November)[17] to the Frankfurt proposals
ignored the terms and merely offered a conference. Metternich, however, insisted on the Frankfurt bases and on 1 December issued a proclamation[18] for the edification of the French public, blaming
Napoleon for rejecting generous peace offers and stating that the allies
wished to see France great, strong and prosperous, with even more extensive territory than under her kings. By then he was in a more com-
manding position, not only because of his success in Germany but
also because he could now hope to improve his relations with Great
Britain. Whereas the Tsar, intent on invading France, was not interested in Castlereagh's alliance proposals, Metternich, particularly
attracted by the idea of post-war guarantees, was prepared to accept
most of them. In any case Caulaincourt (who had become French
foreign minister on 20 November) had made it clear to him that
Napoleon's acceptance of a peace conference was contingent on
British participation. To secure that participation Metternich sought
the assistance of the Tsar who, in return for certain concessions, on 6
December sent his minister Pozzo di Borgo on a special mission to
London, and the outcome was that on 20 December the British
government decided to send Castlereagh as their representative to the
continent.[19] Already Metternich had reverted to his task of securing
Austrian interests: he ordered Schwarzenberg to invade Switzerland

and establish a conservative federal government; in Saxony he aroused popular agitation for the restoration of King Frederick Augustus; and in Naples he recognised the reigning king, Murat, in return for a promise to provide 30,000 troops.[20]

In January 1814, alarmed by rumours that the Tsar was planning to put his protégé Bernadotte, the Swedish crown prince, on the French throne and still fearing a Franco-Russian alignment, Metternich ordered Schwarzenberg to halt the Austrian army at Langres. He still considered Napoleon a lesser evil than the Tsar. He therefore took great pains to be accommodating to Prussia. On 8 January 1814 he agreed with Hardenberg that Prussia should have the whole of Saxony provided she opposed Russian ambitions in Poland. Hardenberg indeed was ready to do a comprehensive deal and he hoped moreover to establish, with British support, a defence league which would include Holland, Switzerland, Denmark, Sweden and Turkey.[21] When on 18 January Castlereagh arrived at allied headquarters, Hardenberg began to increase his demands. Learning that Castlereagh wanted to join Belgium to Holland he demanded territory on the left bank of the Rhine and found a sympathetic response. But Castlereagh's arrival was not unhelpful to Metternich: Castlereagh was strongly opposed to the Tsar's plans for Bernadotte: he agreed with Metternich that the House of Bourbon was the only alternative to Napoleon as the ruler of France;[22] and he conceded that the union of Holland and Belgium should not be allowed to jeopardise the Frankfurt bases, provided it were included in any new terms which might subsequently be presented.

Although Metternich had quickly come to an understanding with Castlereagh, he found the Tsar, who was all for pushing on with the war, difficult to deal with and it took another threat to conclude a separate peace to secure Alexander's consent to join a four-power conference.[23] At this conference, which took place at Langres at the end of January, although he angled for an armistice, he had to accept Castlereagh's demand that military operations be continued. He also had to accept his allies' demand that Napoleon be offered not the 'natural' but the 'ancient' frontiers, it being conceded that a few additions of territory should be offered in order to comply with his proclamation of 1 December and to agree to the principle that France should be allowed to settle her own dynastic problems only provided she had no share in the settlement of Europe outside her frontiers.

As France was to be excluded from any voice in the settlement of

Germany, Metternich was intent on giving nothing away in advance of the final peace conference. He avoided any undertaking to agree to a four-power directory and he secured the principle that Germany should be composed of sovereign states united solely by a 'federal bond', a vague phrase which nevertheless ruled out the restoration of the Reich. Meanwhile he continued to improve his relationships with Hardenberg and Castlereagh, with the result that the Tsar at length agreed to attend a congress at Châtillon.[24]

At this congress, which opened on 5 February, Caulaincourt offered the 'ancient limits' in return for an armistice, but the Tsar announced his intention to march on Paris, depose Napoleon, and convene an assembly of notables to decide on a form of government for France. This plan, along with a threat to withdraw the Russian troops from Schwarzenberg's command, alarmed Metternich and exasperated Castlereagh. Fortunately for Metternich, however, between 10 and 14 February Napoleon inflicted considerable losses on the Russians and Prussians. Not only was the Tsar now ready to sign an armistice but, under Metternich's further threat to sign a separate peace,[25] he was prepared to accept a preliminary peace treaty and to reaffirm the allied terms offered at Châtillon. It was Metternich, then, rather than Castlereagh who kept the Tsar within the Concert. The upshot was that the allies agreed to continue military operations and to reiterate their terms: they also agreed that if Napoleon accepted them he should keep his throne, provided he were not repudiated by the French. In order to make the terms more palatable Castlereagh had specified the colonies that Great Britain would return to France.[26]

On 17 February the allies presented to Caulaincourt a draft of treaty, but Napoleon, following his recent victories, had already withdrawn his emissary's full powers. Caulaincourt asked for time to obtain new instructions. Stadion gave him until 10 March. During the interval Metternich conducted private negotiations with the French, and Castlereagh, learning of these, feared that Austria might conclude a separate peace. Metternich, however, was probably merely out to improve his negotiating position: he had learned that the Polish patriot Czartoryski was back in Alexander's favour and feared that this might mean a Russian attempt to obtain Eastern Galicia. Hence he readily fell in with Castlereagh's demand for a four-power allied treaty to consolidate the separate alliance. By the Treaty of Chaumont (9 March 1814)[27] the Four Powers agreed each to provide 150,000 troops and to continue the war until Napoleon accepted their terms, Britain undertaking to pay £5 million in subsidies. As there was a possibility that Napoleon would retain his throne, the Treaty provided that the alliance should last for twenty years, that each power, after the war, should retain with the colours 60,000 men, and that the allies should jointly resist any French attack upon their European possessions. Secret articles confirmed decisions already reached on Holland, Spain, Italy, Switzerland and Germany and invited Spain, Portugal, Holland and Sweden to accede to the Treaty.

When Caulaincourt failed to give a satisfactory reply to the allied demands, Metternich twice persuaded his allies to extend the time limit. On 18 March, however, negotiations were broken off, Stadion making an allied declaration to the effect that Napoleon was responsible for the rupture. From that point events moved rapidly. By the end of March the allied armies had entered Paris.[28] Early in April Talleyrand convened willing Senators who absolved the French populace from its loyalty to Napoleon, voted a constitution, and restored the Bourbons. By 10 April, the Tsar, acting for his allies, had negotiated the terms of the Treaty of Fontainbleau, having, much to the disgust of Metternich and Castlereagh, shown great leniency.[29] Napoleon was to have the island of Elba in full sovereignty and an annual revenue of 2,000,000 francs, while the Empress was to receive the Parma Duchies. It was not, however, until 30 May that the allies concluded with Bourbon France the First Peace of Paris.[30] By that treaty France obtained approximately the frontiers of January 1792. She agreed to the free navigation of the Rhine, the independence of Switzerland, a confederated Germany, an augmented Holland, the cession of Italian territories to Austria, and the acquisition by Great Britain of Malta, St Lucia and Tobago. Article XXXII stated that within two months the powers should meet in a general congress at Vienna 'to complete the provisions of the present treaty' and in a secret article the French agreed to accept the allied decisions to be made in that congress: other secret articles stated that most of the Austrian Netherlands should go to Holland, that free navigation should be established on the Scheldt and that the left bank of the Rhine should be partitioned among Holland, Prussia and other German states. No indemnity was imposed on France, who was even allowed to retain Napoleon's ill-gotten art treasures, and no provision was made for an allied occupation. At negotiations in London the allies agreed that Britain should pay Sweden for Guadeloupe, which island, earlier promised to Sweden, had been returned to France. They also agreed that Britain should pay Holland for Cape Colony £2,000,000, which sum the Dutch agreed to spend on frontier fortifications, the remaining details of those frontiers being left over for the Congress of Vienna.[31]

Yet at the Congress of Vienna it was not these details that were to become the major problems but Saxony and Poland. If Russia took almost the whole of Poland and if Prussia took the whole of Saxony, Austria's strategic position would have been seriously jeopardised, and if Prussia also obtained the great fortress of Mainz it would have been disastrous. By the end of the war Russia occupied both Poland and Saxony. The Tsar had committed himself to re-establishing Poland as a satellite kingdom and was ready to compensate Prussia with the whole of Saxony. Already on his way to Vienna, Castlereagh, thinking that Alexander might present the allies with a *fait accompli*, called upon Talleyrand in Paris to ascertain whether he could count upon French support against a Russian *coup*.[32] In the event, however, the Tsar decided to appear at the Congress and to obtain by diplomacy what he shrank from gaining by force, and Talleyrand was greatly disappointed on his arrival at Vienna to find himself excluded from the counsels of Europe. Castlereagh's policy was now to check the Russian diplomatic threat by aligning Austria and Prussia in opposition to the Tsar:[33] Prussia could have Saxony provided she claimed for herself and for Austria their former possessions in Poland. On 9 October Hardenberg put in writing an offer to oppose Alexander's plans for Poland in return for the cession of Saxony. It was not, however, until 22 October that Metternich replied, more or less accepting the offer but making acceptance conditional on the cession of Mainz to Bavaria.[34] On 24 October Castlereagh drew up a memorandum[35] for Metternich and Hardenberg to show to their sovereigns who were on the point of leaving for Buda, where Alexander was to join them. But the Buda meeting saw Castlereagh's plans collapse in ruins as, on learning of the opposition of Great Britain, Prussia and Austria to his Polish plans, Alexander denounced Metternich and Hardenberg in the presence of their sovereigns. The timid Frederick William III gave way and ordered Hardenberg to cease co-operation with Castlereagh and Metternich. After this a prolonged exchange of letters and memoranda between Castlereagh and the Tsar brought no change in the Russian position.[36] To all intents and purposes Poland was lost. It was now the

Saxon question that became the focus of Castlereagh's attention, and
he managed to persuade Hardenberg to consider a letter from Metternich suggesting that Prussia should accept only a part of Saxony.
Hardenberg, hoping to discredit Metternich, showed some of his correspondence to Alexander, but Metternich had the better of the encounter for he managed to give the Tsar satisfactory explanations.[37]
In their difficulties towards mid-December both Hardenberg and
Metternich looked towards Castlereagh to help in solving the Saxon
question. Castlereagh's weight inclined towards Austria, for Prussia
was disposed to count on support from Russia. That support, however, was not forthcoming: now that Alexander had virtually established his claim to Poland, he had become somewhat indifferent to
Prussia's interests.

As Castlereagh and Metternich were opposed to Prussia on the
Saxon issue, Talleyrand, who had always had the Saxon question as a
greater priority than that of Poland, was able to come forward with
offers of help. Although he had arrived at Vienna with elaborate instructions of his own making[38] (and they harked back to a pre-
revolutionary French conception of a balance of power), he had failed
to influence the Vienna negotiations. But, as his despatches show,[39]
he had learned a great deal, no doubt from Metternich, who saw that
one day he might have need of Bourbon France, and on 12 and 19
December he wrote to Metternich explaining, in terms of the balance
of power, how vital it was for Austria to resist Prussia on the Saxon
issue. To this approach Metternich responded. Castlereagh, however, for some time held aloof. Although he had earlier contemplated
armed mediation in company with France he was most reluctant to
depart from his policy of bringing Austria and Prussia together and it
was not until, in conferences at the end of the year, Prussia threatened
war that he submitted to Talleyrand and Metternich a draft of a
treaty of alliance which was signed on 3 January 1815.[40] Talleyrand
made no request for a rectification of the French frontier: he was content to have dissolved the coalition.

The immediate consequence of the treaty of 3 January 1815 was the
collapse of the Russo-Prussian front and the settlement of the German
question in accordance with the interests of a balance of power between the two leading German states. It was nevertheless Castlereagh
who took the leading role in this, his aim, like Pitt's, being to create a
strong central Europe as a barrier to France. It was Castlereagh who
turned down a Russian-backed proposal to transfer the Saxon

dynasty to the west (Luxembourg, Trèves, and other Rhineland terri-tory), and who obtained the Tsar's and Metternich's agreement to a compromise on Saxony. At length, having persuaded the Tsar to cede Thorn (on the Vistula) to Prussia and having induced Hanover to give her 50,000 souls, Castlereagh arrived at a solution whereby Prussia received about two-fifths of Saxony's population and about three-fifths of the soil, Leipzig being excluded. Altogether Prussia gained rather more Polish than Saxon territory. She emerged as a relatively powerful state, replacing Austria as the defender of the Rhine.

Once the Polish-Saxon question was out of the way, other Euro-pean frontiers were quickly settled. Bavaria, in return for ceding to Austria her gains of 1805 and 1809, received Wurzburg, Frankfurt and the Palatinate. Mainz, which Austria had promised her, was des-ignated a German confederation fortress and placed under the sover-eignty of Hesse. Hanover, which became a kingdom, was enlarged, principally on the Ems: she obtained East Frisia from Prussia in return for Lauenberg, which Prussia then ceded to Denmark in return for Pomerania and the Isle of Rügen which Sweden had given to Den-mark in return for Norway. To the king of Holland went the Duchy of Luxembourg, which was part of the German confederation, the for-tress being garrisoned by Prussia. Germany as a whole emerged as a confederation of thirty-four princedoms and four free towns, all enjoy-ing independence and equal rights. Under this arrangement Austria was to enjoy, like Prussia, a prominent position in Germany. It was, however, in Italy that Austria obtained her principal compensation. Here the Emperor Francis had already received, at the Peace of Paris, the new Lombardo-Venetian kingdom. The settlement of the rest of Italy (except for Genoa [Liguria] which was earmarked for incor-poration in the Piedmont-Sardinian kingdom) had to wait until cen-tral Europe had been reconstructed. Metternich, in his determination to secure Austrian interests, was prepared to bide his time. Above all, he wished to ensure that French influence should not prevail in Naples.

As we have seen, Metternich had made a treaty (11 January 1814) with King Murat. This treaty had had the blessing of Castlereagh who had contemplated similar action but, owing to the waywardness of his envoy Lord William Bentinck, he had remained free from this entanglement while temporarily benefiting from Metternich's action. At the Congress, Talleyrand demanded that the Bourbon Ferdinand I of Sicily should be restored to Naples in place of Murat, and he could count upon some support from Great Britain, Prussia and Russia. Although Metternich eventually agreed with Castlereagh that Murat must go, he was determined not to desert his ally except as a price for the satisfaction of his aims in Italy which Talleyrand opposed. In the end Castlereagh and Metternich went behind Talleyrand's back and obtained from Louis XVIII and his government an undertaking to agree to Austrian demands in Italy in return for a promise to over-throw Murat.[41] Such was the situation when Napoleon returned to France. Murat, who had been long in despair at the failure of his agents to gain recognition by the European powers, seized the oc-casion of Napoleon's return to attempt to rally general Italian support on his own account, counting somewhat optimistically on popular hatred of the prospects of Austrian rule. But his army failed, he him-self fled to Switzerland, and Ferdinand was restored to Naples, Met-ternich having, in a treaty of 12 June 1815, secured his agreement not to grant a constitution to his subjects. By this time Talleyrand was a cypher and Metternich was able to secure a settlement of central Italy to his liking. The Parma Duchies went to Marie Louise, the reversion being left unsettled. The Emperor Francis's brother was restored to the Grand Duchy of Tuscany and his grandson obtained the Duchy of Modena. The Pope recovered the Legations of Ravenna, Bologna and Ferrara, where Austria retained the right of garrison. Indeed the whole of Italy, except for Piedmont and Lucca (which went to the Infanta Maria Luisa of the Parma branch of the House of Bourbon), was virtually under Austrian control. As a consequence Austria rein-forced the two front-line powers containing France in the South – the Piedmont-Sardinian kingdom which in addition to Genoa incor-porated Nice and Savoy and the Swiss Republic whose frontiers and twenty-two cantons had been settled by a committee of the Vienna Congress. To the new Switzerland the Four Great Powers and France gave a guarantee of neutrality. Another committee of the Congress settled the fate of the former Venetian Ionian Islands. These, which at one time had been considered as suitable compensation for Ferdinand of Sicily in the event of Murat's retention of Naples, were constituted as the Septinsular Republic and were eventually placed under British protection, this arrangement proving satisfactory to Austria and Russia.[42]

Although the Vienna territorial settlement survived Napoleon's hundred days, the First Peace of Paris was revised following Napoleon's second downfall. At the Second Peace of Paris, 20

November 1815,[43] France was reduced to approximately her 1790 frontiers; she was ordered to destroy the fortress of Hüningen; she was subjected to an occupation of certain areas by up to 150,000 allied troops for five years, which period might be (and was indeed) reduced to three; she was compelled to pay an indemnity of 700,000,000 francs and to restore her stolen art treasures. These terms were far more moderate than those which Holland, Bavaria, Prussia and Wurtemberg had wished to impose. For this moderation Castlereagh and Wellington, and to some extent the Tsar and Metternich, were responsible, and they justified their moderation largely on the grounds that a moderate peace best served the interests of a European balance of power. To partition France would only lead to instability and perhaps to another revolutionary phase. Castlereagh indeed (and the same is true of the Tsar and Metternich) set greater store on the complete renewal of the Treaty of Chaumont, which had been only partially renewed when the coalition of the Four Powers had been reconstructed on 25 March 1815 to deal with Napoleon's renewed bid for power. This complete reinstatement of the Chaumont Treaty was in effect achieved by a Treaty of Defensive Alliance signed by the Four Powers on the same day that they signed the Second Peace of Paris.[44] It consisted of a series of identical bilateral agreements: the allies agreed to uphold the Second Treaty of Paris, to prevent by force the return of Napoleon or any of his family, and to repel any attack by France upon the occupation. It contained, however, a significant departure: Article VI provided for periodic conferences of the allied sovereigns or their ministers to facilitate the execution of the Treaty, to consolidate the intimate relations of those sovereigns and to examine those measures most salutary for the repose and prosperity of the peoples and for the peace of Europe. This article, which underlined the fact of the ascendency of the Great Powers, gave a formal basis to the idea of the Concert of Europe and was an attempt to perpetuate the practice of conference diplomacy which had come into use during the final phase of the Napoleonic Wars. It did not, however, define precisely when and for what specific purposes these international conferences should be held – an omission which led to the controversies of the 'conference period'.[45]

Already, before the clause was finally drafted, there had been considerable differences of opinion. Castlereagh had considered that a Russian draft had contemplated too much interference in the internal affairs of nation states, and in his own draft he had chosen his words carefully but without legal precision. At an earlier stage he had had in mind Pitt's idea of a guarantee. Pitt had stipulated a special guarantee by Great Britain and Russia, thus using the term guarantee in a sense well understood in earlier times. Russia and Britain, however, had ceased to be the peripheral and disinterested powers envisaged by Pitt. In the new situation created by the Final Coalition, by the Peace Treaty with France, and by the Vienna Settlement, both Castlereagh and the Tsar (and Metternich and Talleyrand went along with them), began to think in terms of a general guarantee. Eventually on 13 February Gentz, who had acted as the Secretary of the Congress, drafted a declaration embodying the idea, and on that same day Castlereagh in a circular letter to his Ambassadors[46] stated that there was 'every prospect of the Congress terminating with a general accord and Guarantee'. This projected guarantee Castlereagh, Talleyrand and Metternich wished to extend to the Ottoman Empire and Alexander concurred, provided their three governments would mediate in his disputes with the Porte. The Porte, however, refused to co-operate. In the confusion caused by Napoleon's return from Elba the idea of a general guarantee was dropped and Castlereagh never reverted to it, being content with the partial renewal of the Treaty of Chaumont and subsequently with the Treaty of Defensive Alliance of 30 November 1815. There is no written evidence to explain Castlereagh's change of policy but it is probable that he came to realise his government would not stand for the commitments which a general guarantee entailed. He was therefore content to work for a general treaty – to gather into one instrument the numerous agreements reached during the negotiations.

The general treaty bore some resemblance to the settlement Castlereagh had envisaged in his Project of Alliance. France had been hemmed in by a ring of relatively powerful states – Prussia, Holland, Bavaria, Austria and Piedmont. He had failed, however, to secure his projected eastern frontier of central Europe and the German Confederation hardly fulfilled his somewhat vague hopes of a more powerful Germany. Whether a balance of power had been truly established, whether given the Europe of the day it was possible to do so, are matters open to doubt. Many contemporaries, including Gentz, considered that the balance achieved was quite inadequate and even Castlereagh doubted whether the settlement would last very long.[47] That it did last for a very considerable period may not have been due to the settlement itself but to a host of other factors – to the relative stability of Restoration France; to changing economic and political conditions; to the pursuit of different national interests; to the need to consolidate territories acquired; to a widespread desire not to return to a state of war with its unforseen eventualities; and to a growing disposition to pursue national interests at the conference table. This last-mentioned factor may well have derived its strength from the feeling that from 1813 to 1815 the conference diplomacy of the European Concert had worked reasonably well and had established itself as part of diplomatic practice.

Broadly speaking contemporaries discussed, like Gentz, the 1814–15 Peace Settlement in terms of the balance of power. In his reply of 20 March 1815 to an attack by Whitbread in the House of Commons[48] upon his policy, Castlereagh took it for granted that his task was to restore a balance of power and was at pains to show that every detail of the Settlement was conducive to that end. When, just over a month later, Sir James Mackintosh denounced Castlereagh[49] for agreeing to the transfer of Genoa to Piedmont, he too, while upholding the rights of small nations, related his argument to a balance of power theory:

> To destroy independent nations in order to strengthen the balance of power, is the most extravagant sacrifice of the end to the means. . . . In the new system small states are annihilated by a combination of the great. In the old, small states were secured by the mutual jealousy of the great. . . . The Congress of Vienna seems, indeed, to have adopted every part of the French system, except that they have transferred the dictatorship of Europe from an individual to a triumvirate.

Underlying his argument was the assertion that true nations, great and small alike, are the products of time and nature and are animated by a national spirit. One of the errors of the French Revolution and Napoleonic France was 'the fatal opinion that it was possible for human skill to make a government'. That error the Vienna Powers had perpetuated since they had created states composed of irreconcilable elements and in so doing they had sown the seed of further aggression.

These ideas, shorn of the assumption that before the Revolution there was a balance of power which respected the rights of small nations, were taken up by the nationalist historians of the late nineteenth and early twentieth centuries who denounced the Settlement of 1814–15 for its failure to respect national aspirations. Writing with a knowledge of the national revolts and wars of unification they invariably, each one for his own purpose, denounced the so-called iniquities of the statesmen who reconstructed Europe at the Congress of Vienna. Invariably they exaggerated the strength, and failed to discern the exact nature, of early nationalist and liberal movements, and they attributed to nationalism and liberalism a moral quality which they denied to the ideas of the balance of power and to the old order in general. They assumed that the pursuit of nationalistic ends justified every means – even the destruction of a balance of power and a disregard for the public law of Europe.

In the pursuit of nationalist aims the leaders of the wars of unification destroyed the old balance of power and substituted another which was based on shifting alliances and alignments. The new system transformed the main features of the Vienna Settlement, and the nationalist historians justified this outcome by denouncing the makers of that Settlement as unmitigated reactionaries, devoid of vision and humanity. Not until the present century were these facile judgements reversed. Detailed studies of Castlereagh, Metternich, Talleyrand and Tsar Alexander shed a new light upon their diplomacy.[50] Moreover, the problems that faced the peacemakers after the World War of 1914–18 led generally to a much more sympathetic understanding of the aims and accomplishments of their forebears. Above all it was seen that the Vienna Settlement was not a break in historical continuity, that it was not the work of irresponsible people who were out of touch with their age, but that it emerged from prevailing historic forces, the details being determined by wartime plans and agreements, military realities and by a series of compromises between differing views of what constituted a desirable balance of power.

2. Allied Diplomacy in Peacetime: the Failure of the Congress 'System', 1815–23

ROY BRIDGE

BETWEEN 1813 and 1815 the Fourth Coalition had succeeded, where all others had failed, in destroying French hegemony and restoring peace and a balance of power in Europe. Contemporaries attributed this success, at least in part, to the fact that, unlike their predecessors, the statesmen of the Fourth Coalition had been engaged in continuous personal contact. Tsar Alexander, for example, had left Russia with his armies in January 1813 and did not return until August 1814. Castlereagh lived on the continent for the greater part of eighteen months after January 1814; and his experience of what is now called summit diplomacy had left him a firm believer in 'the habits of confidential intercourse which a long residence with the principal actors has established and which gives facilities to my intervention to bring them together.'[1] The question in 1815 was whether these wartime habits of co-operation could survive once the great crisis had passed, or perhaps even be transformed into some rudimentary international organisation to safeguard the peace and the equilibrium.

The fact that France, even after her losses in 1814–15, remained, next to Russia, easily the strongest power on the continent, might point to the need for continuing allied co-operation – all the more so as France was notoriously dissatisfied with the 1815 Settlement. At a time when the draconic treaties of 1856, 1871 and 1919 still lay in the future, most Frenchmen, using the eighteenth century as their yardstick, regarded the 1815 Settlement as both harsh and unjust. The correspondence between the restored Bourbon kings and their foreign ministers[2] harps continually on the theme that France had been pushed back behind the frontiers of the *Ancien Régime* while Britain, Russia, Austria and Prussia had made considerable acquisitions since 1789: France would have to redress the balance, restore her influence in Italy and Spain, reach out, if the chance arose, for Belgium and the Rhine, and challenge Britain's supremacy on the seas and in the New World. The task would not be easy. France's very attempt to challenge Austrian domination of Italy was to force the Habsburgs to resume the role of hereditary enemies of the House of Bourbon; and as the British were determined to uphold Austria in both Italy and Germany as a barrier against revisionist France and ambitious Russia, a community of interest was to arise between Austria and Britain that was to be a formidable factor on the international scene.

Not that the French were without resources. Important people in Paris looked to a Franco-Russian combination, both to disrupt the obnoxious Quadruple Alliance and to further their revisionist aims. The disgraced Talleyrand might scoff at his successor, the duc de Richelieu, 'l'homme de France qui connait le mieu la Crimée'[3]: others expected very real achievements from the man who had served Alexander I as a brilliant governor of Odessa for a decade. And their position was all the more influential owing to the confused political situation in Restoration France. The annual supplementary elections prescribed by the Charter brought frequent changes of government; and the resultant succession of inexperienced political heads of the foreign office relied heavily on their permanent officials, people such as Rayneval, director of the political department and 'nôtre plus grand capacité diplomatique' ('our most talented diplomat'),[4] people who had made their careers under the Empire and who were revisionists to a man.

They were supported in turn by like-minded professionals in the Russian service: Pozzo di Borgo, Alexander's ambassador in Paris and a fanatical advocate of Franco-Russian collaboration; Tatischev, Russian ambassador at Madrid; even the Tsar's foreign minister, Capodistrias, a native of the Ionian Islands, now languishing under British military rule, and always interested in the Near East, where Britain, Austria, and Turkey conspired to hold the Balkan Christians in chains. Besides the revelation in 1814–15 of Russia's own ambitions in central Europe – her acquisitions in Poland, her exploitation of a network of dynastic connections in the German states, the intrigues of her diplomats against Austria in Italy, and the ever-present threat of a Russo-Turkish war, arising out of an albeit minor dispute about the interpretation of the Treaty of Bucharest, but nevertheless threatening to bring a Russian military and naval presence into the Balkans and the eastern Mediterranean – all these developments served to focus attention of the fundamental conflict between Russia's interests and those of Britain and Austria. It was not surprising, therefore, that

these latter powers were preoccupied with the threat of a Franco-
Russian combination.

The danger was undoubtedly real. In the first years of peace
Russian diplomats were searching constantly for a means of establishing a genuine world balance in place of the fraudulent balance of
1815, which, while it held France and Russia in check on the continent, left Britain supreme and unopposed throughout the rest of the
world. The solution they worked for was to bring France and Spain in
to play, and to establish international relations on the basis of the
Tsar's Holy Alliance (of which Britain was not even a member) or of a
general alliance of at least all five great powers. If this could be done,
France and Russia could between them hold the German Powers in a
pincer; and Russia, with the help of the Bourbon navies (and perhaps
of the United States), could set limits to Britain's supremacy overseas.
Against these projects, Castlereagh and Metternich stubbornly
insisted that the Quadruple Alliance of 20 November 1815 remain the
basis of conducting international affairs: its military and precaution-
ary provisions were directed solely against France, who was to remain
safely in quarantine; and the famous Article VI, which pledged the
allies 'to renew their meetings at fixed periods . . . for the purpose of
consulting upon their common interests'[5], could be used to confine
Russia in a strait-jacket and force her to march in unity with Britain
and the German powers.

The conflict between these two interpretations of the international
system was never far from the surface, even in the first years of peace
when the allies' relations with each other and with France were relatively harmonious. Until the summer of 1820 the Anglo-Austrian interpretation on the whole prevailed. At first the French did not dare
challenge it: Richelieu prudently decided that any open attempt by
France to foment strife would only drive the allies closer together, and
that for the present France should assume a studied passivity and wait
for the Alliance to dissolve itself. True, Pozzo di Borgo was intensely
irritated to find himself so often outvoted in the conference of ambassadors at Paris which supervised the occupation of France and the
fulfilment of her Treaty obligations. But essentially the allies were all
agreed on treating France leniently – if only because Britain and Austria did not dare let Russia pose as her sole defender. Wellington and
the Austrians could both see that the continuing occupation was
merely a source of bitterness and instability in French politics; and by
mid-1817 all were agreed that a congress should be summoned in the

following year to complete arrangements for the withdrawal of the army of occupation and to determine the future position of France in the Concert.

This last issue immediately revived the conflict between the Anglo-Austrian and Franco-Russian interpretations of the Alliance; and this was the issue that dominated the Congress of Aix-la-Chapelle (September–November 1818). As early as June, Capodistrias had begun to argue that it was time to return to the 'true principles of the independence of nations' and to abolish 'this kind of directory of four Powers who are arrogating to themselves the right to decide the affairs . . . of the rest of Europe without its participation'.[6] Pozzo di Borgo, too, saw an opportunity to scotch Metternich's efforts 'to keep France and Spain in a sort of political excommunication . . . in order to paralyse Russia'.[7] Castlereagh, however, while prepared to admit to particular congresses powers whose affairs were being discussed, insisted that there could be no question of diluting the Quadruple Alliance itself by admitting other powers to it; and Metternich similarly declared that the peace of Europe was 'intimately bound up with the maintenance of the Quadruple Alliance in its primitive integrity'.[8] By appealing to the Tsar over the heads of his ministers, and by depicting France as a dangerous revolutionary power – a favourite and effective ploy–Metternich even had hopes of getting Russia into line. Richelieu, however, was not so easily defeated. He insisted[9] that he could

no longer consent to receive notes signed collectively by the ministers of the four Powers. This Areopagus sitting at Paris and discussing the affairs of Europe and of France herself can no longer exist unless France forms part of it. If this surveillance is to be tolerable, it must be reciprocal: France may be called on to suppress a revolution in Prussia just as much as Prussia to suppress trouble in France.

He went to Aix with instructions to secure the abolition of the Quadruple Alliance; and his hopes rose when on 14 October Capodistrias proposed the formation of an 'Alliance Generale' of all the signatories of the 1815 Settlement, to control the affairs of Europe and to guarantee to all sovereigns their territories and thrones.

Castlereagh would have none of this. He was aware of the suspicion with which his fellow-countrymen viewed his association with continental statesmen, and he despaired of bringing Parliament to accept any new treaty, even if its political implications had not been so objectionable. He demanded, therefore, the renewal of the Quadruple Alliance unchanged, although, rather than leave France to make trouble in isolation, he was prepared to admit her to any future conferences summoned under Article VI. Metternich agreed. He was tempted by the prospect of an alliance to guarantee all thrones, but he was even more alive to the fact that a general alliance would open the door to Franco-Russian collaboration. Indeed, he went even further than Castlereagh: no general alliance existed, he declared; there had only been a coalition against Napoleon. In the end it was essentially Castlereagh's solution that was adopted; and although he had been forbidden by the Cabinet to subscribe to any system of periodic conferences (which Canning termed 'new and . . . very questionable')[10] he nevertheless joined with the four other governments in signing the Declaration of Aix-la-Chapelle. This established Article VI of the Quadruple Alliance as the basis for any future congresses, and Castlereagh left Aix well content: the Congress, a 'most decided proof of the advantage of bringing together from time to time the principal cabinets', had done much that could not be done 'by the ordinary course of diplomatic intercourse'.[11] Metternich was equally pleased: 'Je n'ai jamais vu de plus joli petit congrès' ['I have never seen a prettier little congress'].[12]

Not so Richelieu. True, he had with Russian help managed to prevent the Allies from actually publishing their renewal of the Quadruple Alliance. But that was about all. He was bitterly resentful of the British – there had been unpleasant exchanges about rights of search to control the slave trade, and Britain and Austria had crushed a French initiative to put economic pressure on the rebellious Spanish colonies; but he was especially scathing about the 'completely absurd' attitude of Metternich, whose devotion to the Quadruple Alliance was solely attributable to his 'fear of Russia . . . an *idée fixe* which preoccupies him incessantly'.[13] The Tsar, however, could not be thanked enough: as Richelieu impressed on Louis XVIII, 'il faudrait baiser les traces de ses pas'.[14] The King would do no such thing. He smarted over the fiasco of Aix-la-Chapelle, and in December replaced Richelieu by the liberal Decazes. Yet this only made France's position worse. Alexander, who took the dismissal of Richelieu as a personal slight, began to listen to Metternich's preaching about the unreliability and demoralisation of France; and as the British stood firm by the Austrian alignment, France fell into total isolation at the end of 1818.

In these circumstances the Anglo-Austrian combination was able to dominate Europe until the summer of 1820. In Germany, for example, it might have been expected that France and Russia, who had a common interest in maintaining the disunity and weakness of central Europe, and who were both guarantors of German liberties by the Treaty of Teschen of 1779, might combine to stiffen the lesser states against Habsburg pretensions. But they failed to co-operate, and Metternich was able to take advantage of a few disturbances both to play on Alexander's fears of revolution and to check what really did worry him in Germany – the move towards constitutionalism on the part of some German governments. The king of Prussia, exasperated by incessant criticism from those whose hopes of the War of Liberation had been disappointed, was beginning to look to Metternich as the saviour of the established order, and from 1819 Metternich was able to secure the appointment of his lieutenants to ministerial posts in Berlin, and generally to get control of Prussian policy.[15] This was shown at Teplitz (29 July–1 August) where he prevailed on Frederick William III to adopt a conservative policy in all German questions; and at Carlsbad (6 August–1 September) where he got most of the other princes into line. Although no formal congress had been summoned, Metternich's diplomatic tactics – face to face negotiations with those who had the power of decision-making – were of a piece with the tactics he had used at Aix and was to use again at Troppau. And the effect was much the same. The French were dismayed to see him dictating to the German states; and Capodistrias, encouraged by wild talk in the British Parliament, summoned the western powers to join Russia in a protest. It was all futile. Although Castlereagh tactfully advised Austria and Prussia to avoid bullying the south German states into Russia's arms, he was in fact well pleased to see Austrian influence strengthened in central Europe.

It was indeed difficult to see what France and Russia could do to wrest control from the Anglo-Austrian combination. Even when they showed signs of becoming active – as in the spring of 1820 when a military revolt in Spain forced Ferdinand VII to restore the extreme constitution of 1812 – they came up against the same blank opposition in London and Vienna. Richelieu, for example, who returned to power in February 1820, ably seconded by the Bonapartist Pasquier at the foreign office, embarked on a bold policy of *expansion de la Charte*,[16] attempting to establish French influence in Spain by persuading Ferdinand to opt for a constitution like that of

France. But in the face of British intrigues in Madrid the plan came to nothing. In April the Russians proposed that the Alliance should take the matter in hand. But Metternich, always fearful lest France use the Spanish Question to break free from the control of the Alliance, and convinced by reports of Russian intrigues in Italy and Germany that any intervention in which Russia had a hand was bound to injure Austrian interests, declared for a policy of 'magisterial inaction': let the revolution consume itself in its own fury.[17] Castlereagh, for his part, was opposed to any intervention whatever in the internal affairs of other states that did not pose a threat to the 1815 Settlement; and his devastating State Paper of 5 May 1820,[18] deploring intervention in Spain and issuing a general warning against attempts to pervert the Alliance for purposes for which it was not intended, heralded yet another humiliating defeat for France and Russia.

But if Britain and Austria could co-operate effectively in a negative sense to thwart French and Russian initiatives in Spain, it remained to be seen whether they could do so when positive action was demanded. In July a military *coup* forced Ferdinand IV of the Two Sicilies to proclaim the radical Spanish constitution of 1812. This, unlike events in Spain, seemed to Metternich a clear threat to Austria. If the revolution were allowed to establish itself in the South, the contagion would soon spread to northern Italy and Germany, undoing all Metternich's work of the last two years. With constitutions established in the Italian and German states, the Austrian monarchy, held together only by an absolutist dynasty, would itself be endangered. The Austrians, therefore, prepared to intervene – as in international law they had every right to do, by virtue of the Austro-Neapolitan Treaty of 1815 which had debarred Ferdinand from introducing constitutional changes without Austrian consent. Yet in so far as the Neapolitan revolt was but one symptom of an international movement and it was important to discourage revolutionaries everywhere, Metternich hoped too for a demonstration of moral support from the other powers. In London he was not disappointed. Wellington told the Austrian ambassador that the time had come to make an example: 80,000 troops would suffice; and Castlereagh, while pointedly insisting that this was no question for the Alliance to take up, readily recognised both the threat to Austria and her clear right in international law to take single-handed action against it.

The French, of course, took a very different view. It might well be that Austria could claim that their motives were defensive: the fact remained that an Austrian military success in Naples would shift the balance of influence in Italy still further in Austria's favour. Even the anti-revolutionary Richelieu found it 'very tiresome to concede to Austria the right to dispose of Italy uncontrolled'.[19] Pasquier warned of the reaction of 'the whole of France'[20] if Austria were allowed to make herself mistress of Italy 'on the pretext', as Pozzo di Borgo put it, 'of punishing the revolutionaries'.[21] It was partly to ward off this danger, therefore, that the French decided to work for a collective intervention. Was not Naples a case, Richelieu innocently asked, 'for one of those meetings envisaged by the agreements of Aix-la-Chapelle?'[22] But there was more to it than this. As a French Circular of 10 August[23] announced, it was France who was primarily affected by events in Naples – owing to the dynastic link with the Neapolitan Bourbons – and it was therefore up to France to propose a congress. '*Expansion de la Charte*' was again in vogue in Paris: if collective intervention could establish in Naples a moderate constitutional regime, Pasquier calculated, France would automatically appear as its protector; and Metternich's whole absolutist structure in Germany and Italy would be shaken. Moreover any collective intervention whatsoever would have the happy result of dividing Austria from Britain, leaving France and Russia to dominate the congress. Metternich, for his part, tried desperately to head the French off, suggesting a simple conference of ambassadors at Vienna to endorse Austrian action in Naples; but a French mission to Warsaw won Alexander over, and on 31 August the Tsar declared for a full congress on the model of Aix-la-Chapelle.

This brought the conflict between the British and the Franco-Russian points of view into the open. As Castlereagh complained to the French ambassador on 22 September:[24]

The Emperor Alexander wants to make all questions into questions for the Alliance. The five Powers would thereby become a general government of Europe. . . . The terms [*cas*] of the Alliance have been determined [*prévus*] at Paris and Aix-la-Chapelle and cannot be extended. To apply them to all revolutionary events . . . is to pervert the principle. It is the Holy Alliance as conceived by the emperor and which we cannot adopt.

The powers should try rather to avoid debating principles and concentrate on specific cases: otherwise 'England will be obliged to withdraw from the Alliance.'

Any hopes Metternich may have entertained of securing the united support of the Alliance were now lost, and he was faced with a choice between acting alone and yielding to French and Russian demands for collective intervention. The arguments in favour of the latter course, although unpalatable, were overwhelming. On the one hand, the Tory government in London, even if it survived the crisis over Queen Caroline's trial, could give little more than moral support. On the other, if France openly opposed Austrian policy in Italy, the hydra there would grow; and open opposition from Russia would encourage revolutionaries everywhere – even if it were at all conceivable for Austria to commit forces to Italy with huge and hostile Russian forces on her northern frontier. Moreover a blank rejection of the proposals of France and Russia would simply drive those two powers together. Compliance with their demands, however, would still leave him the chance to practice that personal diplomacy at which he so excelled, perhaps even to get control of Russian policy by appealing to Alexander against his ministers and the French. Not that he had any intention of severing those links with Castlereagh that had served him so well since 1815. But if he could also establish control over the Tsar he could feel even more secure. This thought was to dominate Metternich's policy from the summer of 1820 until it was proved to be a chimera at Verona. Certainly it explains his decision in September 1820 to drop his proposed conference of ambassadors and agree to a full-dress congress at Troppau.

Even so, his opponents – the 'liberal' Capodistrias and both French and Russian exponents of a Franco-Russian *entente* – were not defeated yet. True, the French were in a difficult position, torn between the need to maintain contact with the eastern powers, especially Russia, in order to maintain France's position in the Pentarchy, and the fear that too close an association with reaction might hand to England the *beau rôle* of patron of liberty in Italy and Europe. They decided in the end to imitate the British in sending representatives to the Congress only as observers; but at the same time they instructed them to secure Russian support for a strict control of any Austrian intervention, and for the establishment in Naples of a *'constitution sage'*.[25] Their hopes rose high, therefore, when Capodistrias made his first formal proposal to the Congress in a memorandum of 2 November.

According to this, any Austrian intervention must be preceded by an allied attempt to reconcile King Ferdinand and his people on the basis of 'the establishment of an order of things which would guarantee the realisation of an authentically national desire'.[26]

Metternich's counter-offensive was facilitated by the procedure adopted at Troppau – a series of private meetings between statesmen of the eastern powers with only occasional formal sessions when the French and British observers attended and listened. Metternich was thus able steadily to work on Alexander in long nightly tea-drinking sessions alone with him. The Tsar's recent unhappy experiences with the Polish diet had already dampened his fervour for constitutions, and Metternich skilfully exploited his disillusionment both to discredit the idea of constitutionalist intervention in Naples and to drive a wedge between the Tsar and the advocates of Franco-Russian collaboration. Every day, according to the disconsolate La Ferronnays, Metternich bombarded the Tsar with documents about secret societies and French intrigues in Italy, all proofs that 'the whole of Europe was threatened by the revolutionary spirit that was still alive in France'.[27] Faced with Capodistrias's memorandum, Metternich determined to concede the point of principle to gain the point of substance: while admitting that intervention was a matter not for individual powers but for the Alliance, he sought to eliminate, in the case of Naples, its constitutional overtones. When the Capodistrias memorandum was transformed into the Troppau Protocol of 19 November, therefore, it proclaimed – to the dismay of the isolated British – that it was the business of the Alliance to take revolutions in hand. Metternich even conceded, in the Neapolitan case, an attempt at a mediatory peace overture. But all reference to 'authentically national desires' had disappeared: the aim of intervention would be to free the King 'to consolidate his power so as to offer guarantees of calm and stability to Naples and to Europe'.[28] It remained to be seen at Laibach – whither the Congress now adjourned to meet King Ferdinand – whether Capodistrias and the French would be able to make anything of the peace overture; but Metternich had won the first round.

In fact, once Metternich had won the Tsar over at Troppau, his triumph over the French at Laibach was a foregone conclusion. Already in December the news of a mutiny in St Petersburg had put Alexander in so reactionary a mood that Capodistrias found himself, Metternich was pleased to note, 'like a devil in holy water' at

Laibach.[29] Equally the Neapolitans' rejection of the advice of Ferdinand and the French to opt for the French Charter (which Metternich admitted would have been 'terribly embarrassing'[30]) and their insistence on the extreme 1812 constitution, made it easier for Metternich to scoff at French talk of establishing a 'reasonable and appropriate government in Naples': one could not mediate between vice and virtue; the Neapolitans, 'un peuple a-demi africain et barbare' [a barbarous half-African people] were clearly unfitted for liberalism.[31] Consequently the Congress of Laibach saw no serious attempt at mediation whatsoever. Even the Journal of the Congress, purporting to record negotiations with King Ferdinand, has recently been shown to have been a sham, concocted after the Congress had decided to give Austria a free hand to undertake a simple reactionary intervention.[32] The last despairing attempts of the French to assert their influence – joining with Russia and Prussia in attaching a commissioner to the expeditionary force; currying favour with Ferdinand by appointing his 'tutelary angel',[33] the reactionary Blacas, as minister to Naples, were the merest token gestures. It was in vain that Pasquier rebuked the French delegation at Laibach for their supineness, and complained that France had only participated in order 'to keep the scourge of war from Italy'.[34] Such language only deepened the rift between the French and the Tsar, who was already irritated by French reluctance to follow Austria's example and invade Spain. Well might Boislecomte look back in disgust on the Congress of Laibach, where 'j'ai vu le prince de Metternich dans tout l'orgueil de son triomphe' [I have seen Prince Metternich in the full flush of his triumph].[35]

The aftermath of the Congress saw the culmination of Metternich's triumph as he strengthened his hold on the Tsar, and the final discomfiture of the French. The Neapolitan expedition went off smoothly, establishing Austrian influence – but no constitution – in Naples and an Austrian military presence in Tuscany and the Papal States; and in so far as it provoked a revolt in Piedmont which was suppressed by the Austrians with the approval of the Congress in March, it ultimately established Austrian military surveillance over the whole of Italy. The French, for their part, continued their disastrous policy of half measures, failing to enhance their influence in Italy, but doing just enough to confirm their isolation in Europe. La Tour du Pin in Turin, for example, urged the Regent to adopt the French Charter and pleaded with his government to seize the chance to establish a constitutionalist alliance of Iberian and Italian states against Austria and Russia. But the government in Paris had no stomach for such a confrontation, and the bourse was in a panic until news arrived of the suppression of the Piedmontese revolution. An attempt, encouraged by British parliamentary speeches, to secure British diplomatic co-operation was rebuffed by Castlereagh and used by Metternich to keep Alexander's suspicions of France alive. The issuing of passports to fleeing rebels by the French legations in Naples and Turin was naturally grist to Metternich's mill; as was the news of the Greek revolt, which reached Laibach in April. For, if most of the Italian rebels had fled to France, a number had gone to Greece, 'that vast sewer open to all revolutionaries'.[36] And the Greek revolt itself was, according to Metternich, only another aspect of the work of the direct-ing revolutionary committee in Paris. 'It is at Paris, Sire,' he told the Tsar, 'that the great furnace exists . . . for the most vast conspiracy that has ever threatened the whole of society.'[37] It was not surprising, therefore, that the sovereigns of Laibach assured the Turks that they would give no support to the rebels, who were acting contrary to the principles of Troppau; and that when Alexander and his fellow sover-eigns issued their final pronouncements before leaving Laibach on 13 May, the French were not consulted at all.

It is sometimes argued that Metternich paid a high price for his triumph: he had estranged Britain. Certainly the debate that arose over the general principles enunciated at Troppau lacked nothing in warmth. Castlereagh made it clear that Hanoverian Britain could never endorse the Troppau Protocol with its sweeping condemnation of revolutions; he rejected out of hand the claim that intervention was the duty of the Alliance; and he officially declared the Protocol to be a violation of international law.[38] Yet the significance of this theoretical debate should not be exaggerated. In terms of the practical issues of the day, the fundamental community of interests between Britain and Austria had not been affected at all. The French appreciated this per-fectly, as they contrasted Metternich's reactions to their own and Castlereagh's criticism: Britain 'has the right to say anything; she and Austria are like college friends, who can say anything to each other without breaking up (se brouiller)'.[39] British observers had after all gone to Laibach; Castlereagh had done nothing to hinder Austria's progress in Naples; and over Piedmont he had coldly rebuffed French criticisms of Metternich. As the Greek Question came to the fore in the summer, so did the Anglo-Austrian community of interests. Both Castlereagh and Metternich were determined not to allow the rebellion to exacerbate the long-standing Russo-Turkish dispute over the Treaty of Bucharest to the point of war. Indeed Castlereagh lost no time in reinforcing Metternich's efforts at Laibach, writing a personal letter to Alexander begging him to stand firm with his allies against the Revolution, and to give no countenance to the Greek revolt, which was merely 'a branch of the organized spirit of insurrection'.[40]

This advice was timely. Once back in St Petersburg, Alexander came under other influences: military circles, the Orthodox Church, and the ubiquitous Mme de Krudener, now a fervent advocate of a Holy War to rescue the Greeks. Castlereagh and Metternich were dismayed to learn that on 18 July the Russian ambassador at Constantinople had presented the Porte with a long list of grievances and an eight-day time limit. They would have been even more concerned had they known that on the following day Alexander had sent for the French ambassador to tell him that France ought to abandon her traditional friendship for Turkey: 'c'est la Russie que la France doit avoir comme allié' ['It is Russia that France should have as an ally'].[41] These enigmatic words naturally caused a stir in the French foreign office, where Rayneval urged Richelieu to seize the chance: a war over the Eastern Question would offer plenty of chances for pickings, and France could re-establish herself in Belgium and the Rhineland. Even Richelieu admitted that the moment was favourable to secure for France by diplomacy 'the position that belongs to her'.[42] But in the end his acquaintance with the Tsar's changeable personality determined him to await a firmer offer from St Petersburg. This was wise: although by mid-August Stroganov had demonstrably left Constantinople, Alexander was now fearful that 'if we reply to the Turks with war, the Committee in Paris will triumph and no government will be left on its feet.'[43] Not that Metternich could feel sure of the Russians even now. He was planning a conference, either in Vienna, or in Hanover (where he had arranged to meet Castlereagh in October) in order to 'group' Alexander and the French and control them. But after their humiliations at Laibach the French would not hear of another conference, and Alexander too declined the invitation. The Hanover meeting was thus confined to Metternich and Castlereagh.

Despite its restricted scope, the diplomacy of the Hanover meeting was not qualitatively different from that of the Congress of Troppau.

As with Alexander then, so now with Castlereagh, it was for Metternich a question of co-ordinating policy through direct personal contact with an old wartime colleague: 'I shall achieve more in a few days
. . . than in six months of writing'.[44] And as at Troppau, it was not so
much a question of opposing Alexander as of guiding him, above all of
eliminating the influence of Capodistrias. The upshot was a series of
appeals to Alexander – not too obviously co-ordinated, lest he become
suspicious – in which Metternich emphasised conservative solidarity
and the unity of the Alliance, and Castlereagh concentrated on the
practical dangers inherent in a Russo-Turkish war. At the same time,
British and Austrian diplomats in Turkey struggled to persuade the
Porte to concede most of the Russian demands of July; and a supreme
diplomatic effort by Castlereagh and Metternich eventually succeeded in bringing even the French into line.

This last development naturally exasperated those in Paris who
had seen in the Eastern Question a chance to recover the Rhine frontier, and in December they combined with the Ultras to bring Richelieu down. But although the new Ultra government under Villèle
agreed with Richelieu's critics that France was 'being kept within
narrow limits, while since 1789 Russia, England, and Austria had
expanded by a third', they shrank from the risks of an actively revisionist foreign policy – a new European war would mean 'the ruin of
the social order in the old world'.[45] They decided for the time-being to
follow Metternich's lead. Capodistrias sarcastically congratulated
them on their wisdom: Britain and Austria had after all done so much
for France in the past.[46] But his fury was to no avail. Although in the
spring of 1822 the Tsar was again angling for support in a war against
Turkey, and sent Tatischev on a special mission to Vienna, Metternich gave him only the vaguest verbal assurance of diplomatic support, and even that was conditional on the unanimity of the great
powers – a hopeless prospect. As the French maintained their new
reserve, the Tsar at last gave up. In June he agreed to leave all
decisions on the Eastern Question to a conference which Metternich
was trying to arrange at Vienna in the autumn. Metternich's chances
of containing Russia within the Alliance were further improved when
Castlereagh managed to secure the Cabinet's permission to attend in
person; and when Capodistrias embarked on an extended leave of
absence in August: 'Well, General,' Metternich wrote to the British
governor of the Ionian Islands, 'the principle of evil has been uprooted. Count Capodistrias is buried for the rest of his days.'[47] The

Emperor Francis 'would have cut off his head'.[48]

Although Castlereagh's suicide (12 August) was a blow to Metternich, who had come to count on him as his 'second self'[49] over the past nine years; and although Wellington's late arrival at the Vienna conference meant that its business had to be deferred to the congress arranged to review Italian developments at Verona, Anglo-Austrian co-operation continued, at least in the Eastern question, until the end of the year. Moreover this co-operation was still necessary, despite the fall of Capodistrias: Alexander seemed to favour the admission of the Greek provisional government to the negotiations; and when the Turks started interfering with Russian shipping in the Straits, he angrily declared that 'these affairs shall be ended only by cannon fire'.[50] But Canning continued Castlereagh's policy of separating the Greek Question from Russia's justified grievances about treaty rights; and on the latter point the Verona powers succeeded in calming the Tsar by successfully applying diplomatic pressure on the laggardly Turks. As for the Greek revolt, the Tsar was impressed by Metternich's ample supply of 'frightful information'[51] about the intrigues of philhellene societies all over Europe, and readily acceded to the final Verona Circular which condemned the revolt as a 'rash and criminal enterprise',[52] yet another example of that spirit of rebellion recently in evidence in Naples and Piedmont. Even as late as the spring of 1823, therefore, Anglo-Austrian co-operation to 'group' the Tsar and restrain him from action in the Near East could still succeed.

On this occasion, however, Metternich had to pay a higher price for his success than at Troppau and Laibach. The very emphasis he had placed on Alliance solidarity in order to restrain the Russians, was now turned against him. If Alexander had accepted the Anglo-Austrian argument that war against Turkey would shatter the Alliance and play into the hands of revolutionaries everywhere, he was in turn entitled to demand that the Alliance should prove its usefulness and effectiveness by crushing the nest of revolutionaries in Spain. Moreover, by focusing attention on a practical case of Alliance intervention in the west, he might be able to break up that Anglo-Austrian combination that was thwarting him in the east. The Tsar's decision to abandon Capodistrias and yield to Anglo-Austrian advice coincided with a diplomatic campaign to restore Russia's reputation by greater activity in western Europe.

The king of Spain's incessant appeals to the powers offered plenty of opportunities. As early as February 1822, the French had suggested that the Conference of Ambassadors at Paris keep an eye on developments in Spain. But Britain and Austria, ever suspicious of manoeuvres to increase French influence in Spain, had forbidden this. They also killed a Russian proposal of April for intervention in Spain by an allied army. In this case, the French too were opposed: they would not hear of Russian troops marching through France; and they were now hoping that a moderate regime might after all establish itself in Spain, perhaps with a constitution like the Charter. They were greatly discomfited, therefore, when in July the most extreme elements seized power in Madrid. Clearly Spain would have to be on the agenda for the forthcoming Vienna conference.

The instructions drawn up for the French delegate, Montmorency, on 30 August, show that in the Spanish question Villèle was above all concerned to reserve France's freedom of action, or inaction: 'to emancipate France from the humiliating control of foreigners and to assert her independence and influence'.[53] In no circumstances, therefore, could France accept the role of an agent of the Alliance as Austria had done at Troppau and Laibach. Indeed, Villèle, with an eye on French finances, would have preferred no military action whatever in Spain. But, obviously, a gesture of moral support from the Alliance would be useful in impressing London. Moreover Montmorency, in contrast to Villèle, was resigned to the inevitability of French military intervention, and not too scrupulous about maintaining French independence if it were a question of buying allied support; and Chateaubriand, who joined him at Verona, although inordinately jealous of French independence, was equally warlike. All this meant that French policy would be as confused as at Troppau. The Alliance itself, meanwhile, was in total disarray: the Tsar arrived at Vienna with a plan for an international army to crush the Spanish revolution; whereas the British were pledged to 'a rigid abstinence from any interference in the internal affairs' of Spain.[54] Metternich's chances of preserving the unity of the Alliance were slim.

On the eve of the Vienna conference, which early in October merged into the Congress of Verona, Metternich's dilemmas were indeed appalling. Ideally, he would have liked to see the Spanish revolution crushed, but not by a French military intervention that might see the establishment of the Charter in Spain, with disastrous repercussions in Italy. Equally dangerous, the French army might fail in Spain, whereupon the revolution would spread to France itself. The prospect of Russian troops marching across Europe was, if anything, even more alarming (although France and Britain could probably be relied on to prevent this). Moreover, action of any kind in the name of the Alliance would mean a breach with the British whom he needed to restrain Russia in the east. On the other hand, inaction seemed equally perilous. The Tsar was emphatic that 'if the Congress separates without adopting a common policy, revolutionaries everywhere will be convinced that we cannot agree on one and that our union is broken. The only aim of the Alliance is that for which it was formed, to combat Revolution.'[55] And how long would Alexander remain loyal to an Alliance that simply thwarted his own plans and was itself incapable of taking any effective action?

Metternich's diplomatic campaign at Verona had to be skilfully planned. Essentially he sought to reduce the possibilities for military intervention to one, namely the French plan; then to eliminate that as demonstrably impractical; and finally to demonstrate the unity of the Alliance by some moral gesture strong enough to satisfy France and Russia, but not so strong as to alienate Britain.

He was, of course, only too willing to let others take the lead against Russia, and by 20 October Alexander, faced with a French veto on the passage of Russian troops, and British objections to any intervention whatsoever, had abandoned his plan for international military action. Not that Metternich missed any chances to drive France and Russia further apart: 'Beware of the emperor', he warned the French, 'because he mistrusts you', and only wanted to intervene in Spain 'in order to take away your Charter and your liberties' on the way home.[56] And his language to Alexander about the dangers of French intervention served a similar double purpose: 'How can France talk of war when her army is infected with a revolutionary spirit?' Even if she succeeded in Spain, 'then would not France, intoxicated by her victories, regain a taste for the old ideas of conquests?'[57] He was determined not to allow France a free hand, even in the diplomatic field. While Villèle was insisting that 'we have taken charge of Spain ourselves',[58] Metternich managed to inveigle Montmorency into asking the Congress for its advice; and by 22 October he had got the Russians and Prussians to agree with him 'that France must consider herself the agent of the Grand Alliance, and that the question of Spain is entirely European'.[59] The difficulty still remained, however, that if Alexander were to be kept in line, something would have to be done about 'the question of Spain'.

It seemed that Metternich had squared the circle when he brought the French to agree to join the three eastern powers in a demonstration of moral solidarity. The four powers were to send notes to the Spanish government in such provocative language – the Prussian despatch, for example, spoke of the 'frightful sickness' in Spain[60] – as would 'unfailingly' lead to a rupture of diplomatic relations.[61] But that was the limit of the agreement. Although Alexander readily promised France full support should she be forced to go to war in Spain, Metternich's pronouncements on that subject were so riddled with loopholes as to be meaningless. The whole agreement, in fact, rested on an equivocation: whereas Alexander and the French delegation saw it as a preparatory step towards war, Metternich hoped that the despatches would suffice to overawe the revolutionaries and restore the King's control, thereby averting all need for further action. Moreover, even this moral demonstration was too much for the British, who roundly condemned the 'insulting' despatches and announced that they would henceforth confine themselves to 'allaying the ferment which these communications must occasion'.[62] Metternich's hopes of conjuring up an illusion of Allied unity by means of a moral demonstration had failed.

Worse, the demonstration even failed in its more practical purpose, of fending off single-handed intervention by France in Spain. Metternich might be a consummate master of the closed world of congress diplomacy, but he was not in command of Europe: he might be able to handle a confused and disunited trio of French diplomats at Verona, but that was not to say that he could handle France. On his return to Paris, Montmorency was disavowed by Villèle who felt he had shown himself both too warlike and too subservient to the allies. He was succeeded at the foreign office by Chateaubriand, notoriously a fanatic for the independence of French policy, but also – unbeknown to Villèle – even more warlike than Montmorency. Chateaubriand ostentatiously refused to send the French note to Madrid simultaneously with that of the allies; and from January 1823 worked remorselessly for a war that might establish French control, and even a version of the French constitutional system, at Madrid. Metternich, who had left the Congress of Verona thinking he had limited France to a moral gesture within the framework of the Alliance, found himself confronted with France military action outside the Alliance.

His desperate efforts in Paris, London, and St Petersburg to stave it off came to nothing. France, Russia, and Britain had all escaped him. The Pentarchy itself was now in full dissolution. Assured of the support of Russia, and in defiance of the wishes of three other members, France invaded Spain in April. 'Our true policy', Chateaubriand declared, 'is the Russian policy, by which we counterbalance two declared enemies: Austria and England.'[63] The French view of the world had not changed since 1815. This was clear from the discussions on subordinate issues at Verona. The French were ferocious in their opposition to British proposals regarding the Spanish colonies, or the policing of the seas against the slave trade (according to Chateaubriand a ruse 'to attack with impunity all the navies of the world').[64] Their support for the resistance of the Italians, who, according to the papal delegate 'almost without distinction of sect or party detested Austria and groaned from the subjugation in which she held Italy',[65] was also nothing new.

What was new by 1823 was that Britain and Austria were no longer able to co-operate to hold France and Russia in check. If, at Verona, Canning had had to implement a policy outlined by Castlereagh and approved by the Cabinet, he asserted himself once the Congress was over. Not only was he a complete stranger to the habits of co-operation that Castlereagh, Metternich, and Alexander had established in eight years of personal contact, and which had constituted the essence of congress diplomacy, but he detested Metternich and disliked congresses on principle. Much as he disapproved of the invasion of Spain, he welcomed the fact that it had not proceeded from 'an assumed jurisdiction of the Congress'.[66] 'The issue of Verona', he noted with satisfaction, 'has split the one and indivisible alliance, and so things are getting back to a wholesome state again'.[67] Metternich, for his part, despaired of Britain who, 'gangrenous to the bones with the revolutionary spirit, now shows herself naked to the world'.[68] Anglo-Austrian co-operation, cornerstone of the 1815 system, was dead. And with the entire Pentarchy in such chaos, congress diplomacy itself lost its attractions for Metternich: 'before talking about congresses', he testily reminded Gentz, 'it is necessary to come to an accord on many matters, and the way to do this is through simple conferences'.[69] In 1823 there was no sign of any such 'accord'. The era of the congresses was over.

In relation to the period 1815 to 1823 as a whole, the term 'era of the congresses' is perhaps misleading, in that it focuses too much attention on the congresses themselves. Certainly, the term 'congress system' is a misnomer. The congresses did not constitute a new system of international organisation. Their place in the history of international relations is as precursors of the summit conference, not of the League of Nations. Moreover they were themselves only part of the seamless web of interacting and conflicting interests that make up the substance of diplomacy, and cannot be understood outside that context. Between 1815 and 1820 the chief issue in international relations was the struggle between the Anglo-Austrian and French and Russian interpretations of the international system; and the Congress of Aix-la-Chapelle was simply one aspect of that struggle. Equally in 1820 Metternich decided, congress or no congress, that Austro-Russian co-operation offered a better chance of restraining Russia than Anglo-Austrian resistance, and this was reflected in the emergence of the conservative Neo-Holy Alliance of the three eastern monarchies at Troppau and Laibach. But both the *rapport* he established with Alexander at Troppau, and that which he re-established with Castlereagh at Hanover, failed him in the end; and in 1822–23 he suffered a signal defeat at the hands of a Franco-Russian combination that was to dominate European affairs for most of the 1820s. The congresses of 1818 to 1822 are really of a piece with the round-table talks between the Allies in 1814 and 1815. They were essentially an expression of the desire of Metternich, Castlereagh, and Alexander to manage their differences in peacetime by the methods that had served them so well in the wartime coalition; and their success depended not only on the continuation in power of these personalities, but on the continuance of the wartime diplomatic constellation, above all, the isolation of France. By the mid-1820s two members of the great triumvirate who had made the 1815 Settlement had passed from the scene. Not only were international problems becoming more acute as France revived and the conflict of interests intensified, the statesmen who were called on to deal with them were uninterested in, if not temperamentally averse to, round-table talks with Metternich. After 1823 it was, as Canning triumphantly declared, 'every nation for itself and God for us all'.[70]

3. The Great Powers and the Iberian Peninsula, 1815–48

ROGER BULLEN

In the early nineteenth century the word 'intervention' was used by statesmen and diplomats to describe the use of force by one state in the internal affairs of another. Until 1849 when the Russian army intervened in Hungary, part of the Habsburg Monarchy, to suppress the revolt led by Kossuth, the great powers had intervened only in the internal affairs of their smaller neighbours.[1] Metternich, whose concept of intervention was extremely wide-ranging, admitted that 'it is not by means of foreign cannon that revolution in a big state can be stamped out.'[2] In so far as the principle of intervention was directed against a great power it was formulated by the three eastern powers of Austria, Russia and Prussia in the 1820s to provide a basis for intervention in France. In fact the French, with the support of the British government, claimed immunity from intervention. They were able to do so because they were capable of massive resistance to any attempt to intervene in their internal affairs. The duke of Wellington, the British prime minister, made this perfectly clear after the revolution of July 1830 in France. He warned the three eastern powers that they could not intervene in France, they could only go to war against her. France claimed immunity again in 1848. The following year Austria appealed for Russian assistance to suppress the Hungarian uprising. In 1830 and in 1848 the French governments, overthrown by revolution, had made no such appeals for support. Moreover Austria without Hungary was not a great power; Russian intervention in Hungary was not a diminution of Austria's great-power status but the means by which it could be restored.[3] Between 1815 and 1848 intervention was a device used by great powers to control and assist the governments of weaker states.

There was throughout this period a clear distinction between intervention and war. Although the great powers intervened many times in the internal affairs of small states, none of the acts of intervention were preceded by a declaration of war.[4] Intervention was not an act of aggression against another state but a measure of assistance to a beleagured friendly government. Indeed there was a manifest determination amongst the great powers to establish the principle that intervention by force in the internal affairs of another state was a legitimate and legal act. It derived its legitimacy from the assumption shared by all the powers that they were the self-appointed guardians of the peace of Europe. If it was the obligation of the great powers to maintain peace, it was argued that they had the right to see that it was not disturbed by others. These rights and obligations were based on accomplished facts and binding treaties. It was the four great powers – Austria, Great Britain, Russia and Prussia – who had defeated Napoleon and restored peace and idependence to the states of Europe. The Treaty of Chaumont of March 1814, renewed on four separate occasions before 1818, was the visible expression of their power and unity. At the Congress of Aix-la-Chapelle in 1818 France was admitted as an equal member into the ranks of the great powers and she based her claim for admission on the principle that she might be called upon to maintain order in her neighbouring states.[5] The legitimacy of intervention was therefore grounded in the rights which belonged to the great powers and the assumption that peace between states depended upon the maintenance of order within states. This unity of outlook was undermined in the 1820s and 1830s by disagreement amongst the great powers as to what constituted disorder and whether disorder in a particular country constituted a threat to the peace of Europe.

In the period 1818 to 1822 which was dominated by the three Congresses of Troppau, Laibach and Verona, conflict arose between the great powers on the question of the legal basis of intervention. The three eastern powers were anxious to establish two separate bases for intervention. Firstly they argued that an appeal for assistance from the governments of the state which was unable to suppress opposition to its rule was an essential preliminary to intervention. This, said Metternich, was a 'call for help on the strength of positive treaties' right'.[6] This transformed what would otherwise have been an act of aggression into a measure of police assistance. To this justification the three autocratic monarchies wished to add a second: that intervention should also be carried out in the name of the alliance of the five powers.[7] The case for a dual basis of intervention was enshrined in the Protocol of Troppau which the three eastern powers signed in

November 1820 but which Great Britain and France refused to sign. The two western powers claimed that the right to intervene rested solely on the appeal of the government in distress for assistance. They vigorously rejected the argument that a right of intervention belonged to the alliance of the five powers. Clearly they recognised two or more powers could act together if they so wished, but they could not claim to act in the name of the five. This difference between the powers was never formally resolved. In practice, however, the eastern powers were forced to abandon their claim to act in the name of the alliance when it became clear that the alliance no longer existed. In the Convention of Berlin of October 1833, signed by the three powers, the legal basis of intervention was based solely upon the right of independent sovereigns to call upon fellow monarchs for assistance.[8] In 1834 Great Britain and France acted upon exactly the same principle in the west when they responded to the appeals of the governments of Portugal and Spain for assistance. The Quadruple Alliance of April 1834 and its Additional Articles of July were the western equivalent of the Convention of Berlin.[9] By the 1830s there was no longer any substantial disagreement between the powers on the legal basis of intervention. The dispute between the great powers on this issue, in the decade after the Congress of Vienna, had in reality been about the nature and the purpose of the five-power alliance and a contest for its leadership. There never was a debate about the abstract principle of intervention and non-intervention between the great powers.

This debate was conducted within the political system of Great Britain and France. The three autocratic monarchies of eastern Europe did not tolerate public discussions of their foreign policies, especially when such discussions were likely to be critical of fundamental principles of policy. In Great Britain and France in the 1820s and 1830s the debate about intervention and non-intervention was part of the political conflict between liberals and conservatives. Until 1830 liberals in both countries attacked the policy of intervention as practised by all governments, particularly their own. They claimed that intervention denied the citizens of other states their essential civic liberties; the right to protest against arbitrary government and the right to demand constitutional reform being foremost among them.[10] Their case against intervention was not based on abstract principles of foreign policy but was derived from their political sympathies. Their real aim was to protect reform movements in other countries from suppression by outside forces. In the 1830s when

these same liberals were in power in Great Britain and France they
quickly abandoned non-intervention in order to afford protection to
liberal regimes which, they argued, were threatened by counter-revolution. It was then that the conservatives, who had earlier rejected the non-interventionist arguments of the liberals, adopted
them in the hope that their application would give the reactionary
forces in the small states of western Europe the opportunity to crush
their liberal opponents without fear of restraint by liberal great
powers.[11] It was only in the 1840s, when radicals began to attack the
concept of the balance of power and the traditional methods of great-
power politics, that there was a genuine debate about intervention
and non-intervention, but this was virtually confined to Great Britain.

The practice of intervention by the great powers reflected the fact
that at the Congress of Vienna the victorious allies had divided
Europe into informal spheres of influence; each great power was responsible for the maintenance of order in its own sphere. Conflicts
over intervention arose from fears of encroachment. In 1822 the Tsar
Alexander I offered to send a Russian army across Europe to suppress
the revolt in Spain. This was opposed by all the other powers; their
opposition was grounded in the fear that a Russian army passing
through central Europe to the west would undermine the influence
exercised by the other powers. It was the French who paid the least
respect to the spheres of influence of the other powers. At the Congress of Vienna the victorious allies had contained France in the west
by surrounding her with strong hostile states. Unless France
encroached upon the influence of the other powers she could not
create client states for herself. Once the French had established
preponderant influence over some of their smaller and weaker
neighbours, as they did for example in Spain in 1823, they were
equally anxious to ensure that other powers did not attempt to
weaken the position they had established. In the Convention of
Berlin of 1833 the three eastern powers clearly linked the practice of
intervention to their rights over their spheres of influence. They described themselves as the 'most appropriate powers to render aid'
in eastern and central Europe and asserted that no other power
could 'interfere with the aid which had been requested and
offered'.[12] This was an attempt to keep France out of Italy and
southern Germany. Great Britain and France were equally determined to exclude the eastern powers from intervention in the west.
Their real problem in the 1820s and 1830s was that they could not

agree on a satisfactory division of responsibility for intervention in this area between themselves.

By the 1830s Europe was divided into two zones; an eastern and central zone where the three autocratic monarchies intervened, and a western zone where Great Britain and France intervened. The practice of intervention was much the same in both areas. The only significant difference was that Great Britain, as a naval power, was not in a position to contemplate the prolonged occupation of another state. It was only the purpose of intervention which was different. The autocratic monarchies were determined to prevent political change in their spheres; to create a strong barrier against the eastward spread of western liberal and reforming ideas which they were convinced would destroy both respect for and the institutions of absolute monarchy. In the 1830s the British and the French manifested their determination to protect reform movements in the west from destruction by counter-revolution. In fact, therefore, both great-power groupings used exactly the same means to promote completely opposite ends. It was not surprising that hypocrisy should prevail in their attitude towards each other's interventions. The British and French condemned Russian policy in Poland and Austrian policy in Italy.[13] Similarly the eastern powers condemned western intervention in Spain and Portugal.[14] It was not the practice of intervention which was being attacked but the political ends it was designed to achieve.

For all the great powers intervention was the policy of last resort. None of them consciously set out to create in their neighbouring states the conditions which would justify their intervention. The great powers used force only when their regular means of controlling and regulating the internal affairs of their client state had failed. The normal means of exerting influence and, if necessary, control were diplomatic. The sovereigns of the great powers, their foreign ministers and their diplomats abroad regularly advised and guided the monarchs and governments of friendly smaller states on internal questions. The aim of this was twofold: to preserve the close connection between the great power and its neighbour and to maintain political stability in the small state. Queen Victoria's constant advice to the Queen of Portugal in the late 1830s and 1840s, and Palmerston's exhortations to the governments of Spain and Portugal in the same period, on the need for moderate reform were no different in kind from the advice which Nicholas I gave to his fellow autocrats, or from the guidance which Metternich offered to the governments of the lesser

German and Italian states. Intervention was a response to a political crisis over which both the great power and the government of the small state had lost control. It was disliked by the great powers because it involved considerable expense and its outcome was uncertain. The great power which sent a military force into another state could not predict the degree of resistance it would meet. It was therefore impossible accurately to assess the size of the force which would be needed. There were also problems of finance and supply for an army operating away from its home base but lacking the rights of requisition and billeting which normally operated in time of war. It was thus impossible to predict how long it would take to fulfil the purpose of the intervention, or, indeed, whether a prolonged period of occupation would be necessary. The occupation of a foreign country reduced the number of troops available for the maintenance of order at home. For some of the great powers, for example France in the 1830s, this was a very important consideration. In fact intervention raised many of the hazards of war; it was not lightly embarked upon.

The decision of a great power to intervene in a neighbouring state was sometimes forced upon it. Once they had established the principle of not allowing a friendly state 'to go to the dogs' as Palmerston put it[15], they presented the often inept and corrupt rulers of small states with a way out of difficulties of their own making. Intervention was demanded by the governments of the small states more often than it was offered by the great powers. The rulers of these states came to see intervention from outside as an alternative to political concession and compromise with their domestic opponents, or as a cheaper, easier and quicker military solution than the raising and organising of a force of their own. In a very real sense intervention was the price which the powers paid for their great-power status. In the years between 1815 and 1848 Great Britain and France intervened with either miitary or naval force five times in the internal affairs of Spain and Portugal. These five interventions created some and reflected other problems associated with intervention. They reveal the constant interaction between the crisis of order within the small states of Europe and the diplomacy of the great powers which was one of the most distinguishing characteristics of early nineteenth-century diplomacy.

In both Spain and Portugal the monarchies, restored in 1814 as a result of the British expulsion of the Napoleonic Army from the

Peninsula, attempted to reconstruct the old order in government and society. They were thoroughly imbued with the spirit of legitimism, zealous crusaders against change and the doctrines of change. This was a bold programme. They set themselves the tasks of wiping out the memory of military defeat, political collapse, popular agitation and liberal reform. Restoration at home was combined with the ideas of imperial recovery overseas and the reconquest of their lost empires in South America. These ambitious schemes of reconstruction at least required sound systems of public finance, efficient ministerial government and popular confidence in the restored regime, none of which they possessed. As far as imperial recovery in South America was concerned both governments needed the support of Great Britain, who could make or break any expeditions from Spain or Portugal to suppress colonial revolts by virtue of her command of the seas. The Spanish in particular refused British attempts to mediate between them and their rebel colonies. The government of Ferdinand VII was determined to reimpose Spanish sovereignty in South America in its entirety and by Spanish force alone. In 1819 the government at Madrid began to gather together in Andalusia a small force which it planned to send to South America in ships it had already purchased from Russia. It was at this point that the programme of domestic and imperial recovery collapsed. In January 1820 two junior officers in the army intended for South America 'pronounced' for the liberal constitution of 1812 which had been dismantled when the Bourbons returned in 1814. Spain was in revolt. The Restoration government proved incapable of destroying this challenge to its authority. For the next three years the five great powers continually discussed what they should do about the Spanish revolt. Spain, Canning said, had begun 'a war of opinions in Europe'.[17] This was only partly true; it was as much a question of great-power rivalry. The crisis in Spain became bound up with the Anglo-Russian struggle for the leadership of the new Europe, and with the efforts of France to break out of the limits imposed upon her in 1815. The political disturbances in Spain did not cause these great-power conflicts; they merely reflected them.

In the years between 1815 and 1820 Great Britain and Russia conducted a diplomatic contest on many fronts for the leadership of Europe. Although they had reached agreement on the making of the territorial order in 1814 and 1815, they subsequently began to look at what had been achieved at the Congress of Vienna from very different viewpoints. The essence of Castlereagh's policy was enshrined in the belief that the peace of Europe could only be preserved by the containment of France and Russia. Anglo-Austrian co-operation was the device he used to achieve this end. In his view the alliance of the four victorious powers – and after 1818 the extension of the alliance to include France – was useful in so far as it kept alive the spirit and practice of co-operation and could be dominated by Britain and Austria. The Russians resented Castlereagh's attempt to control them by his *entente* with Austria and were determined to expose the inconsistency between the British policy of the balance of power in Europe and the unrestrained naval dominance of Great Britain on the high seas. This was why the Russians sold ships to the Spanish for their expedition to South America. If Spain could recover her naval and colonial power she, with the co-operation of France, could begin to challenge the Atlantic supremacy of Great Britain. The Russians were equally anxious to create a new power grouping in Europe which would act as a counterweight to the Anglo-Austrian *entente*. Russian policy towards the Spanish revolt was thus determined by her anti-British bias. At the Congress of Troppau this was given a new twist when the Russians saw the opportunity of separating Great Britain and Austria on the right of intervention. The British rejected the existence of a general right belonging to the alliance and insisted that it was for individual powers to act according to their interests.[19] From the Congress of Troppau to the Congress of Verona the Russian government used the Spanish issue as a means of driving a wedge between Great Britain and Austria and as a means of upholding the principles enshrined in the Protocol of Troppau, in the hope of creating a new great-power combination of autocratic monarchies which Russia would lead.

To European conservatives the Spanish revolt revealed the conspiratorial nature of revolution and its contagious character. The revolt was led by officers who exploited the grievances of the people and exposed the fragile nature of authority in poor and weak states. The fact that the rebels had declared for the constitution of 1812 clearly demonstrated that the revolt was inspired by the ideals of the French Revolution. This confirmed the belief of conservatives that they had not completely destroyed the monster of revolution when they defeated Napoleon in 1815. In their view the suppression of revolution was not a new task for the alliance of the great powers; it was dealing with unfinished business arising out of the war against the French Revolution. Moreover, they argued, just as the French Revolution had infected the rest of Europe with its pernicious ideas so did the Spanish revolt. In Naples in 1820 those who took up arms against the King used the Spanish constitution of 1812 as their rallying cry. In 1821 liberal army officers in Piedmont and Portugal followed the example set in Spain the previous year. To conservatives Spain was providing a model for revolution; in their view the continued existence of the revolt was an affront to order.[20]

The French government saw the difference between Great Britain and her continental allies over Spain and the alarm of European conservatives as developments which it could exploit to further its own interests.[21] Since 1815 French governments had felt constrained by the limits imposed upon them by the Second Peace of Paris and humiliated by the subsequent allied military occupation. Although the restored regime in France was bound by treaty not to attempt to renew the Family Compact between Bourbon France and Bourbon Spain, which in the eighteenth century the British had regarded as an alliance directed against them, it had not abandoned its aim of recovering for France a dominant position in western Europe. Even before the revolt of 1820, France had tried to establish close links with the restoration regime in Spain. The revolt and the rivalries with which it was bound up seemed to the French to afford them the opportunity of recovering their position as the great-power patron of Spain. Thus, from the summer of 1820 onwards, there were three distinct policies on the Spanish revolt. The British were anxious to keep Spain out of great-power discussions; this would prevent a further breach between Great Britain and Austria on the general problems raised by intervention and keep the French out of Spain. The Russian policy was to make Spain a European question because this would be embarrassing for Great Britain. French policy was to make it a purely French question; an issue on which Bourbon France would assist Bourbon Spain in whatever way it thought appropriate.

It was the British view which initially triumphed, although more by default than by successful diplomcy. In his State Paper of May 1820 Castlereagh condemned any effort by the alliance to intervene in Spain. Privately he warned Metternich that any attempt by the powers to regulate the internal affairs of Spain would result in French interventions and he was convinced a French army in the Peninsula would be more dangerous to the peace of Europe than the continued existence of an insurrection in Spain. Castlereagh believed that the revolt would either peter out or soon be settled by agreement. The other powers would not follow the British lead and agree to abstain from interference in Spain. At the Congresses of Troppau and Laibach they merely postponed discussions of Spanish affairs until after they had dealt with the problems raised by the Italian revolts. Moreover the Protocol of Troppau was an explicit rejection of the principle put forward by Castlereagh in May; the case for intervention was stated in the name of the alliance and in general terms. It was clear that after Austria had suppressed the Italian revolts the Russians would demand the application of the same principle to Spain.[22] The Russians were perfectly well aware that this was what the British feared. It would further weaken the Anglo-Austrian *entente* and directly challenge British predominance in the west. The only weakness of the Russian position was that it assumed that France would act in Spain in the name of the alliance and under Russian direction. Alexander and his advisers envisaged an agreement between the four continental powers on Spain which would permanently separate Great Britain from the alliance and severely damage her prestige. In order to ensure that the Spanish revolt did in fact become a European question and was not brushed aside by Britain and Austria, the Tsar offered to send Russian troops across Europe to act for the alliance.[23] In fact Metternich was by no means reluctant for the five powers to discuss Spain. He was anxious that the principle enunciated at Troppau should be applied to Spain in such a way as would satisfy the Russians, but at the same time give the British little cause for disquiet. At the Congress of Verona he seemed to succeed.

The Villèle government in France sent representatives to the Congress with instructions to avoid overt co-operation with the three eastern powers on Spanish affairs. Metternich soon cajoled them into treating it as a question of equal interest to all the powers. His solution to the problem of Spain was that the four powers would send similar and simultaneous notes of protest and disapproval to their representatives at Madrid who would present them to the liberal government. In this way the principles of Troppau would be upheld, the Russians would be satisfied that Spain had been treated as a European question, the French would be limited to acting with their allies and the British would be relieved that no action other than verbal protest was contemplated. This was agreed by the four powers at Verona.[24] The British, who sent only an observer to Verona, took no part in the discussions and were not party to the agreement. It was only when the four powers came to act upon their agreement that it collapsed. In late

1822 and early 1823 the French government repudiated the principle of co-operation and Montmorency, who as foreign minister had attended the Congress of Verona, was replaced by Chateaubriand. One of his first acts as foreign minister was to refuse to send the French note of protest simultaneously with the other three powers.[25]

The assertion by the French government of its right to act alone with respect to Spain was not initially accompanied by any firm indication of what its action would be. The French cabinet was divided between those who thought that France should suppress the Spanish revolt by force and those who argued that the risks of intervention were too great. While the French vacillated, Canning, who had replaced Castlereagh as British foreign secretary, tried to persuade the Spanish liberals to compose their differences with the King and to produce a constitution acceptable to themselves and to the monarchists. This they refused to do, a refusal which made their destruction inevitable.[26] By late March 1823 the advocates of intervention in the French cabinet had triumphed over their more timid colleagues. France, said Chateaubriand, must act decisively, quickly and alone. On 7 April 1823 a French army of 100,000 men crossed the Pyrenees. It met with little resistance and within a few months Ferdinand VII resumed control of the government.[27]

The invasion of Spain was a great triumph for France. Her government had dramatically asserted French military power in the west. Eight years after its defeat at Waterloo the French army had crossed the Pyrenees. Canning admitted that 'the entry of the French army into Spain was . . . an affront to the pride of England'.[28] To many Englishmen it seemed as if the British victory in the Peninsular war had now been reversed. War against France to secure the independence of Spain was, Canning acknowledged, an impossibility; Great Britain had no army ready for war and in the circumstance no continental allies with which to threaten the French. All Canning could do was to attempt to impose limits on the actions of the French army in the Peninsula. He sought three assurances from the French: firstly that their occupation of Spain was temporary and that the army would be withdrawn after it had achieved its political objectives; secondly that the French would rigidly abstain from any interference in the internal affairs of Portugal; and lastly that the French government would make no attempt to assist Spain to recover her former Empire in South America. These assurances were demanded in Canning's despatch of 31 March 1822.[29] What he was doing, in fact, was to oppose French military power with British naval power; the British already had a squadron stationed in the Tagus and if necessary a British fleet could prevent a Franco-Spanish expeditionary force from reaching South America. Implicit in Canning's demands was the assumption that if French influence was to predominate at Madrid then the French must respect British predominance at Lisbon. It was, therefore, with the diplomatic consequences for Great Britain, rather than the political consequences for Spain, of the French invasion that Canning was concerned. He had never attempted to pose as the friend of Spanish liberalism. Nor was his South American policy a defence of republicanism and colonial revolt; it was Great Britain's trade with South America which he sought to protect.

While the French were willing to reassure the British government that their occupation of Spain would be a temporary measure and that they would respect the independence of Portugal, they were evasive about their intentions in South America. Canning then turned to the United States of America for support. The American government was unwilling to act with Great Britain on South America; it was jealous of British trade with the former Spanish colonies; it suspected the British themselves of harbouring imperial ambitions and, unlike Great Britain, its republican sympathies were open and acknowledged. Convinced that the British would prevent any European intervention in South America, the American government decided it could appear to act alone. Canning's search for an ally against France in the west thus failed. Eventually the French gave the assurance the British demanded; in the Polignac Memorandum of October 1823 the French agreed, with some protest, not to attempt to restore Spanish rule in South America.[31] What Canning did was to transform what the French claimed was an exclusively Franco-Spanish question into a Peninsular issue in which France was forced to accept Great Britain as an equal, and a colonial question in which, through superior naval power, the British could dictate. After the Polignac Memorandum the colonial question was solved. The Peninsular question, however, moved into a new and Portuguese phase.

The political and imperial crisis in Spain was almost exactly paralleled in Portugal. In August 1820 a military revolt in Oporto challenged the authority of the Council of Regency which was governing the country in the absence of King John VI who was in Brazil. This was followed by a military revolt at Lisbon, and in October the two military juntas called for a national Cortes which was to be elected on the basis of limited suffrage and which was to be charged with drawing up a constitution. The eastern powers were, in theory, as alarmed by events in Portugal as they were by those in Spain. In practice they did not accord them the same importance. The Russians, and for that matter the French, realised that they could not hope to treat Portugal as they did Spain. The treaties of alliance between England and Portugal and the British squadron in the Tagus stood in the way of any overt intervention by other powers. They therefore confined their Portuguese policies to written and verbal protests delivered through their envoys at Lisbon. Britain's naval power and the reluctance of the other powers to encroach upon Britain's sphere of influence protected the Portuguese revolt at the same time as that in Spain was being destroyed.

The triumph of the counter-revolution in Spain after the French invasion altered the Peninsular context within which the Portuguese reform movement had to operate. The Portuguese absolutists believed that henceforward they could count upon the assistance and protection of Spain. The eastern powers encouraged them to do so; by opening her borders to the Portuguese conservatives and by supplying them with arms Spain could do by stealth what the other powers could not openly attempt. Canning's response was to revert to the same tactics as he had earlier used in Spain: encouraging the parties to settle their differences and offering to mediate in the dispute between Portugal and Brazil. The aim of these measures was to protect and preserve the special relationship which existed between England and Portugal. What the Spaniards and the other great powers needed to know was how far the British would go to secure these objectives.

In 1824 Dom Miguel, the second son of King John, who had emerged as the leader of the absolutist faction, attempted to organise a military *coup* against his father and the constitution. Thornton, the British minister in Lisbon, believed that the *coup* was inspired and organised in Spain. He offered British troops to protect the King and the constitution, fearing that if he did not do so the French would intervene. Canning was clearly embarrassed by his offer. He warned Thornton that the British government could not commit itself to such a course without parliamentary approval. Canning therefore substituted a demonstration of naval power for full-scale intervention; he augmented the naval squadron of the Tagus and increased the number of marines on board British ships in Portuguese waters.[34] For Canning the issue at stake was British prestige; the protection of the

Portuguese constitution was the occasion but not the cause of a demonstration of British power. He privately admitted that he had no admiration for 'paper constitutions'.

In March 1826 King John VI died. His successor Dom Pedro, who was already Emperor of Brazil, abdicated the Portuguese throne in favour of his infant daughter Dona Maria, and bestowed on Portugal a Regency and a Charter of limited monarchy. The eastern powers and France were alarmed by these developments. They could not openly condemn the constitution in Portugal as Pedro had granted it through proper exercise of his regal power. They therefore concentrated their attack on the possible international repercussions of the new arrangements. A Conference of Ambassadors of the four continental powers was held in Paris and resolved to ensure that the Portuguese constitutions in no way undermined 'the security of Spain'.[35] Canning rejected these attempts by the continental powers indirectly to supervise the internal affairs of Portugal. In his view their efforts to protect the restored absolutism in Spain were in fact an attempt to subvert the liberal order in Portugal.

This suspicion was confirmed in August 1826 when absolutist deserters from the Portuguese army crossed the Spanish border. The government at Madrid refused to disarm and disperse them. Both the Portuguese and the British governments were convinced that Spain, acting as the agent of the continental powers, was preparing an army of invasion, composed of Portuguese dissidents, which would march on Lisbon and Oporto and dissolve the Cortes. Metternich suggested reconvening the Conference of Ambassadors at Paris to discuss the dispute between the two Iberian monarchies, and invited Great Britain to attend. Canning refused; he was determined not to allow the other powers to claim equal rights with Great Britain in Portugal. Instead he demanded in October 1826 that the Spanish government should take the necessary measures to disarm the Portuguese deserters. The Spanish reply was extremely evasive and it soon became apparent that they were supplying the Portuguese rebels with arms. On 14 November Portugal appealed to Great Britain for assistance against invasion from across the Spanish border. Canning was convinced that assistance was necessary; 'the *casus foederis* has occurred' he wrote on 9 December. Four thousand British troops were immediately despatched to the Tagus and as a consequence the Spanish government took the appropriate measures of restraint and surveillance on the border. For the time-being at least, the Portuguese constitution was saved by British intervention.[36]

In the years from 1823 to 1826 Great Britain and France established a pattern of control in the Peninsula which was to last for the next two decades. Although both powers claimed exclusive rights of intervention in their respective client states, they were both forced to acknowledge each other's interests in the Peninsula. In 1823 the French had no alternative but to give the British definite assurances about the limited nature of their military operations in Spain. In 1824 the French government withdrew their ambassador from Lisbon because of his embarrassingly overt anti-English activities. In 1826 Canning went to Paris where he discussed Portuguese affairs with the French government, although he had earlier refused to send a British representative to a five-power conference on Portugal. Both powers came to recognise their joint dominance of the Peninsula and, after the British had recovered from the set-back of the French invasion of Spain, they evinced a willingness to avoid any direct conflict on Peninsular affairs.

The revolutions of July 1830 altered the position of France in Europe. To the suspicions which the other powers already entertained, of the revisionist objectives of French foreign policy, were added the fear that France would now pose as the champion of revolution. Fear of France drew the three eastern powers together; in September 1833 the Russians and Austrians concluded the Münchengrätz agreement on the Near East, and in the following month the three powers signed the Convention of Berlin which provided the basis for their future co-operation in Europe. The clause in the Convention of Berlin of 1833, in which the three agreed to assist each other in case of counter-intervention by an unnamed fourth power, was in fact directed against France.[37] In 1823 the French had been able to intervene in Spain because they realised that the British could not prevent it and because the eastern powers would not mobilise their armies on the German–Italian borders to protect a revolution in Spain. Liberal France could no longer count on the neutrality of the eastern powers if she now attempted to destroy absolutism in the west. Moreover the new French regime relied upon the goodwill of Great Britain to prevent a revival of the four-power coalition against them. As a result of these developments the French, in the early 1830s, lost their freedom to act as they saw fit in Spain. The British, however, were determined to maintain their exclusive influence at Lisbon. Lord Palmerston, the British foreign secretary, saw in these changes an opportunity to destroy the exclusive position which France had gained in Spain in 1823. Behind the façade of Anglo-French co-operation in the Peninsula in the early 1830s there was a determined attempt by the British to exploit the weakness of France.

After the British intervention in Portugal in 1826 the Portuguese constitution fell victim to those forces from which the British had tried to protect it; namely the Portuguese absolutists, assisted, supplied and encouraged by Spain. Whereas in Spain the destruction of the constitution by the French army was followed by a prolonged occupation during which order was restored, the British withdrew their force in 1826 after the immediate danger had passed. In 1827 Dom Miguel usurped the throne of Dona Maria, destroyed the constitution and began ruthlessly to persecute the Portuguese liberals. In these acts he was fully supported by the Spanish government. The second British intervention in Portugal in 1834 was no more than an attempt to establish the new order of succession of 1826 and Pedro's constitution on a firm and secure basis, which had not been achieved when Canning first ordered intervention. To the Canningite assumption that it was Great Britain's duty to protect Portugal's independence Palmerston added a further assumption that Great Britain was committed to the defence of Portuguese liberalism.[38] He was convinced that the absolutist forces in the Peninsula were the paid agents of the eastern powers. Palmerston linked the struggle between liberalism and absolutism in the west to the attempt of Russia to pursue an ambitious and agressive foreign policy in eastern Europe and the Near East.[39] Whereas in the 1820s Great Britain and France acted separately to exclude the eastern powers from the Peninsula, Palmerston was, in the early 1830s, convinced that they should do this together. This and their common commitment to liberalism provided a basis for co-operation. It was on the form of co-operation that Palmerston revealed his determination to exploit the weakness of France.

From their assumption of office Palmerston and the Whigs were determined to destroy Dom Miguel and his absolutism. The object of this policy was to reassert British influence in Portugal on a permanent basis, an influence which would be exercised through a new and friendly government at Lisbon. Palmerston hoped that if the two Peninsular absolutisms could be separated, either by threatening Spain or by reaching agreement with her, the British could destroy Dom Miguel and restore Dona Maria.[40] His several attempts to influence the government of Ferdinand VII failed. However, the King's death in

September 1833 dramatically altered the Portuguese policy of the Spanish government. The accession of his daughter Isabella was followed by the attempt of her uncle, Don Carlos, to raise an army in Portugal for the invasion of Spain in order to assert his right to the throne. The co-operation which Palmerston had hitherto failed to gain was now anxiously offered. The Queen Regent of Spain threw in her lot with the Spanish and Portuguese liberals because her daughter's throne was threatened by the combined forces of the Spanish and Portuguese absolutists. In this way the conflict of ideologies in the Peninsula became bound up with disputed successions, and both became enmeshed in great-power rivalries.

Palmerston's solution to these problems was to create a 'Western Confederacy' for the defence of liberal institutions and the female successions in Spain and Portugal in which Great Britain would lead and France follow. The two powers would present a united front to the encroachment of the absolutist powers, but in Portugal itself Great Britain would act without France. Palmerston drew up a Treaty between England, Spain and Portugal whereby Spanish land and British naval forces would intervene in Portugal to destroy the armies of Dom Miguel and Don Carlos. France could accede to this Treaty, although she would play no part in the actual operations. The French realised that the British were attempting to place them in an inferior position in the Peninsula. To this British claim that she alone had the right of intervention in Portugal the French replied that they could not allow Spain to act with Great Britain without their concurrence. The fact was, however, that the Spanish government would do so because its very existence was at stake. The Queen Regent would not sacrifice her daughter's throne in order to satisfy the *amour-propre* of France. A compromise was reached when Palmerston agreed to admit France to the Treaty as a full contracting partner, and to insert a vaguely worded clause to the effect that France could participate in the intervention if her assistance were needed by the other parties. It was agreed that no such French assistance should be asked for. From these discussions emerged the Quadruple Alliance of April 1834.[41]

The British fleet and the Spanish army quickly destroyed the Miguelite and Carlist bases in Portugal. The operations were begun in April, immediately after the agreement was signed, and were over by June. Palmerston, like Canning in 1826, sought quick and decisive results and was anxious to avoid any prolonged occupation. Dom Miguel admitted defeat and signed the Convention of Evora Monte which stipulated he would live in permanent exile in return for a pension. Don Carlos surrendered to the British rather than the Spaniards and he accepted voluntary exile in London. As Carlos was a Spanish subject and there had been no British declaration of war he was not a prisoner of the British government. It was assumed by the British that he would eventually seek exile in a more congenial capital of an absolutist state. Palmerston was well pleased with the results of his Treaty. As far as he was concerned the fact that the letter of the Treaty was fulfilled by the expulsion of the two pretenders from Portugal did not mean that it had ceased to be of any importance to the four signatory powers. From the outset Palmerston distinguished between the letter and the spirit of the Treaty. In his opinion the spirit of the Treaty enshrined three objectives. Firstly it would enable the two Iberian monarchies securely to establish under British and French patronage liberal institutions and to follow a programme of reform and modernisation. Secondly it openly identified Great Britain and France with the liberal cause in Europe; it created a western liberal combination as a counterweight to the eastern autocratic powers.[42] Lastly by creating a secure order in the west it would enable Great Britain more effectively to oppose Russian expansion in the Near East.

It proved impossible for Palmerston long to sustain this lofty and extended view of the Treaty. In fact the spirit of the Quadruple Alliance became a source of bitter conflict between the four signatory states rather than the outward expression of their unity. For more than a decade there was constant disagreement between them on their rights and obligations arising from the Treaty. Two questions dominated the discussions. What exactly was the purpose of the Treaty and what were the obligations of the signatories? The debate on these questions took place on two distinct levels between Great Britain and France, the two great-power patrons of the new order in the Peninsula, and between them and the Spanish and Portuguese governments. The two small states were determined to insist that the Treaty of April 1834 made the two great powers responsible for their internal well-being. Between 1834 and 1847 the governments of Spain and Portugal together asked for British and French military and naval intervention on six separate occasions. For them intervention had become the easiest and quickest means of solving their internal problems. Whereas in the early 1820s the French had tried to keep the British out of Spain and the British had similarly attempted to keep the French out of Portugal the Treaty of April 1834 had made this rigid separations of responsibility no longer possible. From 1834 onwards the British government claimed the right to an equal influence with France in determining the future of Spain. The French retaliated by claiming equal right in Portugal. In the long run the Treaty exacerbated the rivalry of the two powers in the Peninsula.

In July 1834 Don Carlos, unknown to the British and French governments, left England and returned to Spain. He joined the revolt in the Basque provinces in the north. Carlism thus became identified with a provincial revolt against the government of Madrid. Carlos fought for the crown, the Basques for their provincial privileges; the two rebel groups had very different objectives but at least they had a common enemy. The return of Carlos to Spain immediately raised the question of the obligations of Great Britain and France to the Spanish government. The Treaty specified that Carlos and Miguel should be expelled from Portugal, but both Palmerston and the French government were agreed that the intention of the Treaty was to make the Peninsula secure for liberalism. Moreover both governments were convinced that the eastern powers were sending supplies of arms and money to the Carlists. They agreed that some further measures to fulfil the spirit of the Treaty were necessary. Whereas in April Great Britain and Spain had intervened in Portugal with massive force to destroy the rebels, in July 1834 Great Britain and France offered Spain not an overwhelming force but 'moral' demonstrations of support. The French agreed to prevent arms crossing the French border to the Carlists and the British government agreed to sell 'arms and warlike stores' to the Spanish government. These measures were linked to the Treaty of April in the form of Additional Articles.[43] They fell far short of intervention. Palmerston and Rigny, the French foreign minister, hoped that they would undermine Carlist morale by convincing them of the hopelessness of their cause. Both governments admitted that they had a moral responsibility to assist Spain but at the same time asserted that this responsibility did not oblige them to intervene.

The Spanish government took a different view of the situation.[44] By the summer of 1835 it was clear that the Queen's army in the north could not destroy the challenge of Carlism. The government at Madrid therefore decided that it was the duty of Great Britain and France to do for Spain what she could not do for herself. It argued that intervention was a necessity and that the two great powers were morally obliged to provide it. In August 1835 the Spanish ambassador in Paris formally requested the intervention of the French Army to be

combined with British naval assistance. In 1835 the French government considered many of the same arguments for and against intervention in 1835 as the Villèle government had done in 1823. In 1823 the
advocates of intervention triumphed, in 1835 they were defeated.
Broglie, the prime minister, argued that the position in which France
was placed was not analogous to that of 1823. Carlism was associated
with a provincial revolt; it possessed a complex and effective military
organisation and could count on the loyalty of the Basque peasantry.
In 1823 the radical constitutionalists were concentrated in the large
towns, they did not have massive support in the army and they did not
enjoy the confidence of the peasantry. Whereas the French army
could destroy an urban movement, it could not quickly crush a provincial revolt backed by guerillas. What Broglie was in fact saying was
that the great powers could intervene in conflicts between political
parties within their client state but that they could not deal in the
same way with civil war. This was true; the other great powers had
successfully intervened to destroy urban revolts in small states but not
one of them had been involved in a prolonged and provincial civil war.
This was not the only respect in which the circumstances had
changed. In 1823 the British alone opposed the entry of the French
into Spain. In 1835 the eastern powers not only supported Carlism but
regarded the July monarchy in France as the enemy of order.
Moreover the British would not guarantee to support France if she
was attacked on her eastern border after her army had crossed the
Pyrenees.[45]

Although the French attitude towards intervention in Spain had
changed significantly since 1823, the British had not. Palmerston
was just as determined as Canning had been to prevent it. He emphasised the need for Spain to suppress Carlism by her own efforts,
but what he really meant was that the British were opposed to a
recovery by France of her preponderant influence at Madrid, which
would inevitably follow the suppression of Carlism by a French
army. In 1835, therefore, both powers opposed the Spanish request
for intervention. On the other hand they were equally anxious to
demonstrate their solidarity with the Spanish government. Not to
do so would imply that they were no longer determined to support
liberal regimes in the west, and this would be interpreted by the
eastern powers as a sign of weakness. Once again they agreed upon
further measures of assistance to Spain but still fell short of intervention. They offered small British and French forces to fight

alongside the Spanish constitutionalists in the north. These were token forces. The French agreed to allow the Foreign Legion to serve in Spain and the British government suspended the Foreign Enlistment Act to enable the Spanish government to recruit in England and Ireland.[46] In Madrid these measures were regarded with disappointment; the Spanish government was convinced that the two great powers were attempting to evade their treaty obligations.

In 1836 the Spanish government renewed this accusation in a different form. They claimed that the French government was failing faithfully to fulfil even the limited obligation it had incurred under the Additional Articles – to prevent supplies reaching the Carlists across the French border. Palmerston accepted these Spanish charges at their face value. In 1836, therefore, he tried to ensure that the French fulfilled their actual obligations under the Treaty and, at the same time, that they did not attempt to extend the scope of their assistance to Spain by full-scale intervention. He suspected that the French wanted the limited measure of assistance to fail in order to provide a case for intervention. In the summer of 1836 Thiers, who had replaced Broglie as French prime minister, sought a spectacular success in foreign policy which would strengthen his government at home and secure for France the independence of action and the prestige which she had lacked since the revolution of 1830. He sought to emancipate France from the role of playing second fiddle to Great Britain in the west. Initially he tried to establish dynastic links with Austria; France would then be free from British control and Austria relieved from her dependence on Russia. When this failed Thiers turned to Spain. He hoped to repeat Chateaubriand's triumph of 1823: once again Spain would become the theatre of actions for the French army.[47]

Thiers's argument was that full-scale French intervention in Spain was the logical culmination of the Treaty of April 1834 because both the Additional Articles and the further measure of assistance provided in 1835 had failed to end the war. In effect he sought to extend the spirit of the Alliance beyond even Palmerston's conception of it. The British could not object to France doing in Spain what they had done in Portugal. Thiers was convinced that the eastern powers would not take any hostile steps against France; Spain was outside their sphere of influence and they would take comfort from the fact that French intervention in Spain would be a source of conflict between the two western powers. Thiers's plan was therefore to take one step further along the path to intervention; he proposed to send a

French force of about 10,000 men across the Pyrenees to assist in the struggle against Carlism.[48] Unlike Broglie in 1835 he did not consider the provincial character of the revolt and the guerilla nature of the warfare to be serious obstacles. If this force did not succeed in destroying Carlism then it would have to be increased. The British could not oppose the initial plan for a small force as this would be no more than an extension of measures agreed upon in 1835. Thiers's policy was intervention by stealth by a slow build-up of the French army in Spain. There were good reasons why he should pursue this course rather than full-scale intervention. The King was opposed to intervention and it was thought there was a majority of deputies in the Chamber determined to prevent expensive military adventures. Moreover the Cabinet was divided on the issue; some of its members feared the government would be defeated by a motion of censure in the Chamber if it sent part of the French army across the Pyrenees. In the end it was the opponents of intervention who triumphed; the King dismissed Thiers and found no difficulty in forming another government committed to a policy of non-intervention in Spain. As a consequence two further Spanish requests for intervention were rejected and Molé, the new French prime minister, insisted that it was the letter and not the spirit of the Quadruple Alliance which should determine France's relations with Spain and with Great Britain on Peninsular questions.[49] By 1836 Palmerston's grandiose vision of the Alliance was completely shattered. As far as the Spanish government was concerned the Alliance had failed to provide the security and assistance which it at first thought the Treaty offered.

The collapse of Anglo-French co-operation in Spain was followed by a decade of rivalry. At first the British managed to secure a dominant position at Madrid by exploiting Spanish resentment at the French retreat into the letter of the Alliance. In 1844 this position was reversed when the pro-French Moderado party managed to oust their pro-British rivals, the Progressistas, from power. Lord Aberdeen, foreign secretary in the Conservative government of Peel, was content to allow the French to enjoy their new ascendancy at Madrid as long as they did not blatantly exploit it. For this reason he permitted the French government to take the lead in organising marriages for the young queen of Spain and her sister, the heiress to the throne. In 1846, when Palmerston returned to office, he reversed Aberdeen's policy; he insisted that the Spanish government should have perfect freedom of action over the marriage question and should not be dictated to by France. The government of Guizot in France was alarmed by this British change of policy and hastily concluded a marriage agreement with the Spanish government which was intended to strengthen French influence at Madrid and perpetuate the Moderado ascendancy in Spanish politics. Palmerston retaliated in Europe by attempting to secure anti-French agreements with the eastern powers, and in the Peninsula by supporting the anti-French forces. It was the latter measure which raised in a new form the obligations of the Quadruple Treaty of 1834 and eventually resulted in intervention in Portugal.[50]

In 1846 and 1847 there were radical protests in Portugal against Queen Dona Maria and her government. The protests were both civilian and military. The initial British attitude was that the Portuguese government, by its arbitrary methods, had brought these misfortunes upon itself. Palmerston believed that a programme of reform would reconcile the radicals to the government and create a genuinely liberal and stable regime in Portugal. The French and Spanish governments saw in Palmerston's sympathy with the Portuguese rebels a veiled attack upon themselves. They believed that he was encouraging the Portuguese radicals in the hope that they would triumph in Portugal, and thus provide an example to the Spanish radicals and if necessary a base from which they could operate against the Moderado regime. If the Moderado government was brought down, then French influence would collapse with it. The Portuguese government, in an attempt to avoid giving the concessions to its opponents suggested by the British government, claimed that the revolt had assumed a Miguelite character. There was probably some truth in this; given that both radicals and Miguelites were opposed to the Queen's government, it was natural that they should combine against it. The Portuguese government saw the advantages of exaggerating the Miguelite character of the revolt; it not only avoided the necessity of concessions, it also enabled them to call upon the support of the other signatories to the Treaty of April 1834. Once again they appealed to the spirit rather than the letter of the Treaty. Both the Spanish and French governments supported the demands of the Portuguese for assistance. The Spanish did so because it feared the consequence for itself of a radical regime at Lisbon; the French because it saw in Portuguese radicalism a force which could be used by the British to undermine French influence at Madrid. Prompted by the French the Spanish government claimed that the Treaty of April 1834 gave

Spain the right to intervene in Portugal to suppress Miguelism. It was made clear to Palmerston that if England did not herself take some action in Portugal it would be 'difficult for the other powers to recognise England's predominant influence and Spain might feel herself in danger and thus intervene'.[51] In February 1847 the Portuguese government formally requested the intervention of her allies under the Treaty of April 1834.

Both the French and Spanish governments supported this request. The Spanish government went further than offering its assistance under the Treaty; it began to supply the Portuguese government with arms and to move troops to the frontier. The object of these measures was twofold; firstly to frighten the Portuguese rebels and secondly to make it clear to the British government that if necessary Spain would act on her own. When Palmerston informed the French and Spanish governments that he regarded the Treaty of April 1834 as 'worked out', the French replied that if that was the case there was nothing to prevent the Spanish government from acting on its own in Portugal.[52] From Madrid, Bulwer, the British minister, reported to Palmerston that unless the British government took the lead in pacifying Portugal he could not guarantee that Spain, encouraged by France, would not do so. Like Canning in 1826 Palmerston was forced to act to preserve British influence at Lisbon. In April he made a last attempt to avoid intervention by offering mediation. The Portuguese government tried to foil this by objecting to the conditions which Palmerston was determined to impose. It was the rebels at Oporto who finally destroyed the British initiative by an outright refusal to compromise. This made intervention inevitable. On 21 May the representatives of France and Spain were called to the Foreign Office by Palmerston and a Protocol was drawn up whereby intervention was to be effected by British and French naval forces and Spanish land forces. Palmerston reluctantly agreed to the French request that the grounds for assistance should be based on the Treaty of April 1834.[53] In June and July 1847 the combined forces of the three states destroyed the rebel army and their strongholds. Once again the British government was determined to ensure that intervention was swift and decisive and Palmerston inserted in the Protocol of 21 May a clause which stipulated that the Spanish army should withdraw from Portugal not later than two months after the rebel forces had capitulated. For him as for Canning the real purpose of intervention was to preserve the independence of Portugal. He had worked with France and Spain because he feared that if he did not they would work against him.

In 1847 Palmerston admitted that the intervention in Portugal was a 'very unusual measure for the British government to take' and was 'much more after the fashions of Austria and Russi.'.[54] Hitherto he had always argued that Great Britain's practice was to intervene to protect the independence of states and not to regulate their internal affairs. This conviction ill accorded with the evidence; both in 1834 and 1847 the British government had intervened to protect a particular form of government in Portugal. It was true that in both cases the British government believed that this form of government could best preserve Portugal's independence. The British yardstick of independence was a government which looked to England for support, and the only Portuguese governments which did this were liberal. In the end, therefore, the British approach to intervention was not very different from that of the other powers. Despite Palmerston's protest that the Treaty of April 1834 was not a 'standing engagement'[55] by Great Britain and France 'to give military aid' to the Peninsular monarchies, it was interpreted as such in the Peninsula. Moreover the treaty rebounded on Palmerston in another sense. He had intended it as a measure which would keep the French army out of Spain and give the British equal influence with the French at Madrid. In 1836 Thiers and the Spanish government were using the spirit of the Treaty to do the very thing which Palmerston hoped it would prevent. In 1847 the three other signatories again used the spirit of the Treaty to force the British to intervene in Portugal. In 1834, immediately after the conclusion of the Quadruple Treaty, Palmerston wrote that he had felt for some time that 'morally the alliance must exist'.[56] By 1847 he had good cause to regret its existence. By his own admission the 'moral' distinction between British intervention and the interventions of the other powers had ceased to exist.

4. Russia and the Eastern Question, 1821–41

MATTHEW ANDERSON

In March 1821 Alexander Hypsilantis, a member of a leading Phana-riot Greek family and an officer in the Russian army, crossed the river Pruth from Russian territory into Moldavia with a small force in the hope of leading a large-scale rising against Turkish suzerainty in the Danubian principalities. He thus began a new phase in the develop-ment of the Eastern Question, already during a span of at least two generations a fertile source of diplomatic complications for the governments of Europe. Within a few days revolt, national and still more religious, had erupted in the Morea. By the end of the year almost all that area was under the control of the rebels, though Hypsi-lantis, severely defeated in Wallachia by the Turks early in June, had been forced to take refuge in Austrian territory. A decade of struggle for Greek independence had begun.

This new eastern crisis was most unwelcome to Alexander I and faced him with a difficult and embarrassing choice. Russia had by now a long tradition of territorial expansion to the south, at the expense of the Ottoman Empire, a tradition which dated at least from the capture of the port of Azov by Peter I in 1696. In 1774 the greatest of all Russo-Turkish wars had ended in a crushing victory for Catherine II and the gain by Russia of a permanent outlet on the Black Sea. In 1783–4 the Crimea had become Russian territory; in 1792 the foothold on the Black Sea had been expanded; the first years of the nineteenth century had seen a great forward movement of the Russian frontier in the Caucasus. Finally in 1812, after a six-year struggle, Alexander had gained most of Bessarabia and pushed his south-western boundary as far as the Pruth. Thus, by 1821, enmity between Russia and the Otto-man Empire had become a deep-rooted tradition on both sides. In Constantinople the incessantly expanding northern neighbour was rightly seen as the greatest of all threats to the rickety structure of Turkish power. To Russia the economic value of the newly acquired territories was rapidly increasing. Moreover a feeling of fellowship with the Orthodox Christians of the Balkans was slowly developing, though as yet it counted for little in practical terms; efforts by both Peter I and Catherine II to use the Balkan peoples and their religious and sometimes linguistic affinities with Russia as a weapon against the Porte had been failures.

When the Greek revolt erupted, however, there were more specific and concrete reasons for strained relations between St Petersburg and Constantinople. Alexander I and his ministers claimed that some of the clauses of the Treaty of 1812, signed at Bucharest, had not been observed by the Turks, and rejected the Turkish interpretation of others. They insisted that the *hospodars* (Turkish-appointed governors) in the principalities should hold office for a seven-year term and not be dismissible at the whim of the Sultan. More important, they refused to admit that, under the terms of the Treaty, Russia was obliged to withdraw from the Caucasian principalities (Imeretia, Mingrelia, Abkhazia and Guria) which had placed themselves more or less voluntarily under her rule before 1812. This meant that Russia still retained about 120 miles of Black Sea coastline to which the Porte claimed she was not entitled; and protracted negotiations completely failed to end this important dispute. Both sympathy with an Orthodox people misgoverned and illtreated by infidels and material interest thus seemed, in 1821, to point towards active Russian intervention on behalf of the Greek rebels. Such a course, moreover, would have been widely popular in Russia, especially in military circles. One leading Russian soldier complained that 'The Turks behave towards us as if we were Tatars under their rule', and in the summer and autumn of 1821 the general staff began work on plans for a campaign against the Ottoman Empire. Nevertheless for several years Russia took no effective action.

This was because of the personal attitude and outlook of Alexander I. His feelings were decisive because he alone, in the last analysis, decided Russian policy. A ministry of foreign affairs had been set up in 1802 (though it was not until thirty years later that it finally supplanted the old collegiate organisation for the conduct of foreign policy established by Peter I). But this was no more than an administrative organism; it did not make policy and often had little influence in its making. An official report of 1837 on its work quite correctly described it as 'merely the faithful executor of the intentions' of the ruler, and claimed that under Alexander and his brother and successor

Nicholas I 'its every action was carried out under the orders and direction of the tsars themselves'. By 1821 Alexander was well accustomed to acting as his own foreign minister, a fact illustrated by his role at the Congress of Vienna and in the international meetings of the following years. 'Everyone knows', he told the French ambassador in St Petersburg, 'that I do business myself and never by delegation.' It was only by influencing the Tsar and obtaining his support that a minister could hope to put into practice a policy of his own; this remained true throughout the reigns of both Alexander and his brother. Karl Robert, Count von Nesselrode, who had been state secretary for foreign affairs since 1814 and was to remain in office until 1856, did not regard himself as more than a high-ranking bureaucrat; it is significant that he was not given the higher titles of foreign minister or state chancellor. Count John Capodistrias, the Tsar's most important adviser on eastern policy, was himself a Greek and a stronger personality than the colourless Nesselrode; but as events were to prove he was quite unable to carry out any policy which Alexander did not support.

The Tsar had no doubt that his attitude to the Greek revolt must be one of strong disapproval. His first reaction to it was summarily to dismiss Hypsilantis from the Russian army. He took this attitude because in his eyes the supreme necessity was to preserve the structure of conservative and monarchical solidarity which had, he believed, been created at the end of the struggle with Napoleon I. Of this the Holy Alliance of 1815 was the greatest statement of principle and the 'congress system', as seen in operation at Aachen and Laibach in 1818 and 1820, the practical expression. However oppressive Turkish rule might be (and Alexander had few illusions on this point) intervention on behalf of the Greeks was support for rebels against their legitimate ruler. To this the Tsar was deeply opposed. 'If we reply to the Turks with war', he told Capodistrias, who was urging action by Russia, in 1821, 'the Paris directing committee[1] will triumph and no government will be left standing. I do not intend to leave a free field to the enemies of order. At all costs means must be found to avoid war with Turkey.' Moreover unilateral action by Russia would undermine, perhaps fatally, the unity of the great powers which guaranteed peace in Europe and was already threatened by the independent attitude which Britain had been taking for some time.

Both Metternich in Vienna and Bernstorff, the Prussian foreign minister, in Berlin, pressed on Alexander the need to preserve this unity and sacrifice to it the local and secondary issues at stake in the Near East. Such arguments made a deep impression on the Tsar; it was very reluctantly that he was driven to the conclusion that some unilateral Russian action was inevitable. His attitude shows a large element of genuine idealism, a real sense of European responsibilities and a willingness to make sacrifices to meet them. Such factors were also to influence his brother Nicholas. Both showed, in their attitude to the Eastern Question, a width of view and a freedom from merely national and selfish considerations which could be matched by no other European ruler of the period. To them, and particularly to Alexander, ideological loyalties were more important than material advantage. Recent Soviet historical writing has tended to play down this element in Russian policy and to stress rather the external forces which, allegedly, made it impossible for Russia to act in support of the Greeks as the great majority of politically conscious Russians wished. Faced by the hostility of the other great powers, notably Austria and Britain it is argued, for several years after 1821 Russia was hamstrung: the protracted sufferings of the Greeks must thus be blamed on the selfishness of the western powers rather than on the conservatism of the tsars.[2] This view is one-sided. There is no doubt that the attitude of the other powers helped to tie Alexander's hands; but this was only because, in the last analysis, he was willing to have them tied. Under his successor Russia found no great difficulty, in 1828–9, in taking drastic and far-reaching unilateral action.

In one important way Russia's material interest in the fate of the Ottoman Empire was increasing rapidly by 1821. The settlement and development of the fertile lands of the Black Sea steppe was bringing with it a spectacular growth in grain exports to western Europe. Odessa, by far the greatest centre of this trade, was in the second decade of the nineteenth century the most rapidly growing port in the world. All this increased sharply for Russia the importance of free movement of her merchant ships through the Straits; and the point was driven home when, in the 1820s, the Turkish government began impeding that movement by administrative delays, by searching Russian vessels and sometimes by pre-empting their cargoes. (These tactics had a good deal of justification in that most of the ships passing through the Straits under the Russian flag were in fact Greek-owned.) Soviet historians writing on this period have paid much attention to grain exports and other economic factors in the Near Eastern situation[3] and have usually at least implied that they were in some way decisive in the making of Russian policy. Traditional non-Marxist historiography of the Eastern Question, it is true, has often been couched in too exclusively political and diplomatic terms. None the less the decisive factor in the situation so far as Russia was concerned was her ruler; and there is no evidence that Alexander was influenced by these commercial considerations.

In the early stages of the war he adhered firmly to his refusal to give any practical help to the Greeks. 'Nothing, without doubt', he told Chateaubriand, the French representative at the Verona Congress in the autumn of 1822, 'appeared more agreeable to my interests, to the interests of my peoples, to the public opinion of my country, than a religious war with Turkey. But in the outbreaks in the Peloponnese I saw the signs of revolution – and refused.' At the Congress the Greek delegates who had come to present their case were refused a hearing. Already in August, Capodistrias, unable to persuade Alexander to adopt a more active and pro-Greek stance, had gone on leave to Switzerland. The Tsar was none the less sincerely anxious to co-operate with the other great powers in ending, by diplomatic means, an increasingly vicious struggle. But all his efforts in this direction were failures. A proposal in 1822 for a confidential agreement with Austria and Great Britain and later for a conference in Vienna had no practical result; nor had a meeting in the following year with the Emperor Francis I at Czernowitz in the Bukovina. An international conference on the Greek Question, yet another effort to assert the principle of great-power co-operation, opened in St Petersburg in June 1824; but it was suspended after only two meetings since both the Turks and the Greeks refused to accept a Russian proposal, put forward in January, for the creation of three autonomous Greek principalities on the model of the Danubian ones. When the conference resumed its work, in February 1825, Nesselrode produced a Russian demand for an armistice and concerted diplomatic action by the powers to force the Porte and the Greek rebels to come to some agreement. In April Russia, Austria, France and Prussia signed a Protocol calling for an end to the fighting. But this again had no effect; and by now Alexander was becoming very bitter about the obstructive attitude of the other powers. In August Nesselrode, in a circular despatch, said flatly that it would be quite useless to become involved in new discussions with Russia's allies over the Greek Question, and complained that the other powers seemed to wish merely to paralyse Russia in the Near East.

The situation was now clearly changing. In February 1825 a powerful Egyptian army sent by Mehemet Ali, the semi-independent Pasha
of Egypt, and commanded by his son Ibrahim, landed in the Morea.
This seemed to threaten the devastation and depopulation of much of
Greece. In December Alexander I died. Even before his death there
had been active discussion in St Petersburg of a possible agreement
with Britain, hitherto, of all the powers, the one most distrustful of
Russia, to deal with the increasingly difficult Greek situation.
Nicholas I was anxious to ensure British neutrality in case of a war
with Turkey. The British government was beginning to see in an
agreement with Russia the best hope of exerting some control over her
if a Russo-Turkish struggle should break out. The result was an
Anglo-Russian Protocol of 4 April 1826, signed in St Petersburg.
Britain was to offer mediation with the object of making Greece an
autonomous vassal-state of the Ottoman Empire. If this could not be
done the two powers might intervene 'jointly or separately' between
the Porte and its rebellious subjects. (The Duke of Wellington, the
British representative at the negotiations, did not see the dangerous
possibilities of this provision, which could open the way to unilateral
action by Russia.)

Already, in March, Nicholas had sent to Constantinople what was
virtually an ultimatum, demanding satisfaction for a whole series of
Russian grievances; and under pressure from Britain and Austria,
which were anxious not to give the Tsar any pretext for military
action, the Sultan Mahmud II agreed to send plenipotentiaries to a
meeting on the frontier with Russian ones to discuss these questions.
In October 1826 this produced the Convention of Akkerman which
gave Russia everything she demanded. The privileges of the Danubian principalities, which had been occupied by Turkish forces since
1821, were restored. The Serbs, who had been in intermittent revolt
against Turkish rule since 1804, were granted wide internal self-
government. Russia was to retain all the territory she claimed in the
Caucasus. Ships flying her flag were to navigate freely all the seas and
internal waterways of the Ottoman Empire. Nicholas seemed to have
won a great success: clearly he was a man of harsher and more determined stamp than his brother. But the success was more apparent
than real. The Sultan carried out the Akkerman terms very slowly and
reluctantly; and although the Protocol of April 1826 was transformed
into a formal Treaty between Britain, France and Russia, signed in
London in July 1827, Russia's allies continued to refuse her proposals

for more active measures to help the Greeks. Moreover from June 1826 onwards for two years her attention and resources were partially diverted by a minor but irritating war with Persia. It was only early in September 1827 that Russian pressure forced Britain and France to agree to cut off seaborne supplies to the Turkish forces in the Morea and several of the Greek islands. It was from this action that there sprang the unplanned and partly fortuitous annihilation of the Turkish and Egyptian fleets at Navarino on 20 October.

The battle greatly strengthened the position of the Greeks. But it also made the Turks more uncompromising than ever. By the end of the year Mahmud II had denounced the Convention of Akkerman and summoned all Muslims to a holy war against Russia, his 'great enemy'. By the spring of 1828 Russian money and supplies were being sent to the Greeks. Nevertheless the deep hostility to rebellion in any form, which had so influenced Alexander, carried almost as much weight with his successor. Nicholas wished to increase Russian influence in Greece rather than to achieve national independence there. In fact the central issue for the Russian government had now become the enforcement of the Akkerman Agreement rather than the fate of the Greeks.

The war with Turkey, which began at the end of April 1828, was a difficult one for Russia. Her resources, in spite of her great area and population, were limited. Largely for this reason Nicholas waited until peace had been made with Persia, at the end of February, before embarking on a new struggle. Moreover Russia, as always in the nineteenth century, was short of money: the finance minister, Count Kankrin, was horrified by the estimated cost of a war with Turkey and insisted on its being reduced. There was also a good deal of uneasiness in St Petersburg over the possibility of Austrian military intervention or even, in the early stages of the fighting, of a British attack on the Russian squadron in the Mediterranean. It was at least partly through fear of Austrian hostility that Nicholas steadily resisted any suggestion that the Balkan peoples, under Turkish rule or suzerainty, and particularly the Serbs, should be brought into the struggle as auxiliaries of Russia. Nor were the military operations themselves easy. Mediocre leadership, deficiencies of organisation and supply, the ravages of disease – all these meant that the campaign of 1828 in the Balkans was disappointing. The following year produced better results. By August 1829 Russian forces had entered Adrianople, while the Caucasian army had pushed forward to within about fifty miles of

Trebizond, on the north coast of Asia Minor. The Porte had now little choice but to sue for peace.

The Treaty signed at Adrianople on 14 September was in many ways moderate. In Europe Russia gained merely a small area of territory at the mouth of the Danube, though she also obtained a renewed guarantee of free passage for her merchantmen through the Straits and the setting-up in the principalities of a new system of administration supervised and guaranteed by her. In the Caucasus, however, territorial questions had always, since 1812, bulked larger than in the Balkans in Russo-Turkish relations. In January 1828 Nesselrode had written that 'in Europe Russia wishes for no territorial gains at the expense of the Ottoman Empire', whereas 'in Asia it is necessary to obtain two strategic positions: Anapa and Poti, with the territory around them.' This scale of values applied also to the Turks: a Russian observer noted that in the Adrianople negotiations 'it was visible that their Asian possessions lay nearer their hearts than those in Europe.' Anapa and Poti, ports on the east coast of the Black Sea, were indeed retained by Russia, while the Porte recognised Georgia and eastern Armenia as Russian territory and the Russian government began to claim, in virtue of the Treaty, suzerainty over Circassia. These were really important gains; the significance of the Caucasian aspect of the Eastern Question, which tends to be underestimated in much writing in western languages, was always very great to both Russia and Turkey and should never be forgotten.

The signature of the Treaty of Adrianople coincided with the most searching examination hitherto made of the lines along which Russian policy in the Near East should develop. A special committee of six high-ranking officials and diplomats was set up by the Tsar with Count V. P. Kochubey, one of the most experienced of Russian statesmen, as chairman, to consider the future of Russo-Turkish relations. In the middle of September it produced a report whose main recommendations were to be followed for the next two decades. Its conclusions were notably cautious and conservative. The central one was that from Russia's point of view 'the advantages of the preservation of the Ottoman Empire outweigh its disadvantages.' If the Empire collapsed, which seemed all too possible, an international conference should be called to arrange a peaceful partition of its territories among the European states; and Russia must take 'the most energetic measures to ensure that the exit from the Black Sea is not seized by any other power whatever'. But any further Russian territorial expansion at Turkish expense, at least in Europe, was likely to have very unwelcome results. It was argued strongly in the discussions of the committee that if Russia seized the Straits and Constantinople Austria would occupy the western Balkans, Britain Crete and some of the other Greek islands, and France Egypt. This would establish powerful rivals in unwelcome proximity to Russia and probably lead to a great international war. A proposal by Capodistrias (who had now become president of a short-lived Greek Republic), for the reorganisation of the Balkans as a confederation of five new independent states with Constantinople, transformed into a free city, as its capital, was unhesitatingly rejected. The thinking which underlay the committee's conclusions had already a considerable history in Russia; a generation earlier, in 1802, when he left the Ministry of Foreign Affairs to become minister of the interior, Kochubey had drawn up a memorandum urging that a partition of the Ottoman Empire be avoided if possible, since it was a relatively weak and harmless neighbour and Russia had no further need for expansion. Moreover in 1828 D. V. Dashkov, the most active member of the committee, had argued that the destruction of Turkish power in Europe might lead merely to the creation in Asia Minor of a strong and largely national Turkish state, able to resist Russia more effectively in the Caucasus.

The main characteristics of the report – moderation, restraint, a desire that any important territorial change in the Near East should take place by international agreement – were to bulk large in the thinking of Nicholas I throughout the 1830s and 1840s. His deeply legitimist instincts and intense fear of revolution were strengthened by the upheavals of 1830, above all by the collapse of the restored Bourbon monarchy in France and its replacement by the upstart Orleans line. This meant that he became more anxious than ever for co-operation with Austria, and even with Britain which he in many ways admired and correctly saw as a force making for stability in international affairs. This attitude found little response in Vienna and for long even less in London. A Russian approach to Austria in February 1833 for agreement on joint action in the Near East, and in particular on the enlargement of the independent Greek kingdom which had come into existence in May of the previous year, produced a discouraging response. From London there was, at least for the time being, even less to hope. The crushing of the Polish revolt of 1830–31 and the repressive regime in Russian Poland which followed raised popular fear and dislike of Russia, which had been growing in Britain for several decades, to an unprecedented pitch. So far as the Near East was concerned, this Russophobia was to find new apparent justification in the events of 1833.

Mehemet Ali, secure in Egypt, had for long hoped to add to his dominions the three pashaliks of Syria. Moreover, by the later 1820s, there were clear signs that his willingness to accept any control from Constantinople was wearing thin. In November 1831 war broke out between him and Mahmud II. By the beginning of 1833 the Egyptians, led by Ibrahim Pasha, had overrun Syria and were advancing deep into Asia Minor. There seemed little to prevent their pressing on to the Straits and Constantinople. At this, the most critical moment of his reign, Mahmud II appealed for help to Britain; but without result. Britain could intervene actively in the Near East only through her navy, and the ships available were already fully occupied elsewhere. Many were being used to compel William I of Holland, by a blockade, to agree to Belgian independence. Others were employed in supporting Queen Maria of Portugal against her deeply reactionary uncle, Dom Miguel, in a struggle for power which had been going on for several years. If extra ships were to be commissioned for use in the eastern Mediterranean this would offer the opposition a welcome pretext for attacks on the government – a significant consideration in a period when domestic political tension was acute and a general election clearly in the offing. Moreover many British statesmen, including the prime minister, Lord Grey, were by now very sceptical about the prospects of survival of the Ottoman Empire. French opinion, influenced by memories of Napoleon's Egyptian adventure of 1798 and by the fact that Mehemet Ali had many French officers and experts in his service, was strongly favourable to the Pasha; while the difference of outlook between the relatively liberal west-European powers, Britain and France, and the conservative ones of eastern Europe, which had sharpened markedly in 1830–32, meant that any co-operation between Britain and Austria was now a good deal more difficult than in the 1820s.

For all these reasons Mahmud was, in effect, left to his fate by the powers whom he might, with some justice, regard as traditional friends and allies. This forced him, in a remarkable *volte-face*, to turn to his greatest traditional foe, Russia. As early as the summer of 1832 Butenev, the Russian minister in Constantinople, had been sounded on the possibility of Russian military help against the Egyptians. At the end of November Nesselrode told him that a Russian naval squadron would be provided immediately should the Sultan ask for it. There were two obvious reasons why Nicholas I should be willing to rescue the Sultan from his desperate situation. Mehemet Ali was ambitious; his army was strong; his reign had been, in general, highly successful. He might well create a powerful 'Arab empire' covering not merely Egypt and Syria but also Arabia (much of which he already controlled), Mesopotamia and a large part of Asia Minor. Such a state would be a far more dangerous neighbour to Russia than the still decaying Ottoman Empire. Moreover it would very probably be under strong French influence; and after the 1830 revolution in Paris, France was to Nicholas more than ever the obvious centre of the infection which threatened peace and stability throughout Europe. Most important of all, Mehemet Ali was a rebel. As such he must incur Nicholas's dislike and hostility, while Mahmud represented legitimate authority threatened with violent overthrow by a disloyal subject. When, therefore, General N. N. Muraviev was sent to Constantinople in December 1832 to prepare the way for Russian military and naval intervention, he was told that the Tsar's objective was 'to maintain Turkey in the stagnant state in which it finds itself'. In his first interview with the Sultan he assured Mahmud that 'the emperor is the enemy of rebellion and the friend of your highness', and that 'if the pasha [Mehemet Ali] continues to prolong hostilities he will have Russia to deal with.'[4]

By early February 1833 Ibrahim was only about 150 miles from Constantinople. The Sultan now formally invited Russian military and naval help; and on 20 February nine Russian men-of-war cast anchor at Buyukdéré on the Bosphorus. Six weeks later a force of 5000 Russian soldiers landed there, asked for by Mahmud to defend his capital against any new attack which Ibrahim might launch. By the end of April there were 14,000 of them. This demonstration of strength came too late to be of much use to the Turks: at the end of March the Sultan had been forced to recognise Mehemet Ali as ruler of Syria and early in May the Adana district, which he had also demanded, was placed under Ibrahim's control. Nevertheless it was not until the end of June, when the Egyptians had recrossed the Taurus mountains, that the Russians withdrew. A few days later on 8 July, Count A. F. Orlov, who had been sent from St Petersburg in April to supplement the rather ineffective Butenev, signed with the Turkish government the Treaty of Unkiar-Skelessi.

Both in St Petersburg and in Constantinople the idea of a defensive alliance had taken root in the previous weeks. Turkish suggestions for something of the kind had been tentatively put forward at the beginning of April. When he reached the Turkish capital early in May, Orlov had the task of combating British and still more French influence there, and of opposing any suggestion of collective action by the great powers in the Near East, persuading the Porte to rely completely on Russian support and thus legitimate the sending of Russian forces to Constantinople. A fortnight later, on 20 May, Nesselrode gave him instructions for the conclusion of an alliance. Its defensive character, however, was made very clear. Such a treaty, Nesselrode wrote, would restrain further aggression by Mehemet Ali and thus preserve, for a time at least, the *status quo* in the Near East. It would check French influence in the Ottoman Empire (again we see the unquestioning assumption which Nicholas and his minister shared, that France was the great political and ideological enemy) and its conservative bias would reassure the other powers as to Russian intentions there. However, Nesselrode went on, it would also give Russia a leading position in the Near East and allow her to take the lead either in new action to preserve Turkish power or, if it became unavoidable, in a partition of Turkish territory. In return for her services she was entitled to ask the Sultan for help in protecting her southern coasts in case of war; this he could give only by closing the Straits to foreign warships, a principle which was not new and which was in any case in the interests of the Porte.

These instructions bring out well the essential characteristics of Russian policy at this crucial moment: a genuinely conservative and defensive attitude combined with a determination to exclude so far as possible hostile influences from the Ottoman Empire and ensure Russian predominance there. The Treaty of Unkiar-Skelessi reflected accurately these characteristics. It provided merely for the confirmation of the Adrianople Agreement and the Greek Settlement, and for each of the two signatories to aid the other in case of attack by a third party. In a secret article which was the really significant part of the arrangement, however, Russia declared that in case of such an attack she would not call for Turkish naval or military help. Instead she would require merely that the Porte close the Straits to foreign warships, 'not allowing any foreign vessels of war to enter therein on any pretext whatever'. Nesselrode, in a circular despatch of 17 August intended to explain and justify the Agreement to the powers, argued with much truth that this made no real change in the situation at the Straits. The Treaty placed no new obligations on the Porte; for the closure of the Straits to foreign warships was already an accepted rule of international law, embodied for example in an article of the Anglo-Turkish Treaty of 1809. The provisions of the Unkiar-Skelessi Agreement, he claimed, merely stated an existing fact, 'the fact of the closure of the Dardanelles for the military flag of all foreign powers; a system which the Porte has maintained at all times and from which, indeed, it could not depart without injuring its most direct interests'.

In western Europe, however, the Treaty, apparently dictated by Russia at a moment of great danger for the Ottoman Empire, aroused deep suspicion and hostility. Of course the closure of the Straits to foreign ships of war while the Ottoman Empire was at peace meant that in any war with Russia in which the Turks were neutral the British and French fleets would be unable to attack her Black Sea coast. What alarmed and enraged many western statesmen and diplomats, however, was the fear that the Treaty, as well as closing the Straits to their own men-of-war, gave those of Russia free passage through them. This belief had no foundation. When, early in 1838, Nicholas I and his minister of marine wished to send a Russian naval squadron from the Baltic to the Black Sea, which meant its passage through the Dardanelles and Bosphorus, Nesselrode made it clear that this would be an infringement of international law. 'In the present state of our relations with Turkey', he wrote, 'the treaties oblige the latter to *close* the entrance to the Dardanelles to any foreign war flag, but these transactions by no means oblige it to *open* it to us. . . . No stipulation authorises us to demand in the Bosphorus the admission of our war-ships.' Nevertheless statesmen such as Guizot in France and Palmerston in Britain, diplomats such as Ponsonby and Roussin, the British and French ambassadors to the Porte, shared in varying degrees the belief that Russia had now gained the power, in case of need, to send her warships from the Black Sea into the Mediterranean, with all the dangerous strengthening of her strategic position which this involved. Both Britain and France, therefore, protested in Constantinople against the conclusion of the Treaty and made unsuccessful efforts to prevent its ratification.

They had reasons for alarm, moreover, which went further than the specific issue of the regime of the Straits. The whole sequence of events in February–July 1833, the unprecedented demonstration it had provided of Turkish weakness and apparent dependence on Russia,

seemed very threatening. Russia appeared to have reduced the Ottoman Empire to a mere protectorate or vassal-state. If this were so, it
meant a very ominous growth of her power. There is no doubt,
moreover, that a tilting of the Near Eastern balance of this kind was
hoped for in St Petersburg. Nesselrode claimed, once the Treaty was
signed, that 'our intervention in the affairs of Turkey has acquired a
basis of legality.' It was now expected in Russian governing circles
that the Porte would in future enter into no agreements hostile to
Russia and that if it should again need aid of the kind given in 1833 it
must look for it in the first place to St Petersburg. On this wider
canvas, therefore, the fears of British and French statesmen are more
easily justified than in the context of the Straits alone.

Nevertheless Russian policy was still dogged by the contradictions
which had marked it since at least the latter part of the Napoleonic
wars. On the one hand it sought to serve purely national interests; and
this it seemed to have achieved in 1833 by gaining for Russia a new
status and potentialities in the Near East. Yet at the same time
Nicholas I, like his brother, was genuinely anxious to co-operate with
the other powers and to do nothing to weaken their unity or to provide
openings for the forces of revolution and international discord. This
meant in practice co-operation with Austria and Britain, even at some
sacrifice of Russian interests.

Thus, in September 1833, little more than two months after the signature of the Unkiar-Skelessi Treaty, Nicholas agreed with Francis II
of Austria, in a meeting of the two monarchs at Münchengrätz in
Bohemia, to maintain the existence of the Ottoman Empire under the
existing dynasty, to protect it if necessary against renewed pressure
from Mehemet Ali and to take concerted action if it seemed about to
collapse. To speak of this agreement, as Soviet writers have done, as a
self-inflicted defeat for Russia is a great exaggeration. Nevertheless it
showed clearly Nicholas's desire to co-operate in the Near East with
other reliably conservative powers. To this end he was clearly willing,
within limits, to sacrifice some of Russia's own freedom of action. In
1834, again, Russian garrisons were withdrawn from the Danubian
principalities where they had been maintained since the war of
1828–9, even though the war indemnity promised by the Turks in the
Adrianople Treaty had not yet been fully paid. This too was a gesture,
and quite a substantial one, towards co-operation with Austria even
at the cost of some sacrifice by Russia.

Moreover, by the later 1830s, the Tsar was becoming increasingly anxious to improve his very strained relations with Britain. To this there were many obstacles. The allegedly threatening growth of the Russian navy had aroused intense though short-lived alarm in Britain: in 1833 and 1838 her naval strength was increased to meet this rather unreal danger. In November 1836 the seizure of a British ship, the *Vixen*, by the Russian naval force blockading the coast of Circassia led to a new and sharp outburst of Russophobia. In 1837–8 the apparent growth of Russian influence in Persia and perhaps also in Afghanistan provoked a British response culminating in the unnecessary war with the Afghans which broke out early in 1839. On the other hand the Anglo-Turkish commercial treaty of August 1838 was suspected in St Petersburg of containing secret clauses which weakened Russia's position in the Ottoman Empire. Yet both Nicholas and Nesselrode sincerely wished for an end to this disagreement and bad feeling. The isolation of France, the weakening or breaking of the Anglo-French *entente* which had developed in the middle and later 1830s, the defeat of the forces of anarchy and disruption throughout Europe, seemed to justify some sacrifice of Russia's immediate interests. In June 1837 the French ambassador in St Petersburg said of the Tsar that 'good relations with England seem to him among the conditions imposed on his situation.' By the following year Nesselrode had decided, in spite of pressure from expansionist elements which were strong in military circles, that Russian policy in Asia should aim merely at the creation of buffer zones in Persia and central Asia between the British and Russian Empires which would reduce the danger of conflict and competition; this idea continued to be a significant element in Anglo-Russian relations in Asia until 1843.[5] Moreover, as the Turks in the later 1830s turned increasingly to Britain for help in strengthening themselves for a second round with Mehemet Ali (for example by trying unsuccessfully to raise a loan in London in 1838), it began to appear that the privileged position which Russia claimed to have won in 1833 was hardly worth very much after all. Certainly it was not worth defending at the cost of continued friction with other great powers, especially as Austria's wavering attitude now made her seem a very uncertain ally.

The desire of Nicholas and his minister for co-operation with Britain in the Near East was made clear by the outbreak of a new Turco-Egyptian struggle in April 1839. Within a few weeks the Turks, heavily defeated in northern Syria and faced by the death of Mahmud II and the desertion of the bulk of their fleet, which sailed

to Alexandria and joined the Egyptians, seemed on the point of collapse. On 27 July, when the Turkish ministers, in desperation, were
about to give way to Mehemet Ali's demands that Syria and Adana,
as well as Egypt, be made hereditary possessions of his family, the
representatives in Constantinople of Britain, Russia, Austria, France
and Prussia presented to the Porte a collective note which claimed
that 'agreement among the Five Great Powers on the Question of the
East is secured' and invited the Turkish government to 'suspend any
definitive resolution without their concurrence, waiting for the effects
of the interest which these powers feel for it'. In fact agreement between the powers was far from complete; but for the next year interest
was to centre not on fighting in the Near East, of which there was
hardly any, but on the diplomacy of the great European states. In particular the situation was to be transformed by a surprisingly successful *rapprochement* between Britain and Russia.

Moves in this direction had begun as soon as news of the fighting in
Syria reached St Petersburg. On 23 April Nesselrode warned the Tsar
against sending another Russian expedition to the Bosphorus because of the danger of conflict with Britain which it involved, and
urged an Anglo-Russian agreement for the delimitation of spheres of
influence in the Near East. In mid-May Pozzo di Borgo, now Russian
ambassador in London, was ordered to explore the possibilities of
such an agreement; and in another report in mid-August Nesselrode
pointed out bluntly that the Unkiar-Skelessi Agreement, which on
paper had still another two years to run, had lost all practical significance and should be abandoned. On this, as on so many aspects of his
policies, Nesselrode has been severely criticised both by nationalist
historians before 1917 and by Soviet ones since the revolution.
Goriainov, for example, in what is still in western Europe the best-
known Russian work on the Straits problem, wrote bitterly that
'deceptive arguments drew Russia into a mistaken course of action'.[6]
But there was much to be said in favour of Nesselrode's attitude. The
complete unreliability of the Ottoman government, the limited forces
which Russia could deploy at the Straits, above all the hostility of
Britain and France to any unilateral action by her – all these pointed
towards caution and an effort at co-operation with Britain. The
strength of these arguments has impressed many later writers;[7] it
proved decisive with Nicholas I.

In September the Tsar decided to send to London on a special mission Baron E. P. Brunnow, Russian minister in Stuttgart. For the task

of establishing better Anglo-Russian relations he was extremely well suited. A protégé of Nesselrode, like him German and Protestant by origin, an anglophile and partisan of free trade, Brunnow believed firmly that Russian policy should foster general rather than merely national interests, those of the European family of states. These interests were perpetually threatened by war and revolution and could be secured only by the unity of the great powers. Inevitably, however, this cosmopolitanism has seemed to many Russians a betrayal of their country's true interests which lay in retaining a free hand for Russia and not allowing her to be deluded into a co-operation with the other great powers in which all the sacrifices were made by her. Brunnow has been attacked, like Nesselrode, as a foreigner who, weak and almost treacherous, in effect betrayed the country of his adoption.[8] From the beginning of his talks with Palmerston, however, he made it clear that if Russia once more had to protect the Sultan against his rebellious vassal she would do so as the representative of Europe and not for any selfish purpose of her own. She was quite willing to allow the Treaty of Unkiar-Skelessi to lapse in 1841, at the end of the eight-year period for which it had been concluded; but in return Britain must agree to an international guarantee of the closure of the Straits to foreign warships, and must also guarantee 'the existence and repose' of the Ottoman Empire. An agreement along these lines had much to offer both sides. To Russia it gave protection for her Black Sea coast and the promise of a strengthened concert of the conservative powers and the possible isolation of France. To Britain it offered escape from the nightmare of an exclusive Russian treaty relationship with the Ottoman Empire and the Russian dominance of the Near East which this might lead to. Palmerston showed from the beginning of the negotiations that in all essentials the Russian proposals were welcome to him.

There were long, and to the Tsar, irritating and incomprehensible delays before this agreement in principle could be made effective in practice. But these delays arose from Anglo-French, not Anglo-Russian, tensions. Any agreement between Britain and Russia directed against Mehemet Ali was certain to encounter deep hostility in France, the one power which now supported the Pasha in his demands. Open *rapprochement* with Russia thus meant a serious breach between Britain and the only other great European state which could claim to be in some sense liberal. This the majority of Lord Melbourne's Cabinet were long unwilling to face. 'The particular obstacle,' Brunnow told Nesselrode at the end of January 1840, 'is that France will not join in the common action, and Great Britain will not act without her.' Only by a threat of resignation was Palmerston able to obtain Britain's accession to the International Convention of 15 July 1840 which provided the basis for a solution of the Near Eastern crisis. The details of the terms which this Convention offered Mehemet Ali are scarcely relevant here. Much more important was the fact that the Sultan, Abdul Medjid, agreed to declare explicitly that henceforth the Straits would be closed in peace-time to the warships of all foreign states; this 'ancient rule' of the Ottoman Empire was thus given an international status clearer and more formal than ever before. Moreover it was now obvious that Russia, by playing an ostentatiously 'European' role in the crisis and successfully wooing Britain, had for the time being destroyed the Anglo-French *entente*. Soon Nicholas I was even to offer the Russian Baltic fleet to defend the British coasts against a possible French invasion.

A year later, on 13 June 1841, after the Egyptians had been decisively defeated in Syria by a native rising and British naval action, the powers, including France, signed the Straits Convention. This, as well as finally confining Mehemet Ali to Egypt, of which his family were to become hereditary rulers, repeated the provisions of the agreement made a year earlier regarding the Bosphorus and Dardanelles. The Straits were thus made, explicitly and unmistakably, an object of European concern; their status was now regulated by an international agreement which was to last until the First World War. Clearly this ruled out the sort of unilateral action by Russia which had resulted in the Russo-Turkish treaties of 1805 and 1833.

Was then the whole sequence of events in 1839–41, a great defeat for Russia, one which meant her abandoning any claim to a free hand in the Near East and adopting a humiliatingly passive attitude there? Some historians have so argued. 'We offered up as a sacrifice,' wrote Tatishchev of the crisis of these years, 'all the best traditions of our history, the principle of the non-intervention of foreign powers in our relations with the Porte, and the Treaty of Unkiar-Skelessi, signed only six years before and providing a brilliant example of the above-mentioned principle.'[9] It is true, moreover, that the Russian government showed its uncertainty about the value of the Convention of 1841 by trying unsuccessfully to limit its life to a mere eight or ten years. On the other hand it could well be argued that the new situation gave Russia a more effective guarantee than any merely bilateral agreement ever could against attacks on her southern coastline, at least in any war in which the Ottoman Empire was not a belligerent. 'The London convention', Nesselrode claimed in his long year-end report to the Tsar on the events of 1841, 'served no other end than to prevent the entry into the Black Sea of ships of war other than our own, and this guarantee of safety which was given us in 1833 only for eight years and not recognised by other cabinets, was given general recognition as part of international law.'[10]

Many materials for a comprehensive history of Russia's Near Eastern policy during the period 1821–41 are still lacking. In particular we have no collection of the letters of either Alexander I or Nicholas I; and though the works of Shil'der, Schiemann and Tatishchev provide much valuable information they are all written from an official and rather impersonal standpoint. A full and rounded picture of these rulers, whose influence on every aspect of Russian policy was so decisive, is still lacking. The question of how far the economic development of south Russia and the growth of its trade with western Europe influenced government policy is also perhaps still an open one, though it seems unlikely that this will ever be proved a factor of much importance. But the central point is clear. These two decades saw a struggle between the conservatism and the genuine feeling for the unity of the great powers which in the last analysis dominated the thinking of the tsars and their closest advisers and, on the other hand, the nationalist, expansionist and isolationist forces represented by many Russian soldiers and by some diplomats. Against Nesselrode were ranged the military leaders who had expected war with the Turks in 1821–2 and who had hoped in 1833 that Muraviev might be able to establish Russian garrisons at the Straits. The diplomacy symbolised by Brunnow was challenged by that represented by Pozzo di Borgo, who in 1821 urged the destruction of Turkish power in Europe and in 1828 demanded a Russian occupation of Constantinople and the Straits. In spite of the war of 1828–9 and its results, in spite of the events of 1833, this period as a whole saw a victory for the first of these tendencies. Probably this benefited both Russia and Europe, a suggestion borne out by the disastrous results of Russia's unplanned and largely unintentional abandonment in 1853 of the attitudes which had been predominant in the 1820s and 1830s.

5. The Metternich System, 1815–48

ALAN SKED

W AS there really such a thing as a 'Metternich system' and, if so, what was it? The question is posed for two reasons: first because Metternich himself consistently denied the existence of any such system, and secondly because, although historians are wont to refer to one, they rarely get round to defining it. The result is that students are very often confused by the term when it is employed in the secondary literature. The subject is such, moreover, that wider reading can serve to create greater confusion. For Metternich – who used to boast that he could bore men to death – very seldom wrote to the point either. Thus his own allusions to the subject do not necessarily shed much light on his position, although his explanation that his policies rested not upon a 'system' but on immovable, fixed principles may serve as a starting point for discussion. Finally the monographic literature on Metternich has still not brought general agreement among historians as to how much room for manoeuvre the Chancellor had in applying his policies, or for that matter, as far as the Habsburg domains themselves were concerned, to what end his policies were directed. The student might well conclude, therefore, that talk of a 'Metternich System' would be better avoided. None the less there is a case to be made out that a Metternich system existed and that its operation can be described. Essentially it is that Metternich strove to uphold the interests of an aristocratic, European social order through maintaining the 1815 Settlement by means of a repressive alliance of monarchical states, whose internal and external security were to be preserved by military and police co-operation as well as by efficient and centralised bureaucratic rule. In this way he hoped to exorcise the threat of revolution and so maintain the *status quo*.

His system was a European one, and this on two accounts. In the first place he completely identified the interests of Europe with those of the Austrian Empire. The latter he saw, with her nationalities, as a sort of European microcosm, but in other more important ways, she was a 'European necessity'. Territorially satiated, she upheld the sanctity of treaties and the European balance of power. Moreover she was the only power which could be trusted to maintain stability in central Europe. Her very existence as a state depended on the maintenance of peace and order in Europe. This is what Metternich was really saying when he told Wellington in 1824 that Europe was like a fatherland to him.

In another sense, however, he was saying that as a member of the aristocracy he felt at home anywhere in Europe. Indeed his utter determination to preserve the way of life of Europe's aristocracy provided the basis for a system of thought which in practice amounted to an ideology, and it was his ideological crusade against the enemies of aristocracy which gave his work an unusual coherence. It also allowed him to talk about his 'principles' which he would like to have applied systematically, and meant that he had fixed ideas not only about relations between states but about the constitution of the ideal state itself. Thus he had a clear idea of how he would have liked the Habsburg monarchy to have been governed and was prepared to advise other governments to conduct their affairs along similar lines.

Metternich assumed, given the experience of the French Revolution, that the only natural form of government was monarchy. The sovereign at the head of the social pyramid represented the principle of social order and the principle of order, therefore, required monarchical government. To deny this self-evident truth was to invite the chaos of revolution again. Thus monarchy was to be supported against all rival theories of government, and supporters of rival theories of government were to be regarded as enemies of monarchy. By monarchy, moreover, Metternich meant pure monarchy rather than the consitutional brand. The latter might be acceptable in Britain after centuries of adaptation, but even there he distrusted it. In France he saw it merely as a front for revolution. Thus when he spoke of monarchy he meant one in which the ruler ruled. A sovereign who did not exercise sovereignty, he held, was a contradiction in terms. Metternich, on the other hand, was no supporter of arbitrary or absolute monarchy. A sovereign had to be advised and had to follow orderly government practices. He had to uphold the law and social order and, of course, the laws of God. If he were not to lose respect he would have to demonstrate his capacity to exercise justice as well as authority. In practice this meant that there should be a powerful sovereign whose wishes, formulated in consultation with his advisers, should be enforced by a centrally organised judicial and civil service. This was the system of stern paternalism which Metternich would have liked to see prevail in Europe as a whole.

In the Habsburg monarchy itself there were many obstacles in the road to achieving it. Francis I for a start – and he was monarch until 1835 – had little sympathy for organised government. His central administration lacked direction, while in various parts of the monarchy the diets sought to increase their powers. Finally there was the problem of personalities which became acute after the accession of the mentally retarded Ferdinand I. All these factors meant that Austria during the Metternich period was, in Metternich's phrase, 'administered' rather than 'governed'. This had direct consequences for Austrian foreign policy. Before listing them, however, it is necessary to examine Metternich's domestic position since in the first place this is a controversial area historiographically, and secondly, in the light of the general argument, one can best see what types of government he would like to have seen established in Europe generally by working out what kind of government he sought to establish at home.

Care has to be taken, however, in describing Metternich's position in the domestic politics of the Austrian Empire. Not a great deal is known about the exact nature of his working relationship with Francis I, but what there is suggests that there is no need to take at face value many of his own statements on the matter. Thus, although he told a Russian general on one occasion that were he to 'diverge' from the Emperor's will 'Prince Metternich would not remain Foreign Minister for twenty-four hours'[1] and despite his famous statement 'I may have governed Europe occasionally but Austria never',[2] there can be little doubt that he played a very powerful role in the Empire's domestic as well as foreign affairs. One would hesitate on the other hand to endorse Constantin de Grunwald's claim that he stamped 'every branch of the administration with his own personality' and 'enjoyed the privileges of a Prime Minister without being called upon to bear official responsibility'.[3] The truth seems to be that, although there were occasions on which Metternich was prepared to quarrel with Francis, on many if not most issues their views were much the same. Both were horrified by change and both were absolutely committed to the struggle against the revolution. Thus, as the Russian ambassador commented, 'Austrian politics [were] based on Francis's character and guided by Metternich's spirit.'[4] Or as

Metternich put it: 'Heaven has placed me next to a man who might have been created for me, as I for him. The Emperor Francis knows what he wants and that never differs in any way from what I most want.'[5] The question is often posed, however, 'why did Metternich not threaten to resign when Francis failed to remodel the imperial administration?' There are several possible explanations for this: probably Metternich believed that it was impossible for the Emperor to change his working habits; maybe he himself lacked sufficient determination with which to pursue his plans; perhaps he simply did not believe that he had the right to demand his own way over everything. What is very difficult to maintain is that a threat to resign on Metternich's part would have led to his instant dismissal. Francis for one thing, had far too high an opinion of his Chancellor; moreover it is known that his rival Kolowrat threatened to retire on no less than twenty occasions.

Metternich, however, was certainly less than satisfied by the way in which the Empire was run. The trouble was, as he complained, that 'the Empire did not have a government'[6] – or rather one which actually worked. Under Francis I the so-called *Kabinettsweg* prevailed. This meant simply that Francis, who could take years to reach a decision on any matter, however trivial, – and who insisted on reading innumerable written reports on anything which had to be decided – would take advice from anyone he chose. Metternich did not deny him his right to do so, but he greatly deplored the waste of time and administrative chaos produced thereby. Thus, whenever he was asked for his advice on the administration, he would advise the Emperor to reform it in the interests of efficiency. He had no desire – as some historians have maintained – to decentralise the bureaucracy or to federalise the monarchy; his plan was to create a strong, efficient central government which would deal with all parts of the Empire in a uniform way – even if (against the inclination of Francis I) he was prepared to tolerate the traditional presence of emasculated provincial estates.

Basically the system which Metternich wished to devise for the Habsburg monarchy (and which, as will be seen, he recommended elsewhere) was that the government should consist of a council advising the Emperor (i.e. the *Staatsrat* or if a few representatives from local diets were to be added – as Metternich advised in 1817 – the *Reichsrat*) which would have a purely consultative role. In other words it would advise only on those issues which were presented to it, and its advice could be accepted or rejected by the monarch. Moreover, as Metternich devised it, it would not deliberate as a full body but in sections which would deliberate orally. This, appearances notwithstanding, was in order to expedite its business. Once the monarch had received its advice however, he was then to come to a decision on any particular issue in consultation with his Ministerial Conference [*Ministerkonferenz*]. This in Metternich's ideal form would have consisted of a number of executive ministers who would have supervised the *Hofstellen* or administrative departments and who would have been responsible to the Emperor alone for enforcing imperial policy. Much of this was derived from Napoleonic administrative practice since Metternich, as ambassador to France, had been highly impressed by the more despotic aspects of the Bonapartist regime. Napoleon, in fact, had won his eternal admiration for having imposed order on the chaos of revolutionary France.

In Austria, however, Francis I could come to no decision about reform so that, for the whole of his reign, the Austrian foreign minister was forced to operate within a system of administrative chaos. Indeed, instead of a sharp division in functions and in personnel between the *Staatsrat* and the *Ministerkonferenz* which Metternich wished to see established, an overlapping of both was prevalent in the system operated by the Emperor Francis, and the *Staatsrat* functioned as the principal council advising the Emperor. The *Staatsrat* itself, however, never became an executive body but operated rather as another part of the bureaucracy. Represented on it were most of the heads of the *Hofstellen* so that in practice it became a sort of co-ordinating body for the higher civil service. Francis, however, still managed to impede its work by demanding individual written reports from every member concerned with each and every piece of advice, and very often by consulting people who were not even members of the body. To Metternich's particular chagrin, he also refused to develop a proper Ministerial Conference. In fact, by 1830, Metternich himself was the only 'Minister' in the government (the post of finance minister had been abolished in 1829; that of minister of the interior had fallen into disuse almost as soon as it was created in 1818), and when the 'Ministerial Conference' met it was not really an executive conference at all. Apart from Metternich it would be attended by the police chief as well as by the head of the political and financial sections of the *Staatsrat*; in any case, it was not summoned very often. Metternich, therefore, was forced to accept that the '*Kabinettsweg*' would continue. The best he could do was to develop *ad hoc* ways himself to get around the muddle created.

His initiative, however, was circumscribed by the emergence after 1828 of Count Franz Anton Kolowrat-Liebsteinsky as the dominant figure in the *Staatsrat*. Kolowrat is sometimes portrayed as a Liberal and an ideological opponent of Metternich within the Austrian administration, but such a picture must be modified. Kübeck, a senior Austrian civil servant of this period and one of the few of bourgeois origins, bitterly pointed out in his diaries how Kolowrat used his influence with the Emperor to have his Bohemian aristocratic relatives and protégés appointed to the best administrative posts. He also quoted Kolowrat's description of his differences with Metternich as he explained them to the Chancellor. Kolowrat said:

> You are completely wrong about me and the people with whom I mix. You think that my principles are different from yours. That is wrong. I am an aristocrat by birth and by convictions and completely agree with you that people must strive for conservatism and do everything to achieve it. Yet we differ about means. Your means consist of a forest of bayonets and a fixed adherence to things as they are: to my mind, by following these lines we are playing into the hands of the revolutionaries. . . . Your ways will lead us . . . not tomorrow or next year – but soon enough – to our ruin.[7]

Kolowrat, in other words, was merely a more subtle conservative than Metternich.

His opposition to Metternich's 'forest of bayonets', however, stemmed from more than subtlety alone. Kolowrat's influence rested on the fact that he was head of both the political and the financial sections of the *Staatsrat* (he later surrendered the latter post, but only to take charge of an all-powerful financial commission entrusted with the control of government expenditure), and as such he found himself in a constant battle with the Chancellor to balance the budget by reducing the costs of the army and the police. Given Metternich's natural inclination to expand both these bodies, not to mention his apparent lack of economic sense (the Chancellor was constantly getting into debt and arranging 'state' loans on his own behalf through the Rothschilds; he also received a pension from the Tsar), it is not surprising that he should have encountered Kolowrat's resistance. Despite the support of the

Emperor's adjutant and head of the military section of the *Staatsrat*, Count Charles Clam-Martinitz, however, Metternich was unable to weaken Kolowrat's control of the purse strings and of the police and army estimates. As will be seen, this undermined Austria's position in foreign affairs.

The lack of administrative cohesion became immeasurably worse after the death of Francis I. If the Empire had lacked direction under Francis, it lost much of what it had under the 'rule' of the retarded Ferdinand I. Incapable of reading documents or following an argument, the Emperor should never have been allowed to accede to the throne. Metternich, however, had agreed with Francis to arrange for a normal succession in the interests of 'legitimacy' and in the hope of achieving supreme power himself. He certainly conspired to secure this through Francis's last will and testament and by his manoeuvrings in 1836 to circumscribe Kolowrat's influence in internal affairs. The latter had returned to his estates on grounds of ill health (Metternich said he had 'piles going up to his head') and had given Metternich his opportunity to restructure the system of government. A strong Ministerial Conference was, therefore, set up and separated from the *Staatsrat* whose status was much reduced. Metternich was to preside over the former (which would function in fact as a council of regency) and Kolowrat was given the choice of either becoming a member of the Conference or of remaining merely a section chief of the *Staatsrat*. He was told that he could not be both. Metternich, in fact, was clearly intending to establish himself as the director of Austrian affairs.

The Chancellor, however, had reckoned without the influence of the imperial family. At this crucial moment, the Archduke John, who, like his equally competent brother the Archduke Charles, had been excluded from power by Francis and Metternich for years, returned to Vienna and upset Metternich's plans. To accommodate Kolowrat, the Archduke negotiated a scheme whereby a new Conference came into being, presided over by the Emperor and with a permanent membership of Metternich, Kolowrat, the Archduke Louis and the Archduke Francis Charles. Kolowrat was promised control of the Empire's financial affairs and internal matters on condition that he surrendered his membership of the *Staatsrat*. Kolowrat agreed and Metternich, clearly admitting defeat, offered neither resignation nor resistance. Thereafter the Conference in practice came to be headed by the Archduke Louis who proved even more reluctant than Francis I to reach decisions and whose preference for separate written reports soon reduced the flow of business to a standstill. Moreover, according to Kübeck, the Archduke Louis soon fell under the influence of Kolowrat whose position became unassailable. The Archduke John, as Kübeck interpreted it, had therefore, 'effected a compromise that [was] little different from a complete defeat of Prince Metternich'.[8] He continued: '[Kolowrat] in effect is supreme head of the Staatsrat, master of the money power, of all employments and of the fate of all officials (through the police), head of the entire *camarilla* and – through his position – the deciding spokesman in the conference'.[9] This has recently led one historian to conclude that

> Kolowrat had thus regained the greater part of the influence and power he had wielded before the crisis, with the additional advantage of being officially confirmed in much of what had been vague, undefined and even contrary to regulations. He now essentially fulfilled the functions of a prime minister, an office regarded by his rival as 'quite impossible' for Austria and suitable for 'no sensible servant of the state'.[10]

Such a conclusion, however, not only displays a certain naïveté regarding Metternich's ambitions in 1835–8, but vastly over-estimates the extent of Kolowrat's influence. It is true that he held control of the purse strings of the monarchy but, as before 1835, the man who really controlled the 'higher' imperial police was Metternich who likewise had the leading voice in matters, regarding Italy and Hungary. There is a strong case to be made out, therefore, that given his control of defence and foreign policy also, Metternich's position was stronger than Kolowrat's.

Metternich's policies towards Hungary and Italy will be treated in more detail presently, but at this point it is necessary to show the consequences of Kolowrat's financial control and of the lack of government cohesion on foreign policy.

Financial control meant in the first place that the military budget was curtailed. Kolowrat described it as a 'shield which weighed down the rider'[11] and made determined efforts to reduce military expenditure whenever possible. He was determined to keep Austria's budget balanced (he had first achieved this in 1829), and to reduce the state debt which was enormously high. In fact he was determined if possible to destroy Austria's reputation of being something of a credit risk, a reputation established during the Napoleonic wars.

In 1811 the monarchy had had to declare itself bankrupt, but in spite of this it had incurred enormous debts between 1813 and 1815. In the following period some order was restored in the monarchy's finances, but during the period 1815–48 the annual interest paid on the state debt amounted to roughly thirty per cent of the entire state revenue. If, according to one French observer in 1846, Austrian finances were nonetheless 'in a truly remarkable state of prosperity' (taking the figures for 1840 he calculated that the public debt amounted to not much more than one year's revenue if the sinking fund was subtracted),[12] this was not a view which was widely shared. As Kolowrat perceived matters the army budget for most of the period before 1848 accounted for nearly forty per cent of the state revenue and was the largest item of government expenditure. In years of crisis (or rather of intervention) it rose enormously, with the result that an active (or interventionist) policy on the part of the monarchy threatened once again to undermine the credit-worthiness of the state. Treasury opposition to policies which raised the military budget from fifty-five million florins in 1819 to eighty million in 1821, and from forty-six million in 1830 to seventy-seven million in 1831 had therefore been expressed with vigour. Stadion wrung his hands in 1824 on discovering that the costs of the Naples expedition had brought about a deficit of thirty-five million gulden which in turn had made necessary a loan of thirty million gulden. Nor did his anger abate on hearing that Metternich had had to agree to the part-repayment of an English loan of forty million gulden which the British government was now demanding in a show of disapproval. During the Greek War of Independence, therefore, Kolowrat (despite Metternich's boasts to the Powers) had informed Prince Winchischgraetz, the later field marshal, that Austria (whose military budget in 1827 had been again reduced to forty-eight million florins) was 'armed for eternal peace'.[13] He continued: 'we must do everything possible to prevent hostilities: and can only pray that people don't believe our threats. Our hopes rest on the divergence of interests of the three powers who are at present so unnaturally coalesced.'[14] The Austrian army, in other words, as far as Kolowrat was concerned was to be used only in the last resort. Metternich realised the implications of such an attitude and at the end of the Russo-Turkish War demanded that more money be spent on rearmament. But Kolowrat retorted:

If the military authorities have not yet succeeded, during a period of fifteen years of peace which has been interrupted only by one short campaign against Naples and Piedmont, to place the army and our other means of defence on such as footing as to be able to defend the Monarchy against whatever threat . . . one begins to fear that a military expenditure which already exceeds the financial resources of the Monarchy has hitherto been insufficient to fulfil its task. It is difficult, therefore, to answer the question how the annual 38–46 million gulden, which sum it is now recognised is insufficient for defence purposes and for protection against internal threat, could have been spent'.[15]

The army, however, had certainly not squandered its money. Officers and men alike were paid miserable wages and endured hard conditions of service. Nor could it be accused of investing its money in stockpiling: it often found that its room for manoeuvre was limited by its shortage of supplies. In fact, according to one statistician, the army only survived economically by sending one third to one half of its troops home: 'In peaceful times it is usual for a third or even a greater part of the men to be on leave and to keep only those who are indispensable for duty. In particular the peaceful years 1816–29 allowed so greatly extended a use of this system which is occasioned by economy and industrial considerations, that in each of the years, 1825, 1826 and 1828 almost one half of the men were on leave'.[16] The army in fact was so run-down, demoralised and ill-led that it could scarcely be described as battle-worthy. Thus, when Metternich invited the Archduke Charles in 1831 to lead the imperial forces against France, the Archduke made it abundantly clear in his reply that neither the financial state of the Empire nor the condition of the army would allow this. The Emperor himself realised this. When Radetzky asked him why there had been no war against France, Francis told him: 'I held a camp this year near Münchendorf where my troops displayed themselves so badly and apathetically that the Prussians voiced their dissatisfaction. We, therefore, recognised Louis Philippe as King of France at the same time as England. *Isolated, I could not undertake war*'.[17] Radetzky was despatched to Italy to reform the army there but, despite a number of measures he introduced and despite considerable mythology, there is little evidence that he produced outstanding results. In any case his efforts to consolidate his position against the looming threat from Piedmont before 1848 were also undermined by

treasury control. The Emperor told the President of the Imperial War
Council at the end of February 1848: 'In future no proposition which
entails additional financial expenditure is to be presented to me
before a preliminary agreement has been reached with the treasury
praesidium.'[18] Radetzky at the same time was informed that he would
only receive more troops if a 'significant rebellion' had already broken
out in Lombardy or if the French or Sardinians attacked. This,
despite the fact that the field marshal's strategy was based on attack-
ing the enemy first.

Metternich, therefore, was conducting the foreign policy of an
Empire whose lack of united leadership and whose financial weaknesses meant that it was in no position to take a strong or independent
line in foreign affairs. The wider implications of this will be discussed
presently. However, given the 1815 Settlement and his control of the
police, Hungarian and Italian policy, he was in a strong position to
impose his 'system' on a very large part of Europe.

Inside the Empire itself he did his best to ensure that the kingdoms
of Lombardy-Venetia and Hungary were run as Austrian provinces
as far as possible. In the case of Lombardy-Venetia this was easy to
engineer since Francis I in 1818 had given his viceroy there, the Archduke Rainer, such little power that it was immediately clear to everyone that this was how the kingdom was supposed to be administered.
The viceroy could only mediate in (but not resolve) disputes between
the governors of Lombardy and Venetia and all important decisions
were taken in Vienna. Essentially, therefore, Rainer's was a ceremonial role – as was that of the Central Congregations (diets) whose
wishes were consistently ignored until they lapsed into passivity from
the early 1820s onwards. Austrian Italy was ruled from Vienna
through the *Hofstellen* and *Staatsrat* which gave the governors their
orders. The governors in turn ran their provinces through delegates
and district commissioners. Metternich approved of this but merely
regretted the fact that the *Staatsrat* and *Hofstellen* as usual took ages to
reach decisions and clogged the administration with endless reports
and paperwork.

In Italy, however, Metternich succeeded in short-circuiting the
bureaucratic system. From 1826 the Emperor allowed him to attach a
special agent from the Foreign Ministry at the governor's office in
Milan. Ostensibly his job was to expedite business with the other Italian states, but in fact his position was more important than that. His
real function was to make sure that Metternich had direct control of

Italian policy. Instructions drafted by Metternich[19] made it clear that 'while paying attention to the usual diplomatic formalities and rules', his agents were 'to take note of the general political situation and do what [was] necessary in that regard'. Thus they were to act as a channel between the governor of Milan and the state and Court Chancellery (the Foreign Office) on all matters of mutual concern and especially on police affairs. Metternich underlined, however, that although they were being attached to the Governor's office and would be expected to work with him, this 'in no way [altered] [their] relationship to [him, i.e. Metternich] . . . ' and that they '[did] not cease to remain directly under [his] orders'.[20] Metternich used these men henceforth as his main source of information on Italy and it was on their regular – sometimes daily – reports that he based his policies.

Most of their correspondence consisted of regular surveys of Italian opinion and of police reports on the sects, and for most of the period 1815–48 the reports sent in were complacently optimistic. There was no attempt to deny that the Austrians were disliked by the upper classes (i.e. the local aristocracy and the bourgeoisie) and by Italian liberals, but it was always pointed out that the vast majority of the population had no political opinions and that the sects were far less active in Austrian Italy than in the rest of the peninsula. Metternich himself took pride in this. The government also consoled itself with the belief that the Italians were divided amongst themselves and that what Metternich referred to as a *Munizipalgeist* – inter-city rivalry – would prevent any general anti-Austrian movement from emerging. There was even a reluctance to believe that Charles Albert represented a threat to Austrian rule, a reluctance which prevailed, in fact, almost up until the outbreak of revolution in 1848. Thus Metternich's agents advised the Chancellor to follow a policy of bread and circuses respecting Italy: 'At the time of the Romans, the circus was the state secret that rendered Italians submissive to the government and modern Italians are no less difficult to please or less manageable in this respect.'[21] Metternich consequently saw little need to change things. As far as he was concerned he now had direct control of events in Italy without having to worry about the bureaucratic channels of the *Hofstellen*. He therefore fobbed off Italian requests for change with his usual clichés, telling one visitor: 'I have not time to bother about details of administration. My job is more important than that.'[22] Another visitor, the mayor of Milan, was greeted by the Chancellor in 1845 as follows:

Metternich was most amiable and received him with great courtesy, yet always avoided saying anything definite about our country. He always embarked on generalities and what he said had no more importance than talk about the weather. If Casati [the mayor] mentioned anything regarding administrative affairs, it did not make any impression.[23]

With the accession of Pius IX to the Papal See and the growing anti-Austrian feeling due to social, economic and political causes in the years 1846–48, Metternich took slightly more interest in the administration of northern Italy and sent his right-hand man, Count Ficquelmont, on a special mission there in the autumn of 1847. Ficquelmont, who was certainly under no illusions about federalising the Empire, devoted himself to the problem of 'How we can go on running the Kingdom as a province but organise and above all govern it in such a fashion that we might present it as an Italian State to the hostile movement that the other Italian States want to stir up against us.'[24] Unfortunately the solution he arrived at was too radical for Metternich who simply ignored his requests to bolster the viceroy's position and to strengthen the viceregal council. He complained instead that 'the police department [in Vienna] [was] receiving nothing or the equivalent of nothing from Milan'.[25] The panicky reactions of Ficquelmont and the viceroy to the Tobacco riots in Milan in January 1848 served only to increase the Chancellor's contempt for the proposed reforms. At the price of driving Ficquelmont to submitting his resignation he made it crystal clear that a little initiative on the part of the local authorities would serve Austrian interests much better than administrative change.

Ficquelmont, at this point, informed the Chancellor in the bluntest possible way that he was deceiving himself. Despite his agents' reports from Milan, Ficquelmont told Metternich that he was 'unaware of the most essential and serious matters which concern[ed] the general interests of the country as well as particular administrative, financial and judicial ones, matters which governors [had] been submitting to the competent authorities for years but which were still unexamined and unanswered'.[26] Metternich would have none of this. He did not want to give more power or even more prestige to the viceroy in Italy and naturally would not accept that Austrian policy had been based on ignorance. He told Ficquelmont:

'Only by centralising the action of the various branches of authority is it possible to establish its unity and hence its force. Power distributed is no longer power.'[27] He consoled himself with the knowledge, after February 1848, that the viceroy, Ficquelmont, the governor and Field Marshal Radetzky were having daily conferences in Milan in order to co-ordinate whatever measures were necessary to restore order in the wake of the riots. His principle of centralising authority was being heeded at last. He wrote: 'Here is what is needed: that what we order this side of the Alps should be carried out on the other; that people there should not seek to weaken our directives but to put them into effect exactly as advised.'[28] To devolve power to Lombardy would be 'dangerous' – 'the same thing would be immediately demanded by other parts of the Empire'.[29] Thus, right until the end, Metternich was striving to ensure that Lombardy-Venetia would be treated as just another province of the Austrian Empire.

It was the Hungarians most of all, however, who, inside the Empire, were affected by Metternich's centralising tendencies, since Hungary was the only part of the Habsburg dominions after 1815 to retain a constitutionally anomolous position thanks to her ancient constitution. This meant that her laws had to be passed by the Hungarian Diet – albeit with royal approval – before the Vienna government could secure the Hungarian troops and revenue it required. Hungary also retained an elective system of county administration and representatives to the Lower House of the Diet were subject to recall by county assemblies. All this meant that the work of the Hungarian Chancellery in Vienna and the Palatine's Council in Pest could encounter stiff and vocal opposition from Magyar public opinion. Moreover public opinion in Hungary was a genuine force to be reckoned with. In the period 1815–48 a greater percentage of the population (*circa* ten per cent of the adult male population) had the vote in Hungary than in England before 1832 or in France before 1848.

This was a situation which Metternich intensely disliked and one which he was determined to alter. During the Napoleonic period he had toyed with the idea of using French troops to stage a *coup d'état* against the Hungarian constitution, and his proposals of 1817 to strengthen the central government of the monarchy were presented as a means by which to bring the Hungarians into line. He wrote: '. . . as a result of this reorganisation [centralising the administration under a Minister of the Interior] the Hungarian and Transylvanian Chancelleries will sink from the high level at which they stand today to that of the administration in general'.[30] Finally he opposed the programme of the Hungarian reform movement in the 1820s, 1830s and 1840s, root and branch. Its proposals would have brought about a liberal and semi-independent Hungary and it, therefore, had to be crushed. Metternich told the Palatine, the Archduke Joseph: 'The Opposition today is a subversive one which exploits moderate constitutionalism in order to overthrow the government and the constitution. The Hungarian polity is a monarchical–aristocratic one. It cannot be accommodated to democratic institutions. Such institutions are in contradiction with the existing order.'[31] The Chancellor himself took the initiative against the reform movement both in the Diet (which financial needs forced the government to call in 1825, 1832–36, 1839–40, 1843–4, and 1847–8) and in the counties, boasting to his son in 1825 that he had taken 'things into his own hands'.[32] He was to continue to do so up until 1848. The policies he pursued, based on total opposition to Hungarian independence or initiative, took many forms: county elections were influenced, the press was muzzled or controlled, the secret police was widely employed and in the 1830s pure terror tactics were resorted to. Leading opponents of the regime were charged with treason and imprisoned. Wesselény was sentence to three years in jail, Kossuth to four and Lovassy to ten. However the public outcry was so great that such terror tactics had to be abandoned. Metternich, thereafter, attempted to control Hungary by backing the 'neo-Conservative' party of Aurél Dessewffy whose 'reform' programme amounted to an attack on the Hungarian county system. In 1841 he told the State Conference: 'If it is impossible to govern Hungary without a constitution based on the Diet, we are faced with the unavoidable task of so manipulating this constitution that it will become possible to govern Hungary in the regular fashion'.[33] He then outlined a plan by which to remove the counties from the control of their elected officials whom he sought to replace by paid administrators appointed by Vienna, administrators who could rely if necessary on military backing. Further proposals included the abolition of county instructions to deputies and the presence of police in the Diet during sessions. In this way the Chancellor hoped that the opposition could be broken. Aware that there was a risk of provoking a national uprising in Hungary by such proposals he was prepared to meet it. It was better, he told his colleagues, that the government should take the initiative in this respect and arm itself for the clash rather than allow the opposition to choose the place and time of the final encounter. Once again, therefore, Metternich intended to exert the greatest possible control from the centre. His proposals were partially introduced in the counties in the 1840s and helped prepare the ground for 1848.

At the centre of Metternich's beliefs regarding forms of government, was the principle that the monarch should be advised by a strong central government responsible only to himself and capable of administering all parts of the state in an orderly and uniform fashion. Although his class consciousness persuaded him that the aristocracy should be allowed to play a ceremonial role in emasculated estates, the Chancellor had no intention of compromising with the representative principle which he regarded as a revolutionary one. Public opinion he believed could be consulted and manipulated through the 'higher state police' and those of his energies which were not expended on foreign affairs were chiefly directed at controlling police matters. He completely dominated the president of the *Polizeihofstelle*, Count Sadlnitzky, and his State Chancellery controlled the censorship. Indeed the police reports from all over the Empire had to be sent to Metternich personally and most of the key decisions regarding the censorship of the press were taken by the Chancellor himself. He prided himself that his intricate system of censorship, spies, subsidies and *cabinets noirs* ensured stability of the monarchy and boasted that within it nothing could happen without his knowledge. Outside, he corresponded with the Chiefs of police of France and Russia. His greatest fear in fact was that the system of government which he had striven for years to build up – despite his failure regarding Kolowrat – would be toppled not from within but from without.

One final point has to be made about his efforts to consolidate the Habsburg monarchy itself. Although he was often dispirited by the opposition he encountered in the *Staatsrat* and in Hungary, and although he often voiced a pessimism which despaired of 'shoring up the mouldering structures' of the imperial administration, he had a genuine conviction in the value of his work which at times he could even idealise. He did believe that a strong central government was necessary in post-revolutionary Europe and he was convinced that concessions to liberal reform were the surest recipe for revolution. Finally he would not accept that his policies had in any way disadvantaged the peoples his Emperors had ruled, and as late as October 1847 he told the Austrian ambassador in Rome:

[if] people would only view our Empire impartially: everything

there is progressing; everything that is good and useful is advancing . . . all the reasonable demands preached by progressives have been fulfilled by us. Our Empire acknowledges the perfect equality of citizens before the law; we have no privileges or feudal burdens; in our Empire is found equality of taxation and the independence of justice. All parts of the Empire have assemblies of estates and a municipal system much more liberal than that which exists in countries ruled by the modern representative system. In no other empire are the nationalities more respected than ours; respect for the nationalities is indeed a necessary condition of our existence; nowhere is there less absolutist government than in our Empire, nor could there be any.[34]

The Chancellor was clearly exaggerating, but there is no reason to suspect that he lacked genuine conviction in the essential benevolence of his system.

What was good for the Empire was good for the rest of Europe. Since Metternich regarded Europe as a whole – interdependent politically, and composed of the same class elements – it was only natural that he convinced himself that it too should defeat the common threat of revolution by the methods he employed at home. Strong government – centralised, administratively efficient government – was the key. This meant not only that individual governments should consolidate themselves (if possible on the Austrian model) but that they should combine in a European concert to co-ordinate their defence of the *status quo* as established in 1815. It was Metternich's desire, therefore, not only to get the powers to agree to intervene to crush revolution whenever necessary (albeit in a way that would not undermine the balance of power) but to bring about the creation of a European police network which could reveal the machinations of the sects. Otherwise the *Comité-Directeur* – the secret committee of revolutionaries whom he thought directed the liberal-revolutionary movement throughout Europe – would once more plunge the continent into war and revolution and overthrow the social and political order. The Chancellor's main problem was simply to convince the rest of Europe that such measures were required and that he was the best man to direct them. He also had to create the instruments through which direction might take place – since the unsatisfactory condition of the Austrian army and Austrian finances meant that Metternich was hardly in a position to impose his will on Europe unilaterally.

The countries most susceptible to Austrian influence and Metternichian principles in the period after 1815 were Italy and Germany. The Vienna Settlement had established Habsburg hegemony over both and Metternich had a freer hand in both to practise what he preached. In Italy he began with a number of powerful advantages: possession of Lombardy-Venetia; dynastic links with the Duchies; the fragmentation of the peninsula into a number of weak states; the treaties which allied these to Austria; and their dependence on Austria's economy. In addition there were certain intangible factors: Austria's protection of treaty rights; a common fear of revolution on the part of Italian sovereigns; fear of domination by France; and Austria's reputation for good government. For in Italy Austria could really present herself as a model for sovereigns to follow: her administration in Lombardy-Venetia was by common consent the most efficiently run in the peninsula; her judicial and educational systems were the most advanced of all in Italy; and the standard of living enjoyed by her Italian subjects reflected the most developed economy of the Italian states.

Metternich, in fact, was constantly forced to encourage the Italian sovereigns to reform. The chaotic state of administration in the Papal States and Naples in particular stood in contradiction to his belief in efficiently centralised rule. Worse still it enfeebled the struggle against the revolution in that very part of Europe where the 'sects' were most at home. Thus he advised the Pope to create a centralised, efficently organised administration run by a professional bureaucracy recruited from men of talent; a legal system purged of the confusion, inequity and inhumanity of the Old Regime and incorporating the principle of equality before the law and some guarantee of equal rights against arbitrary procedures; a financial system capable of providing an adequate revenue without overburdening taxpayers, and an efficient police and military capable of maintaining internal order. Similar advice was given to other sovereigns and a programme was put through at the Laibach Congress intended to force all Italian States to reorganise their administration under Austrian supervision. Yet his efforts remained without success and in fact never really came close to achieving any.

The reasons for this are straightforward. There was for a start a certain distrust of Austria in Italy. This was not because – as some historians have alleged – Metternich had designs on Italian territory. The Chancellor resisted pressure to annex part of Piedmont in 1821 and part of the Papal States ten years later. On the other hand there was a xenophobic resistance to Austria in Italy which he exacerbated by his constant tendency to lecture Italian rulers and to insist on his advice being followed. His efforts, moreover, to negotiate postal treaties which would have brought all Italian mail under Austrian inspection and his attempts to establish an Italian secret police system guided by a Central Information Centre, not to mention his sporadic attempts to establish an Italian League, analogous to the German Confederation, under Austria's presidency, created resentment on the part of princes who had no objection to intervention against the revolution but who protested vehemently against the encroachment of their own legitimate rights. Thus the same princes who were all too content to ignore reform in the secure knowledge that Austria would intervene to save them if the worst should happen, rebuffed the Chancellor's attempts to co-ordinate the anti-revolutionary struggle which he was waging on their behalf. Metternich himself very often despaired of them. Thus, although he was determined to intervene in Naples in 1820, by 1847 he was much more reluctant to pull the Neapolitan chestnuts out of the fire. Given the reaction of Sardinia and the Papal States to Radetzky's 'occupation' of Ferrara in 1847 – which Metternich had originally supported – he thought it best to wait for the revolution to reach Lombardy-Venetia in 1848 before he gave the Austrians his orders to smash it. None the less, for most of the period 1815–48, Austria had the Italian situation pretty much under her exclusive control.

In Germany, Metternich's task was at once easier and more difficult. It was easier thanks to the organisation of the German Confederation which could pass all sorts of repressive legislation in the name of German states as a whole; on the other hand, the more developed national consciousness of the Germans plus the growth of representative and constitutional institutions, especially in the southern German states, meant that opposition to his principles was much more articulate and widespread.

Metternich viewed Germany in much the same way as he viewed Italy – as a 'geographical expression'. Significantly he referred to the German Confederation as a 'European institution' – not a German one – and declared that both Austria and Prussia were European powers who just happened to be part of it in much the same way that the kings of Holland and Denmark were represented in it through Luxemburg and Schleswig-Holstein. The Confederation itself in any case had no powers. Austria and Prussia fixed its business beforehand and Metternich used it as much as possible as a mere organ through which to extend his repressive policies through Germany. Prussia for her part was quite content to follow Austria in these matters and even sought Metternich's advice on constitutional reform. Predictably he advised the Prussian monarch not to establish a central parliament and to emasculate the powers of the local diets which the king had unfortunately already promised. This advice was duly taken and in 1828 only a few enfeebled diets were established inside Prussia. German liberalism had received a body blow.

Indeed it seemed at first as if Metternich's policies would succeed in making Germany an integral part of his system by establishing Austrian control of political life there through Metternich's usual methods. The Carlsbad Decrees of 1819 – passed by the Confederation after the assassination of Kotzebue – laid down that university teachers judged to be politically unsound were to be dismissed and that student societies were to be dissolved; a press law empowered governments to control all publications of less than twenty pages; and a central investigating commission of the Confederation was established to investigate revolutionary movements and disturbances. Then by the Final Act of the Vienna Conference of the following year, Article thirteen of the Confederation was modified (it empowered member states to grant constitutions) by a declaration to the effect that all sovereign power in a member state was to be united in the head of state alone and that local diets might advise their sovereigns only to a limited extent. These provisions finally were reinforced by the Six Acts of 1832 which, in the aftermath of the 1830 revolutions, reconfirmed the provisions of 1820 and established a commission to determine to what extent the provincial diets had already encroached on sovereign powers. It was as a result of this commission's findings that several diets and universities were in fact closed down. When the western powers objected to this, the decrees of the Vienna Ministers' Conference of 1834 established an even more repressive censorship and spy network.

Two developments, however, undermined the Metternich system in Germany. The first was unforeseen and the second unavoidable. In the first place the efforts of Prussia to consolidate her territories soon led to the creation of the *Zollverein*, and in the second the war crises of 1830 and 1840 demonstrated Austria's inability to defend Germany against France.

Prussia, as a result of the 1815 Settlement, acquired control of the major waterways and trading routes of Germany. In order to exploit her position as well as to consolidate her territories she therefore launched a Prussian customs union in 1819. This *Zollverein* first covered an area inhabited by only some ten million Germans, but very quickly Prussia's smaller neighbours were forced to accept the Prussian tariff until, by 1833, the greater part of Germany had been absorbed within the union. The threat to Austrian interests which this represented had been perceived by Metternich who had done his utmost to frustrate the Prussian achievement. Yet it was to no avail. Austrian industry was not competitive enough to allow the monarchy itself to join and the rival customs unions which Metternich encouraged – the middle and southern German ones – eventually adhered to the Prussian system. Metternich warned the Emperor, therefore, that a 'state within a state' was growing up inside the Confederation and that Prussia would use this situation 'to weaken the influence of Austria' in Germany and 'to make Austria appear a foreign country'.[35] He predicted 'that the links which bind Austria to the other states of the Germanic Confederation [would] gradually become loosened and in the end break entirely, thanks to this barrier . . . and to those machinations which tend to change a material into a moral and political separation'.[36] His counter-strategy, however, namely to construct a rival system of commerce connecting Germany with the Adriatic through Austria and Northern Italy, never achieved a significant measure of success.

In his memorandum to the Emperor, Metternich had used the words 'without Austria, Germany is incapable of meeting external danger; without the co-operation of the whole of Germany, Austria cannot find the means of developing her power.'[37] Yet only the second half of this statement was true. For when in 1830 it looked as if a war with France was on the cards, Austria could match Prussia's offer of 250,000 men with which to defend Germany with only 170,000. Likewise, in 1840 when war again seemed imminent, it was Prussia who took the lead. Finally the Germans were given to understand that Austrian strategists envisaged a retreat before the French in southern Germany if and when a war should occur. When revolution erupted in France in 1848, it was little wonder, therefore, that it was Prussia not Austria which the Russians encouraged to defend Germany from attack. These manifest weaknesses in the Austrian position, however, were not to become fatal until the 1860s. During the period 1815–48 it should be remembered that Prussia and Austria co-operated closely in the struggle against the revolution.

What then of Austrian policy towards the rest of Europe? Given her lack of military and financial power it is hardly surprising that Metternich's favourite diplomatic weapon should have been the diplomatic congress or conference where he could proclaim the sanctity of treaty rights; it is also no surprise that he should have achieved his best results at private meetings with Europe's statesmen and sovereigns whom he could convince at close quarters of the need to defeat the revolution at any cost. It is no coincidence, therefore, that his greatest triumphs should have been scored at Troppau and Laibach where he not only got the eastern powers to confirm the legitimacy of the 1815 Settlement but got them to support the principle of intervention against the revolution. This indeed was his masterstroke. For at last he had the hope of others fighting his ideological battles for him. Intervention however, was to be used only as he saw it, as a weapon in the service of legitimacy; it was not to be used either to abet the revolution or to upset the balance of power. Thus he could not condone British (or even French) intervention in Iberia or countenance Russian armies in the Balkans or the west. In a sense, however, – and how ironical in the light of British objections to the Troppau Protocol – intervention failed him when the real test came. For in 1830 Louis Philippe was welcomed by the British and recognised by the continental powers who felt unprepared to fight a war. Metternich, who was inclined to favour war with France, was left high and dry and could not even chase the French out of Italy when Casimir Périer sent an expedition to Ancona in 1832. Yet the 1830 revolutions helped Metternich in their own way. Just as the 1820 revolutions had convinced Alexander I of Russia that liberalism should be abandoned for reaction, the outbreak of revolution in Europe in 1830 helped convince Nicholas I of the need to maintain the *status quo*. At Münchengrätz in 1833 the Tsar, who greeted Metternich as his 'master', promised to uphold the integrity of the Turkish Empire in Europe and reaffirmed the principle of intervention against the revolution.

This was very important, for, given that Metternich always believed that France was the home of revolution and given British policy from 1820 onwards, the balance of power dictated that, after the death of Castlereagh, the Habsburg monarchy would become ever more dependent on Russia. Since Russian and Austrian interests clashed in SE Europe, the Russian decision to maintain the integrity of the Ottoman Empire saved Austria from isolation. It may be argued perhaps that that decision owed less to Metternich than to Britain's opposition to Russian expansion and to difficulties encountered by the Russians in the war of 1827–9. Yet the atmosphere of counter-revolutionary hysteria created by the Austrian Chancellor had undoubtedly affected Russian strategy and Metternich's repeated insistence on treaty rights and upon legitimacy had left its mark. Indeed it is possible to argue that in the period 1846–48 his own violation of treaty rights (through the occupation of Cracow and the trade war with Piedmont) undermined his own diplomatic position.

How then does one finally judge Metternich and his 'system'? That he had clear ideas of how it ought to have worked can not be doubted. He believed that strong monarchical states should have been co-operating in every way to uphold the 1815 Settlement and to exterminate the threat of revolution. France, he believed, should have been quarantined after 1815 and punished in 1830. In eastern affairs he believed that the Turkish Empire should have been upheld and he deprecated the fact that he could do nothing to prevent the Russians from undermining it. Critics, on the other hand, point out that his system was a reactionary one which could not possibly have succeeded. Many statesmen of the time informed him of this – not just Canning and Palmerston but also Nesselrode and Bernstorff. It was, they said, impossible to struggle against the spirit of the times. This, of course, was perfectly true and by 1848 there was a great deal of pathos in Metternich's situation. Forced by economic, administrative and financial weakness to witness the defeat of the Sonderbund in Switzerland he could only prepare for Armageddon in Austria. However he was, as he said, a rock of order. He had never compromised with the revolution (or even for that matter with Louis Phillipe) and he found confirmation of the validity of his position in peasant support for the monarchy in Galicia in 1846. He was right, he had always been right, he knew he was right. A doctrinaire to the end, he told Guizot in exile, on the steps of the British Museum, that error had never approached his spirit.

His policies, however, have been criticised, not merely on the grounds that he could not stop the clock, but also on account of various diplomatic errors. It is alleged that he should not have accepted Italian territory in 1815; that he should not have consented to a Bourbon Restoration in France; that he should have opposed

Russian policy towards Turkey more strongly; that he should have done more to support Louis Philippe against his enemies in France. These criticisms, however, fail to carry the slightest conviction in the light of the possible alternatives. If Austria had refused to accept Lombardy-Venetia, would not France have dominated Italy? Perhaps more support could have been offered to Louis Philippe, but if so, how much and at what price? Again it is difficult to see what the alternative to Bourbon rule in France could have been. Would a Bonapartist regency have preserved the peace of Europe? And with what weapons was Austria supposed to fight the Russians, who after all were the most powerful supporters of reaction in Europe? From his own perspective it is difficult to see where Metternich went wrong.

What is really amazing is how much he achieved, albeit in a negative sense. His hold on Germany and Italy, on Austria and Hungary was to leave permanent scars on European liberalism. It is little wonder, in the last resort, that people thought that there really was a Holy Alliance. The document itself may have been scorned by all, but the ideological alliance against liberty which Metternich did his utmost to cement was no figment of anyone's imagination. Thus if he did not actually control events – and who did? – Metternich certainly set the tone in European diplomacy for more than thirty years. The Europe of his day came closer to his ideals than to those of his opponents or his rivals. There is certainly historical justification, therefore, in talking of an 'age of Metternich'.

Can one, however, justify the use of the term 'a Metternich system'? In the final analysis this is an argument not about Metternich but about the use of the word 'system'. If it is used to mean that he controlled events or even reacted to all events in exactly the same way, then the answer is definitely no. However, if it is taken to mean that Metternich pursued a broad political strategy with great consistency, the answer is undoubtedly yes.

6. France and Europe, 1815–48: the Problems of Defeat and Recovery

ROGER BULLEN

THE final defeat of Napoleon by the allied forces at Waterloo in June 1815 was decisive. The westward progress of the Russian and Prussian armies in 1813 and 1814, combined with the successes of Wellington and the British army in the Iberian Peninsula, had already destroyed the Napoleonic Empire in Europe. At the zenith of its power Napoleon's Empire had stretched from the Pyrenees to northern Germany, from central Italy to the Atlantic. Moreover he had surrounded imperial France with a series of satellite states. By the First Peace of Paris of May 1814 the Empire was destroyed and France was confined within the borders of 1792, thus retaining some of the territorial gains made in the early stages of the war between revolutionary France and the first coalition. The victory of the allies over Napoleon's hastily reconstructed army at Waterloo finally destroyed Napoleon's pretensions to imperial power in France itself, pretensions which the powers of the Fourth Coalition had come to regard as incompatible with their own security and the peace of Europe. It was in this way that the Napoleonic experiment in France and in Europe was ended.

The French attempt to dominate the continent and reduce the other great powers to the status of client states was finally thwarted by crushing military defeat. In 1815 France was no longer the greatest of the European great powers but a defeated state occupied by foreign troops. In the autumn of 1815 the Bourbon monarchy of Louis XVIII, restored yet again by the triumph of the allies, was itself a client state of the victorious coalition. When the King and his advisers returned to Paris after Waterloo they did not know what new peace terms the allies would impose upon France, but they did know that they had no alternative but to accept them. Frenchmen of all shades of political opinion did not doubt that the glory of the army was tarnished by its defeat on the battlefield and that the nation itself was humiliated by the disaster which Napoleon had brought upon it. When foreign troops paraded in the Champs-Elysées it was obvious to all French-men that the power of France was broken.

The Second Peace of Paris was signed on 20 November 1815, after the allied powers had completed the reconstruction of the European state system at Vienna. The final Settlement was con-siderably harsher than the first and many Frenchmen were disposed to think that it was unprecedented in its severity. Like most defeated powers they cared only for their own plight; they did not compare the terms of the new Treaty with the terms of the treaties they had imposed on their own victims in the two previous decades. The fact was that the Treaty was less harsh than some of the allies, the Prussians in particular, had demanded.[1] What the allies sought to do was to chasten France and, more particularly, to strengthen the security network which they had already constructed around her. Consequently most of the territorial losses were of stra-tegic significance. By the new Treaty France was confined within the borders of the 1 January 1790.[2] She was thus forced to cede Philippe-ville, Marienbourg and the Duchy of Bouillon to the Kingdom of the Netherlands; Saarlouis and Saarbruck to the Rhineland province of Prussia; other territories north of Lauter to Bavaria and Hesse; and finally Savoy to Sardinia. The departments of the northern and east-ern frontiers were to be occupied by 150,000 allied troops for five years at the most and three years at the least. The cost of the army of occu-pation was to be borne by the French government which was also forced to pay an indemnity of 700 million francs,[3] which was divided among the allies.

French condemnation of the Settlement was total; all parties were united in their opposition to it. For decades to come an attack on the Treaty was a necessary credential for patriotism.[4] Particular aspects of the Treaty were singled out for special criticism. Paradoxically it was those parts of the Treaty least permanent in their effect which were initially attacked with the greatest vehemence, namely the army of occupation and the indemnity. The French regarded the size and cost of the army of occupation, the length of its stay in France and the amount of the indemnity as without precedent in the history of inter-national relations. Frenchmen were convinced that the aim of these measures was permanently to injure France and long delay her recovery. Thus the basic aim of French foreign policy was to rid France of the army of occupation and the burden of the indemnity. The King, the ministry and the chamber were agreed that France could not be regarded as a great power and the restored monarchy could not begin to appeal to the loyalty of the masses while France was occupied by foreign troops and so greatly indebted to foreign governments. It was as much a question of pride as it was of independence. The evacuation of the army of occupation would be the removal of the outward and visible sign of defeat.

The fact that the army of occupation was withdrawn in 1818[5] and the indemnity paid off by 1820[6] did little to alter the attitude of Frenchmen to the 1815 Settlement. So far as the Second Treaty of Paris was concerned the territorial losses were still a bitter blow to French prestige. The demand for their return, the demand for what Thiers amongst others was later to call 'natural frontiers', was one of the most powerful rallying cries of patriotism in the next half century of French politics. But this was not all that the French resented. In the aftermath of the 1815 Settlement, parties and factions in France formulated a case against not only the Second Peace of Paris but also the new international order in its entirety. Between 1815 and 1848 and indeed beyond, the French referred to their humiliation as a result of 'the treaties of 1815' and not just of 'the second peace of Paris'.[7]

French objections to the new international order constructed by the victorious coalition of England, Austria, Prussia and Russia were basically threefold. First they claimed that the allied powers had used the opportunity provided by the defeat of France to expand their territories at the expense of France and of those states which France traditionally protected. It was in this way, Frenchmen argued, that Prussia was able to extend her Rhenish provinces, that Austria was able to acquire Venetia and that Poland was brutally partitioned by the three continental allies. Thus, as far as the French were concerned, the new order in Europe was no more than an attempt by the allies to give legal title to their selfish aggrandisement. In 1830 a radical newspaper likened the policies of the allies in 1815 to a group of drunken soldiers in search of booty after victory on the battlefield. As such it could not permanently be tolerated. Secondly the French claimed that at Vienna the allied powers sought to relegate France to the status of a second-class power by surrounding her with strong and hostile states and excluding her from her natural and traditional areas of influence; in Spain, where the French claimed the government was forced to conclude anti-French treaties with England, in Italy where the Austrians created an anti-French network of alliances and military agreements and on the north-eastern frontier where the Prussians concentrated their army on the Rhine and a series of barrier fortresses was built along the Franco-Dutch border. Thirdly the French believed that the Treaties concluded by the allies at the close of their negotiations in 1815, in particular the Quadruple Treaty of 20 November which was to remain in force for twenty years, were permanent measures for the containment of France. What had begun, the French argued, as a coalition for the destruction of the Napoleonic Empire in Europe was transformed into a perpetual and hostile league against France.[9]

This, then, was the French case against the 1815 Treaties. They as much resented the diminution of France's status as a great power, the loss of influence over her small neighbours in western Europe and the Mediterranean, as the cession of territory. To suggest that all French governments were revisionist and that all parties and factions in France advocated a revisionist foreign policy is not necessarily to suggest that they all sought territorial revision of the Second Peace of Paris. Some certainly did and for many it was the ultimate goal of a revisionist foreign policy. There were others who thought that it was a desirable but unobtainable objective and that the most prudent course was to avoid inflaming public opinion on the issue. They therefore argued that discussion of the question should be postponed until a suitable opportunity for its fulfilment arose. This was one of the reasons why they denounced the Treaties of 1815 in general rather than the Second Peace of Paris in particular. From both the domestic and the international viewpoint it was safer to attack the Settlement as a whole; this implicitly included the territorial question without specifically mentioning it.

In their propaganda and speeches on foreign policy, politicians of the centre and right emphasised the need for a positive rather than a negative approach to the problems of defeat. They usually described their aim as the recovery of France rather than the destruction of the anti-French system.[10] In the language of diplomacy recovery was a more neutral word than either revision or revenge. Moreover in domestic politics recovery was a much more useful and flexible concept. It made possible the repudiation of the Napoleonic legacy of military conquest and territorial expansion.[11] Recovery, French statesmen were keen to emphasise, did not imply renewal of the search for empire and dominance. In a more positive sense it was possible to relate recovery to the ancient traditions of the old monarchy. For the Bourbon monarchy it was associated with the concept of 'Restoration'; it implied a return to the old ideals and traditions of foreign policy.[12] For the Orleans monarchy it was linked to the eighteenth-century notion that France, by her political and social progress, was in the vanguard of European civilisation.[13] It was only the republicans who could afford to use the language of revision and revenge.

The policy of recovery shared by all parties had a quite definite set of priorities. Firstly it was necessary to rebuild the army and the navy. It was only through strength that France would gain the respect of her enemies. Secondly France must exploit the divisions amongst the allied powers in order permanently to destroy the anti-French coalition and end her isolation. From this task followed the third objective of attempting to secure an alliance or working agreements with other great powers which would enable France to pursue her interests without the fear that her actions could again provoke her isolation. Lastly it meant the recovery by France of her influence in areas where she had traditionally played an important role, namely western Europe and the Mediterranean. All governments and all parties shared these objectives. There was, therefore, a common programme of foreign policy which hardly varied despite frequent changes of government and despite the revolution of 1830. Once the first objective had been achieved, which it was by the early 1820s, therewere differences of emphasis between different governments as to which of the remaining objectives was the more important or which was the more easily obtainable. But these were differences of tactics rather than of aims.

In the actual process of foreign policy making there was considerable continuity. A small group of officials at the French Foreign Office, some of whom had received their training under Napoleon, directed the affairs of the ministry and wrote many of the political instructions to French diplomats abroad.[14] Most of the senior diplomats who served the Restoration monarchy also served the July monarchy, and indeed a few survived to serve Napoleon III in the 1850s.[15] Talleyrand's record of service under Napoleon, then under Louis XVIII and lastly as French ambassador in London under Louis Philippe was in no sense unusual. Like Talleyrand, French diplomats prided themselves on serving France rather than a particular regime or government.

Although there was continuity in the conduct of foreign affairs, it provoked continual and fierce debate in the Chambers and in the press. This debate was conducted on two distinct levels. The first was that of principle. Each party and faction believed it necessary to present to the public a distinctive view of foreign policy. In reality these were no more than slightly modified versions of the common programme of recovery. They were different only in the language in which they were expressed and the political ends they were supposed to promote. After 1830 the ideas of the ultra-royalists were strident in tone and aggressive in intent; they invoked the military virtues of honour and glory and stressed the traditions and achievements of Bourbon France in the seventeenth and eighteenth century. Their most persistent theme was the necessity for a Franco-Russian alliance. In the late 1820s and 1830s the liberals argued that recovery could only be achieved by diplomacy; that war would be a disaster for France and a crime against civilisation. France, they claimed, must assume her destined role at the head of the progressive movements in Europe, the natural protector of liberty and constitutional reform against the forces of despotism.[16] The republican approach to foreign policy was to emphasise the vital connection between revolution in France and the liberation of the oppresed people of Europe from the tyranny which had been imposed upon them in 1815. They claimed that after the revolution in France the army of the republic would offer its fraternal support to people struggling to achieve liberty. In this way a new political order would be established throughout Europe under French protection and the map of Europe would be redrawn when Poles and Italians liberated themselves from their oppressors.[17]

This level of the debate was as much about ideals in French politics as it was about foreign policy. It arose out of the need of each party to integrate its attitude towards foreign policy with its domestic programme, and thus to present a vision of an alternative political system which would be significantly different from that which then existed. At the same time they were attempting to claim for themselves a monopoly of patriotism, or at least to set standards of patriotism by comparison with which the existing government could be found wanting. In office the right and the left were just as prudent and circumspect as any other government. Thus the royalists who expressed their outrage at the revolt of the juntas in Spain against their rightful sovereign were willing secretly to encourage opposition to Austrian rule in northern Italy, and to take the side of the disaffected subjects of the central Italian states. In the 1830s and 1840s the governments of the July monarchy annually condemned the oppression of Poland by the three eastern powers, but in 1846 Guizot was prepared to condone the suppression of the republic of Cracow in order to secure Austrian support in the diplomatic conflict with England which arose after the Spanish Marriages[18] In 1848 the republican assembly passed a rsolution of fraternal greetings to the Italians in their struggle against Austria, but Lamartine was anxious to ensure that if war came it would be limited and localised and, moreover, that Nice and Savoy would be the price of French military assistance for the Italians.[19]

The other level of debate was concerned with the means and speed of recovery rather than with its ostensible ends. This was conducted within each government, between the government and the opposition in the Chambers and in the press. This usually focused on the major issues of the day. Many of the governments of both monarchies were divided on questions of foreign policy. There was a prolonged debate within the cabinet in 1822 and 1823 on the question of whether or not to intervene in Spain.[20] In 1836 the duke de Broglie resigned on a question of foreign policy and, later in the same year, Thiers's government collapsed as a result of differences between himself and the King over Spanish problems.[21] Moreover both Charles X and Louis Philippe had firm views on foreign affairs which did not always accord with the policies of their ministers. Louis Philippe was sometimes accused of conducting a secret foreign policy of his own which was conservative and dynastic in its ambitions, and which affronted the liberal principles of his government. In the Chambers a great deal of time was devoted to the discussion of foreign policy. This was partly because on domestic issues there was very little real difference between the factions – this was particularly true in the 1830s – and also because every government believed that its position would be strengthened by a successful foreign policy. This led to frequent comparisons between the policy of the government and that of its predecessors. The debate in the press was essentially an extension of the debate in the Chamber. The governments of both monarchies attached great importance to a favourable press for its foreign policy and many of them established 'special relationships' with particular newspapers, supplying them with early informaion of speeches and foreign news in return for friendly editorial comment.[22]

There was more public discussion of foreign policy in France than in any other great power between 1815 and 1848. Certainly more than in Great Britain, the only other great power with comparable parliamentary institutions. In French society, more than in any other, foreign policy was a devisive issue; it could determine the fate of governments; it constituted an important part of opposition attacks on governments and it was part of the debate about the direction and purpose of politics since the revolution of 1789. Many French diplomats argued that this public discussion made the actual task of recovery more difficult. It sustained the fear amongst the other powers that the French nation was not reconciled to the defeat and the borders of 1815. It helped to create the belief that France lacked the unity of purpose to become a reliable ally.[23] The revolutionary tradition in France, the defeat of 1815, the instability of French politics and the continual debate about foreign policy all helped to create the impression amongst the other powers that France was a pariah among nations.

Despite her defeat in 1815 France remained a formidable power. Some Frenchmen, for example the editor of the *Moniteur de L'Armée*, prided themselves on the fact that it had required the combined forces of all the other powers to defeat France in 1814 and again in 1815.[24] In one important respect France was unique amongst the great powers in that she had both a large standing army and a powerful navy. It was true that her army was not as large as that of Russia, although French soldiers were probably better trained and better equipped than their Russian counterparts. It was equally true that the French navy was no match for the British navy in the number of ships or in the size and quality of trained manpower. But the fact that she was both a military and a naval power gave undoubted strength to her foreign policy. The French were certainly stronger than either the Austrians or the Prussians. In the years after the Congress of Vienna the leaders of the other powers never doubted that France had a considerable potential for disrupting the new international order. From 1817 onwards, with the creation of the Quintuple Alliance, France was treated as an equal by the victorious allies; this was a matter of necessity not of courtesy. French politicians had great confidence in the actual strength of France *vis-à-vis* other individual powers. Casimir Périer did not fear the consequences of war between France and Prussia alone over Belgium, or between France and Austria alone, before he ordered the French occupation of Ancona in 1832.[25] Some politicians even believed that France possessed immense potential. They argued that if necessity demanded then France could field, by the device of the *levée-en-masse*, an army larger, more efficient and more loyal than those of all the other powers combined. The *Moniteur de L'Armée* argued in 1841 that if France adopted a more extensive system of reserves her army would be invincible.[26]

By comparison with the other continental monarchies France had a strong economy and an efficient system of public finance. In these respects she was second only to England. Villèle more than any other minister was responsible for establishing a sound system of public finance, for creating confidence in the Paris Bourse amongst the international bankers and for liquidating the huge debts with which the restored monarchy was initially burdened.[27] French politicians did not doubt that the state could finance a war if war should come. This was not an assumption that all the other great powers could comfortably make; both the Austrians and the Russians suffered from a chronically inefficient system of public finance. It was sometimes alleged that the Russians would not be able to wage war unless they could borrow on western money markets. In France the major financial obstacle in the way of an active foreign policy was that the government had to secure a vote of credit from the Chambers for all extraordinary expenditure not specified in the budget. On the three most important occasions when this was demanded, in 1823 for the invasion of Spain, in 1829 for the expedition to Algiers and in 1841 for the fortification of Paris, the credits were granted. Yet there were occasions when the government believed that they would not receive credit if they asked for it. In 1835 Broglie was convinced that the Chambers would refuse credit for a second intervention in Spain and in 1838 Desages, the director of political affairs at the French Foreign Ministry, stated that the parsimony of the Chamber seriously inhibited an active foreign policy.[28] The absolute monarchies of eastern and central Europe did not have to consider these difficulties; Nicholas I, for example, was only responsible to himself for the movement of his army.

The governments of the early years of the Restoration encountered no real obstacle to their efforts to reconstruct the army and the navy. It was commonplace for French politicians after the Congress of Vienna to describe the new era in international relations as 'the armed peace'. It was always easy to argue that France must have a strong army to defend herself against her enemies. There was relatively little opposition in the Chamber to the proposals for naval and military reorganisation. Some of the Restoration politicians were opposed to conscription but they were forced to accept it as the only possible basis for a large standing army. Expenditure on the army and the navy increased steadily throughout the 1820s and 1830s. The naval estimate which, in 1818 was forty million francs, was eighty-three million by 1828.

By the law of 12 March 1818 the size of the army was fixed at 240,000 men, a new law of 5 June 1824 raised the number to 400,000 and set the number of annual recruits at 60,000. In fact the government did not take full advantage of these provisions, and for most of the late 1820s and early 1830s the army numbered about a quarter of a million men. In the late 1830s and early 1840s there were some increases, but these were largely in response to the demands of the army in Algiers. Throughout the period the number of men liable for military service exceeded the number actually called up. French governments therefore believed that there was a reserve of manpower which could be called upon in a national emergency. This was in addition to the 'official reserve'. By the law of 12 March 1818 conscripts served six years in the regular army and then a further six in the reserves. In an age when mobilisation for war and, indeed, war itself was a comparatively slow process, these reserves of manpower were counted as part of the real strength of France. For the most part the French were well pleased with their military reorganisation; France has an army, wrote one radical journalist, 'just as ready to march against the Holy Alliance as against the Cortes.'[29] Yet Chateaubriand's claim in 1823 that the rest of Europe was 'astounded' by the new power of France was certainly exaggerated.[30] When they removed their army of occupation in 1818 the allied powers were fully aware that the French would rebuild their army. Indeed they were anxious for the monarchy to possess the military strength necessary to discourage and suppress revolutionary activity. By the time France had reconstructed her army the armies of the eastern powers were all stationed to look west against her. The greater part of the Austrian army was in northern Italy, the bulk of the Prussian army was on the Rhine. The Russians were ready to move troops into central Europe in the event of a French attack on the Rhine and British naval plans for war only envisaged conflict with France. The fact was, as one historian has written, 'a new war of France against Europe was the only one for which the strategists planned in the generation between the Congress of Vienna and the revolution of 1848'.[31] The French were aware of this and the governments of the Restoration and July monarchies did not forget that the France they governed did not possess the military power and resources of the Napoleonic Empire at its zenith and that they, unlike Napoleon, faced a united Europe. As one deputy said in 1840, 'our army can defend four frontiers but it cannot advance on four frontiers'.

Although all French governments in the early nineteenth century attached less importance to the navy than to the army, the service and the dockyards which supported it were never neglected. There were many eager champions of naval power from Baron Portal in the early years of the Restoration, the man most responsible for the rebuilding of the French navy, to the duke of Jouiville, son of Louis Philippe, the author of a pamphlet on naval policy in the 1840s which called for further increases in expenditure to place the French navy on an equal footing with that of Great Britain.[32] A strong navy was an essential element in the recovery of French power in the Mediterranean and from the 1830s onwards the French presence in Algiers was as dependent on the navy as it was on the army. The advocates of colonial and commerical expansion, and they included many deputies from the Atlantic seaboard constituencies, always emphasised the need for increased naval and dockyard expenditure. These men and the measures which they championed were associated with a foreign policy which was essentially anti-English. Their aim was to weaken and if possible to destroy the maritime and commercial ascendency which the British enjoyed. It was in that sense that the rebuilding of the navy was associated with the recovery of France and the destruction of the anti-French system in Europe. Under the Restoration it was directly linked to the European policy of France in that it was argued that the navy would secure for France the alliance of Russia because the Russians wanted an ally who could co-operate with them in challenging the naval hegemony of Great Britain.[33] France's dockyards were thus a diplomatic asset. After the revolution of 1830 this belief was abnadoned by all except the ultra-royalists, and during the Orleans monarchy the navalists again reverted to the overtly anti-English argument for naval expansion. During both monarchies it was the Mediterranean rather than the Atlantic fleet which achieved the most spectacular successes and which was regarded as the more important.

Despite the confidence of French politicians in the ability of France to recover from the defeat of 1815 and to play a leading role in great-power politics, there were few Frenchmen who believed that this could be achieved against overwhelming odds. It was assumed in Paris that if France attempted to undo the 1815 Settlement by war then the allies would unite against her. There was ample evidence to support this assumption. Throughout three decades the statesmen of the allied powers were convinced that in 1815 France had been temporarily chastened but that her appetite for conquest and domination remained strong. The maintenance of this belief arose from the fact that many of the political leaders of Europe in 1848, Metternich, Nesselrode, Wellington, Palmerston and Peel, had been active politicicans in the last years of the struggle against Napoleon.[34] Above all the allied powers feared the potential of France to create the twin-headed monster of revolution and war;[35] what one radical newspaper called 'the war of the people of Europe against the kings of Europe.'[36] These fears kept alive the spirit of the alliance against France. Even in the 1830s and 1840s it was common for the four powers to refer to each other as 'allies' and to emphasise their co-operation in what Palmerston always called 'the late war against France.' In 1835 when British, French and Spanish troops were fighting in northern Spain against the Carlists, who were financed and supplied by the eastern powers, the British minister at Madrid informed Palmerston that he had 're-commended a proclamation recalling the ancient glories of English and Spanish armies during the Penisular War.'[37]

The French feared the coalition as much as the coalition feared France. It was assumed that war against Europe would be long and exhausting, that it would result in the defeat of France and that the peace settlement would be harsher than that of 1815. This would be a heavy burden for the nation to bear, but an even heavier one for the monarchy itself. Between 1815 and 1848 the adherents of both monarchies claimed that the defeat and losses of 1815 were the final legacy of Napoleon. In the event of defeat following a war which the monarchy had unleashed it would not be possible to shift the burden of guilt. Many politicians were convinced that the monarchy could not survive such a disaster; war and defeat would be followed by revolution. This was the basis of Guizot's charge against Thiers in 1840; war, he claimed, was the road to social and political collapse, and to spread rumours of war as Thiers had done was to take a step in that direction.[38] Thus the fear of a revived coalition and the belief that the political system in France itself was too fragile an edifice to survive war and probable defeat were powerful restraints on the pursuit of an all-out revisionist foreign policy. For many French liberals these fears were combined with the belief that a full-scale European conflict was a crime against civilisation. Wars of aggression in Europe, liberal propagandists argued, were characteristic of despotic governments and servile societies and Orleanist France was neither of these.

Diplomacy rather than war was the favoured means of recovery and the first task of diplomacy was to break up the coalition of France's enemies. This would end the isolation of France. Once this was achieved then the next task was to find an ally. Herein was the diplomatic strategy of every government from Richelieu to Thiers. It was easier to define than it was to accomplish. The real problem which no French government was able to overcome was that although the erstwhile allies were divided on many issues they all shared two aims: the maintenance of the 1815 Settlement in Europe as a whole and the containment and surveillance of France in the west. The fact was they all feared France more than they feared each other. The major breach in the relations of the four victorious powers was caused by the differences between England and the continental powers in the 1820s and 1830s. As far as the British were concerned this was essentially a conflict between themselves and the Russians. The British consistently maintained that they had no quarrel with either Austria or Prussia but that they were separated from them by the slavish adherence of the two German powers to Russia, which they attributed to their fear of revolution and their military and political weakness in the face of revolution. In the Anglo-Russian conflict two separate issues were at stake. It was a conflict of means and not ends in Europe; the British sought to avoid revolution by reform and to maintain peace in Europe by strict adherence to implicitly defined spheres of influence. The eastern powers thought that all attempts to change legally constituted governments by popular action must be suppressed by force, and that it should be done in the name of the alliance of the great powers. This view was enshrined in the Protocol of Troppau. The second issue of conflict arose out of British suspicions that the Russians were attempting to pursue a forward policy in the Near East at the expense of Turkey. At the same time the Russians had, since 1815, been jealous of the maritime supremacy of Great Britain and were anxious both to challenge it and encourage other powers to do so. In the two decades after 1818 the French attempted to exploit these rivalries in order to promote their own recovery.

A Russian alliance was the diplomatic prize which Restoration governments valued most and which they persistently sought.[39] At first they believed that a Franco-Russian *rapprochement* would appeal to the Russians as a means of counterbalancing the Anglo-Austrian *entente* which emerged at the Congress of Vienna and lasted until the early 1820s. Moreover the French were convinced that the navies of the two powers could begin to challenge British maritime ascendency. It was also argued in Paris that Russian and French interests were complementary rather than conflicting; Russia could expand in eastern Europe and the Near East, France in western Europe and the western Mediterranean. The two powers could divide the continent between them. The French recognised that there were obstacles to such an agreement. They knew that to the Russians an alliance based on a divison of Europe into a French and a Russian sphere was no more than a new Tilsit. What assurances could they offer the Russians that the second Tilsit would not suffer the same fate as the first? In addition French diplomats at St Petersburg consistently reported that the Emperor Alexander believed that the Restored monarchy in France was too unstable to become a reliable ally.[40] These were problems which the French appreciated and which French diplomats did their utmost to overcome. What they did not fully realise was that the fair words and good intentions offered by Capodistria in St Petersburg and Pozzo di Borgo, the Russian ambassador, in Paris reflected only one of the currents in Russian foreign policy under Alexander I. As Nicholas was later to point out, Pozzo di Borgo knew France well but Russia not at all.[41] The supposed overtures to France were made at the same time as the Russians were seeking to establish closer relations with Austria, and indeed contemplating direct negotiations with England as a means of settling the Near Eastern Question.[42] By 1823 the Russians had definitely opted for Austria, and the Neo-Holy Alliance became the cornerstone of Russian foreign policy until the early 1850s. The formation of the new alignment was a setback for France. It ruined the prospect for a Franco-Russian *rapprochement*. Furthermore, it was a conservative alliance of three satiated states, opposed to territorial change and opposed to constitutional change within states. France could never expect to be treated on equal terms by this trinity; they had defeated her, they suspected her ambitions and they despised her political institutions. Not surprisingly the French regarded the Neo-Holy Alliance as a new coalition against them. They were determined to destroy it.

Between 1823 and 1830 French governments never accepted that Russia's choice of Austria and Prussia was final and irrevocable. They carefully watched for any signs of coolness between the three powers. In the late 1820s they regarded Austro-Russian differences over the Greek Question, in addition to Anglo-Russian tensions on the same issue, as an opportunity to revive their suit at St Petersburg.

In September 1829 Polignac, who led the last ministry of Charles X, put forward his plan for a complete revision of the 1815 Treaties in Europe, together with a settlement of the Near Eastern Question.[43] The plan envisaged that France would acquire virtually the whole of what was later to become the kingdom of Belgium. The other powers were also to receive new territories; Prussia and Austria in central Europe, and Russia significant acquisitions in the Near East. The proposed French gains reflected the argument of many French diplomats that as the other powers had acquired large areas of territory in 1815 France should now demand an equal amount. It was as if France had not been defeated in 1815. It was certainly Polignac's intention to remove the losses of defeat at one stroke. He thought that if the Russians were prepared to accept his plan the two powers could impose it on the rest of Europe, if necessary by force. War was the logical outcome of his plan. In fact the Russians regarded the proposals as entirely unrealistic and did not give them the slightest encouragement. Consequently they came to nothing.

After the revolution of 1830 French politicians, except those on the extreme right, believed that there was no prospect of establishing close relations with Russia. Broglie stated in the mid 1830s that Russia was the country with whom relations had changed the most since the revolution.[44] Russia was now regarded as the patron of those political principles which the revolution of July in France had so decisively rejected, and as the power most likely to lead a coalition to destroy the revised Charter. In Russia France was regarded as the very centre of revolution and the patron of those principles which Russia was determined to suppress. For most of the 1830s the two governments conducted their relations through chargés d'affaires rather than accredited ambassadors.

There was no doubt in France that England was to the new monarchy what Russia had been to the old, except that an agreement with England was not expected to result in territorial revision in the west. It could, however, prevent a revival of the anti-French coalition, thus avoiding the danger of isolation. The two constitutional monarchies could protect reform movements in western Europe and together restrain Russian aggression in the Near East; the alliance of principle would be held together by solid national interests. The early 1830s were thus dominated by the search for an agreement with England.[45] Talleyrand, the ambassador in London, was one of the earliest advocates of such an alignment and he hoped to be its architect. He was supported by many of the leading politicians of the new monarchy. The British government was certainly prepared to accept the new order in France and to establish close working relations with it. Grey, the prime minister, and many of his Cabinet believed that there was a close connection between the reform movement in England and the revision of the Charter in France. The two governments were certainly united in their opposition to despotism. But neither Grey nor his foreign secretary, Palmerston, wanted anything more than a working relationship with France. The British government did not want any new alliance obligations but even if it had, France was regarded as too restless and too unstable to be a suitable ally. In the years from 1830–33 Palmerston was more conscious of the need to keep France out of Belgium than Russia out of Turkey. For him working with France was principally a means of restraining her. This was to be his aim in the Peninsular as it had been in the Low Countries. With the formation of the Quadruple Alliance of April 1834, which the French regarded as a British treaty designed to promote British objectives in the Peninsular, they became convinced that the British government was not prepared to work on equal terms with France. By the end of his embassy in London, Talleyrand regarded the British as devious in negotiations as their foreign policy was Jacobin in intention.[46] In 1834 another French diplomat bluntly stated that if the British government wished to maintain good relations with France 'it must resign itself to offering us something more than the affirmation of its maritime preponderance and the confirmation of the treaties of 1815.'[47]

In the late 1830s many French politicians, Talleyrand, Thiers, and Molé in particular, believed that an agreement with Austria would be an acceptable substitute for an agreement with England. They were convinced that Austria was the prisoner of Russia, unwillingly dependent on her for support against the revolution and thus compelled to sacrifice to her Austria's interests in the Near East. France could offer Austria support against Russia's encroachments and unlike Great Britain she would not demand that France should accept a subordinate role in western Europe. Indeed the French believed that it was possible to present themselves at Vienna as the defenders of conservative constitutionalism, with the British support for radicalism as the real menace to order. In this way the July monarchy would assume the part played by its predecessor; the champion of order in the west. In addition an agreement with Austria would break up the Neo-

Holy Alliance and it could be cemented by a marriage between the duke of Orleans, heir to the throne, and a Habsburg archduchess. Thus France would be her own master in the west and the new dynasty strengthened by powerful connections. It was, said Thiers, a revival of the Franco-Austrian alliance of the late eighteenth century.[48] By their agreement the two powers would end the separation of western liberalism and eastern autocracy. The Austrian response to French overtures in 1836 fell far short of what the French wanted. Metternich's aim in leading the French on was no more than to divide France from Great Britain and thus weaken the liberal movement in the west.[49] In fact he sought exactly the reverse of what the French hoped to achieve. He believed that to separate the two liberal powers would lead Great Britain to seek closer relations with Austria. From the outset of the negotiations Metternich had no intention of concluding an agreement with France. He feared her too much to wish to strengthen her.

In the 1870s when Emile Ollivier wrote his *Memoirs*, he looked back over the foreign policy of the two monarchies and concluded that their alliance projects, unlike those of he Second Empire, had all failed.[50] The fact was (and it was one which French governments were reluctant to recognise) that none of the other great powers was willing to assist the recovery of France. They all feared France as a dangerous rival who wished to destroy the 1815 Settlement and who was capable of undermining the European social and political order. It was the Crimean War which destroyed the unity of the anti-French powers. Only when other powers sought to destroy the 1815 Settlement in central Europe could Napoleon III make French revisionism in the west a negotiable question. There was real truth in the French assertion that the new order in Europe was intended permanently to injure France. The coalition, created for the purpose of destroying Napoleon's Empire in Europe, proved a remarkably durable instrument for the containment of the defeated power.

Although most governments of both monarchies believed that an agreement with another great power was the best and surest means of recovery, there were few who thought that it was the only one. By the early 1820s it was an established axiom of French diplomacy that France could assert her interests by independent action. This approach to the problem of recovery was based on two assumptions; firstly, that France had the power and the resources to act in defence of her interests, secondly, that if action was limited in area, in the scale of its operations and in its objective then it would not provoke a military confrontation with all the other powers. In short, the French aspired to a sphere of influence like the other great powers.

The problem for France was that the 1815 Settlement did not actually accord her a sphere of influence. Prussia stood guard on the north-eastern border, Austria had replaced France as the dominant power in Italy and Great Britain regarded the Iberian Peninsula as under her special protection. In order to recover a sphere of influence for herself, France had to encroach on those of others. The policy of independent action was thus recovery by encroachment. The French were resigned to the fact that this would provoke the hostility of at least one power. It was, however, essential to prevent the opposition of them all. In that case they would be forced to retreat, which would be a humiliation for the government and the regime.

The most successful examples of independent action were the French invasion of Spain in 1823[51] and the reoccupation of the papal port of Ancona in 1832.[52] The French took the decision to send in an army across the Pyrenees and restore Ferdinand VII after long and difficult discussions within the cabinet. They were able to act because the continental powers wanted the destruction of the Spanish juntas. Britain alone opposed the French and she did not have the means to stop them. In Italy the French were determined to assert their equality with Austria as a Catholic power. The Austrians could not prevent the French occupation of Ancona as they had no navy with which to do so. The British were reluctant to allow such a dramatic assertion of French naval power but they were not prepared to act against her in defence of papal absolutism. Both these episodes were regarded by the French as spectacular diplomatic triumphs. In a sense they were; by the invasion of Spain, France re-established the old pattern of control in the Peninsula, with Great Britain dominant at Lisbon and France at Madrid; after 1832 they were able to claim the right to be treated as an equal by Austria in central and southern Italy. Metternich never publicly conceded that France had any influence over the central and southern Italian states, but in his actual policy he was forced to recognise that she did. From the mid-1830s onwards Austria was only able to exert complete control over the northern Italian states.

The policy of independent action did not always succeed. In 1830 after the revolt had broken out in the southern Netherlands, the new monarchy in France hoped to intervene. It was envisaged that French intervention would result in the destruction of the barrier fortresses and the return of territory lost to Holland in 1815. Some Frenchmen hoped for more; Thiers wrote of the desire of France for 'natural frontiers' which meant the incorporation of large parts of Belgium into France.[53] Alternatively the southern Netherlands would become nominally independent but in reality under French control. In fact the French were unable to gain either territory at the expense of Belgium or establish their exclusive influence over the new kingdom. They were forced to accept an international solution to the crisis which confirmed, albeit in a slightly modified form, the 1815 Settlement on the north-eastern border. Talleyrand admitted that France was in no position to risk war with England and Prussia over Belgium and that the other powers would fight rather than allow France to act alone. In 1842 Guizot was forced to abandon his plan for a customs union between France and Belgium because of British opposition.[54] Once again the other powers were determined to prevent France from treating Belgium as a client state.

Total failure as a consequence of the opposition of all the other powers was not the only risk which attended the policy of independent action. In Spain in 1823 there was the danger that the presence of the French army might excite the Spanish patriots as it had done after the invasion of 1808. In that event the French would be forced to fight a long guerilla war with its inevitable drain on manpower and resources. Moreover there was the possibility that the British would support and supply an anti-French movement in Spain. Intervention could have developed into an undeclared, expensive and calamitous war. In the mid-1830s the duke de Broglie refused to intervene in Spain for this very reason.[55] Furthermore the fear that intervention could result in war kept the French out of northern Italy throughout the period from 1815 to 1848. They believed that action there would be regarded as a direct challenge to Austria and that Russia and Prussia would probably come to the assistance of their ally. In 1848 Lamartine and Cavignac acted just as cautiously on this question as their predecessors.[56]

The only frontier on which there was no change under both monarchies was the Rhine. This was the area where the French accepted that they were the least able to reassert themselves. The Prussian army on the Rhine, only seventy leagues from Paris, was the great barrier to the revival of French influence in southern Germany. Behind Prussia stood Austria and the armies of the other members of the German Confederation. The Russian army in Poland was in the last resort ready to defend the Rhine against France. In 1828 Polignac argued strongly against any attempt to recover the eastern territories lost in 1815. It would, inevitably, result in military conflict between France and the two German powers. Even if initially successful it would require a large army to defend any recovered territory and to maintain order over a population which was German in language and outlook. France, he suggested, should recognise Prussian ascendency on the Rhine and thus secure Prussian support for compensation in Belgium.[57] This policy foreshadowed the diplomacy of Napoleon III in the late 1860s. It was, however, an unrealistic policy, firstly because Prussia was in no position to offer France Belgian territory and secondly because she felt no need to make sacrifices to secure French recognition of what she already possessed.

To many French politicians and diplomats the constraints which limited French independence of action in Europe did not exist elsewhere. They suggested that France should pursue an active maritime, commerical and colonial policy outside Europe which would strengthen her and in the long run contribute to recovery in Europe itself. The policy later advocated by Jules Ferry after the war of 1870 was in fact a revival of the ideas put forward after the defeat of 1815. It was pointed out that Britain's wealth from overseas trade had enabled her not only to pay for her own war effort against Napoleon but also to subsidise the armies of her allies. By the late 1820s and early 1830s the arguments for an active overseas policy were well developed. Once the navy was rebuilt and had seen action during the Greek crisis, the navalists constituted a powerful lobby. It was argued that France was the only power capable of challenging the naval and commercial supremacy of Great Britain and that if the French did not build up their own navy and begin to penetrate the markets of the world, the British would acquire a naval and commercial monopoly which it would be impossible to destroy. This was an argument for urgency; for immediate and large increases in the naval budget. Furthermore it was claimed that colonial wars would be a source of activity for the army, improving its morale and sustaining popular interest in the martial arts. Lastly it was claimed that adventure overseas would capture the imagination of the people and this would enhance the popularity of the government and the regime. Louis Philippe's cynical description of Algiers as 'our opera box' clearly illustrates how important this consideration was thought to be.

The principal area of French expansion in the early nineteenth century was north Africa. Algiers and to a lesser extent Tunisia, Egypt and the Levant possessed an importance in French foreign policy which was accorded to no other area outside Europe. There were several reasons for this. North Africa was regarded by the French as the backyard of Europe – outside Europe but not distant from it. French expansion in north Africa could be linked to the revival of French power in the Mediterranean, which was regarded as a vital part of the programme of recovery. By the 1830s north Africa was a naval, military and commercial question and the French presence there had the support of many powerful interest groups. Under the July monarchy it was the most important theatre of operations for both the army and the navy. Bugeaud, the commander of the army in Algiers, was perhaps the only national hero of the July monarchy; the first general to capture the public imagination since Napoleon. The French regarded the build-up of their naval strength in the Mediterranean as a counterpoise to British naval power in those waters. French Mediterranean policy was therefore an aspect of Anglo-French rivalry. Lastly the French presence in north Africa was seen in the 1830s and 1840s as a venture which had just begun and with many possible lines of development. There were many Frenchmen who were strongly convinced that France had a civilising mission to fulfil from Algiers to the Levant. Thwarted and confined in Europe, France could export her ideas and culture to the Muslim world. In this way she would find a new role. What the British had done in India the French could do in north Africa.

If rivalry with England provided some of the impetus for French expansion in the Mediterranean, fear of England and the actual opposition of England set its limits. The Anglo-Russian coercion of Mehemet Ali in 1840 and British determination to prevent the French acquiring Tunis limited French expansion in north Africa to Algiers. Nevertheless the British were forced to accept the fact that the French were determined to reassert themselves in the Mediterranean. Both monarchies did so with conspicuous success. The Anglo-French alliance of 1854, the Crimean alliance, was a recognition of France as a Mediterranean power of the first order, and it was under the two monarchies that the foundations of this power were laid.

French policy overseas was not without its critics. There were many Frenchmen, including leading politicians, who believed that the only area for real successes in foreign policy was Europe. 'I would gladly', declared one deputy in 1830, 'exchange Algiers for the most wretched hole on the Rhine'.[58] Alexis de Tocqueville, who was foreign minister of the Second Republic for a few months in 1849, wrote in the 1830s that for France Europe 'is the natural theatre of her power and her glory'.[59] For such men French activity overseas was a mere sideshow which had no real bearing on the recovery of France in Europe. Nevertheless these criticisms were usually directed against French policy in the Pacific, in South America and west Africa rather than in the Mediterranean. Two attempts were made in these decades to link the Eastern Question with France's position in Europe. In 1829 Polignac attempted to connect what he supposed was Russian revisionism in the Near East with French revisionism in the west. Ten years later Thiers attempted to link French interests in Egypt with the question of war or peace on the Rhine. His attempt was a failure and France was humiliated; Great Britain and Russia coerced Mehemet Ali despite French protests and in Europe the German powers and their allies rallied together to meet the French challenge. Thiers's critics condemned his policy as a disaster for France and Guizot, his successor, quite genuinely believed that the major task of his foreign policy was to recover from the setback of 1840 rather than the defeat of 1815.

Guizot was foreign minister for longer than any of his predecessors since 1815. He dominated the making of foreign policy from October 1840 to February 1848. He accepted advice from the King and his colleagues but he was determined not to be controlled by them. Stability and order at home and abroad rather than the recovery of France in Europe were the keynotes of his policy.[60] He tacitly acknowledged that the 1815 borders were those within which France would have to live. In a real sense he was the first French foreign minister to attempt to give the Treaties of 1815 a positive interpretation; they had created a new sense of community amongst the great powers and by 1845 he could claim that three decades of peace had proved that civilisation had advanced. This he saw as a triumph for liberal ideas and values and for the noble restraint of France. Guizot did not seek an exclusive alliance with any other power. He sought agreements for the settlements of disputes rather than revisionist alignments. He was, above all, anxious to preserve what he regarded as the gains made since 1815. Firstly France should be accepted as an equal by the other great powers. He believed that there could be no permanent great-power settlements without French participation; hence the French ratification in 1842 of the Near-Eastern settlement of 1840. Secondly he jealously guarded the position which France had acquired in the Mediterranean and north Africa and the influence she had acquired over her neighbours. His tortuous and ultimately deceitful policy over the Spanish Marriages was grounded in his belief that French predominance at Madrid was threatened by Palmerston's diplomacy. In 1847 similar differences, although not as serious in their consequences, arose between Guizot and Metternich over Swiss and Italian problems.[61] The basic dilemma of the last years of Guizot's foreign policy was that it was based on the premise that the other powers should trust him because he was an honest statesman, determined to reconcile France to her new position in Europe. Metternich and Aberdeen trusted Guizot, but distrusted France; Palmerston and Nicholas I distrusted both. In the last resort, therefore, Guizot's foreign policy became no more than statements of good intentions which the other powers refused to accept.

Guizot certainly achieved his objective of recovering from the setback of 1840 but he failed to reconcile Frenchmen to the new order in Europe. From the revolution of 1848 until the war of 1870 French policy was again dominated by revisionsit objectives. In his diplomacy Napoleon III was much more the heir of Polignac, Chateaubriand and Talleyrand than he was of Napoleon I. He inherited their aspirations and he followed their methods. Indeed all that separated him from his predecessors since 1815 was that for a time he was able to exploit more favourable circumstances. The Crimean war destroyed the unity of the victorious allies. Polignac, Talleyrand and then Thiers had attempted to exploit the Anglo-Russian clash of interests in the Near East to the advantage of France. The British and the Russians ruined these efforts by amicable settlements of differences. In 1853 and 1854 they did not do so. This was the decisive turning-point in French foreign policy after 1848. It was the first step on the road to revisionism, one which led ultimately to Sedan.

The fact was that after 1815 France entered into a slow decline which neither of the two monarchies could avert. Their policy of recovery was designed to do so but the fact that it met with only partial success meant that, as the decades passed, the status imposed upon France in 1815 increasingly came to accord with her power and resources. Napoleon III sought to reverse the decline but by 1870 France was unable even to defend the borders of 1815. Herein lay the measure of France's decline. Thereafter the aim of French foreign policy was to recover the borders of the Second Peace of Paris.

7. Britain and the European Balance, 1815–48

CHRISTOPHER BARTLETT

THE balance of power has been described by Professor Asa Briggs as a concept which begged many questions. Certainly among British politicians and writers there was and has been much disagreement as to its meaning, and also concerning its relevance to Britain. Yet relatively few have agreed with Richard Cobden's assertion in 1836: 'The balance of power – which has . . . served . . . as a pretence for maintaining standing armaments . . . is a chimera.' Some Whigs in opposition argued that it was primarily intended for the defence of the weak against the strong. But this was too idealistic. Ministers responsible for foreign policy between 1815 and 1848 had rough-and-ready ideas about the balance which met their immediate needs, even though they might differ to some extent in their interpretations of Britain's interests in relation to it, and as to how their objectives could best be realised. But whether the bias in British policy was in favour of change or the *status quo*, and whether policy was ambitious or defensive, the existence of a broad equilibrium among the great powers was treated as a fundamental British interest.

Britain was more involved in Europe in the first half of the 1 nineteenth century than the second for a variety of reasons. To begin with there were relatively few distractions outside Europe, the general effect of the Napoleonic wars being to complete the reduction of France to a minor rival overseas. Competition with Russia in Asia was growing, but the vast distances still softened the impact. There was also the United States of America, a nation of rising importance if uncertain potential and intentions, yet of sufficient consequence for British politicians and admirals to reflect at times on the need for a three-power naval standard (against the Americans as well as France and Russia). In practice a much lower level of naval strength proved adequate, with European waters being the key to British and imperial security. Because Britain was experiencing less competition overseas than in the eighteenth century, a major justification for intervention in Europe might seem to have been removed, and support lent to Cobden's claim that with naval and industrial supremacy Britain had no interest in the European balance. Admittedly Palmerston was known to follow policies whose relevance to the national interest appeared somewhat tenuous. There were, too, some sections of opinion in Britain which could become unrealistically excited by ideological conflicts in Europe. Nevertheless what happened in Europe was often of consequence to Britain both as a European and as an imperial power, as will be argued later in this essay. It must also be emphasised that those charged with the conduct of foreign policy down to 1848 had all lived through the perilous years when Napoleon had dominated much of the continent. From the opposition benches in the Lords on 4 November 1813 Grenville insisted that there was 'neither safety nor peace for England, but with the safety and peace of Europe'. Others, apart from Castlereagh, showed some interest in prolonging the alliance against Napoleon beyond the period of the war itself, and if parliamentary enthusiasm for such an expedient soon cooled, those in office did not so quickly forget the years when there was no satisfactory balance in Europe. Such times might occur again if Britain turned her back on the continent.

In practice, between 1815 and 1848, European threats to British security were prospective rather than immediate so that British intervention was perhaps encouraged by the distractions and divisions of the other powers. Indeed, Gavin Henderson argued that Palmerston was great only because Britain herself was great.[1] It is true that Britain was possibly the only power which could afford a major war at this time, but as a parliamentary state the nation's wealth was not easily mobilised – save in periods of obvious danger. Hence British influence was more usually a product of the deficiencies of others, and of astute British diplomacy, than the riches of the nation. Such of the fleet as was in commission could be used, but only within limits. The despatch of 4000 troops to the Tagus in 1826 was exceptional. Spain was allowed to enlist a 10,000 strong 'British Legion' in 1835, and unemployed officers made some mark in fighting in the Iberian Peninsula and Greece. But Britain was usually dependent upon continental armies, even small ones, such as that of the Swiss liberals in 1847 when British diplomats were able to hold the ring while the other powers hesitated.

The British reluctance to spend could also be a constraint upon

policy. Sir James Graham in the early 1830s noted public sympathy
for the constitutional cause in Spain – as long as it did not entail increased taxes. Even naval spending was restricted, though all agreed
that British supremacy at sea must be maintained. Fear of increased
expense was one of the most effective levers ministers could employ
against an over-zealous foreign secretary. In general, interest in Parliament, the press, and among the public fluctuated too much and
contained too many divisions to have any very positive effect on
foreign policy before 1853–4 – the influences were usually negative. If
Palmerston was embarrassed at times in the early 1830s by the
strength of feeling aroused by the harsh Russian suppression of the
Polish revolt, and by the persistence of Russophobia for much of that
decade, his policy was not markedly affected. Earlier, enthusiasm for
the anti-slave trade cause undoubtedly swayed Castlereagh at
Vienna, but British insularity and dislike of European autocracies
could only temper, not prevent his continuing co-operation with wartime allies. It is true that the Tahiti affair with France in 1844
unleashed both Francophobia and Protestant indignation. Peel's
reactions suggest that the government had to take a tougher line than
the trumpery nature of the dispute properly demanded. On the other
hand, both Canning and Palmerston made good use of the diverse
strands of public feeling to strengthen their hands in dealing with
critical colleagues and to impress other states with the firmness of
British intentions. At least they could usually play off the different
shades of opinion against each other.

Economic interests had to be given a place in British policy. Ministers acknowledged this in general but execution was more difficult.
There were many complaints that Castlereagh had neglected
Britain's trading interests during the negotiation of the Peace Settlement in 1814–15.[2] Castlereagh's view was that political considerations
had to over-ride economic hopes. Thereafter ministers only narrowed
the gap between these priorities. Both D. C. M. Platt and Lucy
Brown conclude from their researches into British trade policy that at
best it ran a good second to national security.[3] In so far as economic
interest groups tried to sway British policy, they were hampered not
only by bias on the part of ministers and diplomats, but also by their
own divisions and by the reluctance of most European governments to
reduce tariffs against British industrial products, such was the fear of
British competition. Where they were prepared to make concessions,
it was often for political reasons. Britain might have secured special

privileges from the hard-pressed anti-Carlist factions in Spain in the 1830s, but these were finally declined. The Foreign Office mainly concerned itself with the defence of British interests from discriminatory treatment. Palmerston tried to persuade both France and Portugal that friendly political relations could be harmed by unsatisfactory trading conditions. In practice he allowed political considerations to prevail. In the separation of Belgium from the Dutch one cannot find ulterior British economic motives.[4] Political advantages were expected to follow from the prosperity of both states. In the Near East Palmerston feared that stagnant or declining economies would intensify political problems, internal and external, though Cobden insisted the Near East would never prosper under Turkish rule.

Foreign secretaries had, of course, to carry their policies in the Cabinet. Palmerston was sometimes constrained in his earlier years at the Foreign Office by his ministerial colleagues. But in the Near Eastern crisis in 1840 he won a most dramatic victory against strong opposition in the Cabinet. Melbourne, the prime minister, was preoccupied with the survival of the ministry, but while several ministers, by their resignations, could have brought the government down, none was so determined as Palmerston. Melbourne accepted his policy as the least of several evils. Castlereagh's position in the Cabinet had been remarkably strong, and though the prime minister had been critical of some aspects of his policy in 1814–15, he had bowed to his knowledge and experience. Canning, however, owed much to Liverpool's backing, especially in the face of pressure from the King and some colleagues in 1824–5. Wellington and Grey as prime ministers between 1828 and 1834 were both active in foreign affairs, and the influence of Peel in the 1840s has not always received the attention it deserves. He was well-informed and had ideas of his own, especially on defence and the handling of France. He sometimes found his foreign minister, Aberdeen, too conciliatory and trusting, though he recoiled from the more extreme methods of Palmerston.

Napoleon professed to be unable to understand British policy as directed by Castlereagh at Vienna. 'The peace he has made is the sort of peace he would have made if he had been beaten.' Clausewitz wrote more perceptively: 'Historically the English will play the better role in this catastrophe, because they do not seem to have come here with a passion for revenge . . . but rather like a master who wishes to discipline with proved coldness and immaculate purity. . . .'[5] In 1814 the

British Cabinet readily gave up many colonial conquests, Britain 'being desirous of providing for her own security by a common arrangement rather than by an exclusive accumulation of strength and power'. Castlereagh, indeed, was often prepared to go further than the Cabinet in the conciliation of France and in the search for a satisfactory equilibrium in Europe. Although Russia was able to prevail in Poland, Castlereagh helped to create a reasonable balance between Prussia and Austria in Germany, and to devise a territorial settlement on France's eastern borders which promised much greater military security for the rest of Europe than at any time since the seventeenth century. Britain had interests of her own in assuring the freedom of the Low Countries, the Iberian Peninsula and sections of the shores of the Mediterranean from the influence of any rival power, but Castlereagh also believed that Britain's interests would be best served by the elimination of the main grievances of the powers, in so far as this could be done without any one state obtaining a disproportionate advantage. Above all both Russia and France had to be satisfied and curbed. A lessening of the risk of war should also lessen the threat of revolution.

Similar fears and considerations were at work in most European chancelleries to a greater or lesser degree. Enlightened self-interest was a great pacifier. Further security was sought in the Quadruple Alliance with its provision for mutual aid against further French aggression. There was also agreement on periodic meetings so that the powers could consult concerning their common interests, and discuss matters 'considered the most salutary for the repose and prosperity of nations and for the maintenance of the peace of Europe'. Castlereagh personally did much to shape the congress system, if placing excessive hopes in its working and in the possibility that Europe could escape from many of the worst features of what he called the 'old diplomacy'. Yet his calculation that Britain's advantages in wealth and security over all other powers were so great as to admit of her 'pursuing a more generous and confiding policy' was well conceived, not only for the preservation of peace, but also to discourage the jealousies and fears that could be aroused in Europe by the extent of Britain's power immediately after 1815. As it happened, talk of various combinations (Russia, the Bourbon states and the United States of America were the usual candidates) came to nothing. British restraint and sensible diplomacy could do something to keep possible opponents apart, but these were not decisive. Russia, France and America remained separated because their interests did not sufficiently converge. Castlereagh's important personal relationships with Alexander I and Metternich, however, continued until his death, but his successor, George Canning, made a change of methods, if not always of aims, inevitable.

Canning commented in November 1822: 'for *Europe*, I shall be desirous *now* and *then* to read *England*.' He disliked the congress system as such. He recognised its unpopularity in England, and for one whose future political position owed so much to increasing popularity in the country, it was important that he dissociate himself from it at the outset. Not that he was an isolationist. He appreciated the limitations of Britain's power – her strength was economic and maritime. She could act as a land power only in special or limited circumstances, and usually then only in conjunction with a continental ally. Thus a French army had to be granted a free hand in Spain in 1823, whereas a small British force could be sent to Portugal in 1826 against a lesser threat where the navy could lend effective support. Such circumspection is far more significant than Canning's all too well-known boast that he had brought the New World in to redress the balance of the Old. Sensible as was his recognition of the new Latin American states, they could not affect the European balance. Similarly, without recognition, British economic and maritime power should have ensured a continuing ascendancy in the ex-Spanish colonies. In many ways, as Canning himself recognised, Britain had greater cause to fear the United States as a rival in the New World. Canning once spoke of his fear of a 'universal democracy' led by the United States which could create 'the line of demarcation which I most dread – America versus Europe'.

Canning's flexibility and disciplined analysis of the international scene are reflected in his consciousness of the variety and fluidity of the balance of power. He sought stability as far as possible in existing treaties and settled boundaries, in the preservation of the independence of states, and through the principle of non-intervention. His conservative critics at home and abroad repeatedly misunderstood him. In the conflict between autocracy and revolution, Canning firmly chose the middle position. He disliked both extremes, but was prepared to co-exist with any regime on the right terms. It was no part of Britain's interest or duty, nor did she have the power, to regenerate Europe. Occasions could, however, arise when action was necessary, and the Greek War of Independence was such an instance. For some time Canning waited patiently upon events, protecting local British interests and, still more, keeping a close watch on French and Russian activities. His policy was highly personal and not always pleasing to all the Cabinet, but by 1825 his preferred solution was some measure of Greek autonomy negotiated from the Turks under British guidance. If necessary, moreover, he was prepared to co-operate with Russia in order to control her, and this became the line of action in the face of Turkish intransigence and as a result of Russian overtures.

The historians who attribute the break-up of the congress system by 1825 essentially to the hand of Canning greatly exaggerate. The initial rift between Metternich and Alexander I was very much of their own making. Nicholas I, when he succeeded his brother, was still more independent of Austria. What Canning did was to make the most of this new situation. The Anglo-Russian alignment was soon joined by France. Canning died two months before the Turkish and Egyptian navies were smashed at the Battle of Navarino in October 1827. The battle might not have accorded with his hopes, but it is unlikely that, had he lived, he would have allowed Britain to lose the initiative over Greece to the degree which occurred under Wellington in 1828–30. The duke was fortunate that the Russians were not stronger or more self-confident, though all the powers knew that Britain could not be ignored if any fundamental redistribution of territory occurred in the Near East. Meanwhile Metternich's verdict on Canning was plainly wrong: 'He has shaken everything and destroyed much. . . .' What Canning had done had been to pursue moderate aims by what sometimes appeared to others as immoderate methods, especially with his parliamentary rhetoric and appeals to public opinion. Professor Temperley interestingly described his regulation of the 'balance of opinion' as his most original contribution to diplomacy.[6] That this could cause problems, Canning himself was aware. He learned with considerable relief that his 1826 'New World' speech had not injured relations with French ministers, as it might well have done, at a time when he was anxious to cultivate their favour.[7]

Under Wellington, developments in Europe as well as a certain lack of imagination and finesse in British policy demonstrated how Britain might begin to slip from the centre of the diplomatic scene. It is unlikely, given the fluidity of European rivalries, that a recovery of sorts would have been long delayed – especially with the 1830 revolution in France. But a change of government carried Palmerston – as third choice – to the Foreign Office in 1830. His first rule in diplomacy was that Britain should secure the strongest possible position on all matters of interest to herself, however small: it was 'not fitting that a country occupying such a proud position as England . . . should be a passive and mute spectator.' He also introduced an entirely new dimension in that he was prepared, unlike Canning, to support liberal causes in Europe to some extent in accord with the wishes of certain vocal elements in Britain. He had greeted the July Revolution in France: 'This event is decisive of the ascendancy of Liberal principles throughout Europe.' He particularly welcomed the relative lack of violence: he saw it as a triumph for the principles of free discussion and the diffusion of knowledge. He was to urge the merits of moderate reform on many occasions in the future, confident that this was the best preventive of revolution. There was always the possibility of progress and improvement under constitutional governments, however slight: under autocratic regimes there could be none. He tried to argue that constitutional states would somehow be more compatible with British interests within the European balance, and would do more to promote peace and prosperity. In the last resort, however, Palmerston had no doubt but that Britain's interest in a satisfactory European balance *per se* was paramount. As he informed Lord Holland on 21 May 1831, when that politician urged sympathy for France as a liberal state, small French territorial gains in western Europe would be of much greater consequence to the balance of power than large Russian gains in the Caucasus.[8] Similarly he would have promised support to the autocratic Piedmontese monarchy against Orleanist France in 1831 had his ministerial colleagues not objected. For all his insistence to the House of Commons in 1832 that constitutional states were 'the natural Allies of this country', in the last resort he accepted that Britain had no permanent friends or enemies.

Palmerston's priorities emerged clearly in 1831 during the Italian revolts, but so did the restraints under which he operated. As he explained in March 1831, his most pressing concern was 'the maintenance of peace and the preservation of the balance of power' in the face of a possible Austro-French war over Italy. He added: 'It will be impossible for England to take part with Austria in a war entered into for the purpose of putting down freedom and maintaining despotism; neither can we side with France in a contest the result of which may be to extend her territories. . . .'[9] It is understandable, therefore, that during the more serious revolutions of 1848 Palmerston should have hoped for an Austrian retreat from Italy. Public opinion was unlikely to permit British support of Austria while she remained there, and her presence afforded France a constant excuse for intervention. Even Castlereagh, when supporting the Austrians in Italy after 1815, had been obliged to do so very unobtrusively. In 1831, however, Palmerston could use a strong naval presence to support his diplomacy, mainly directed against France. The British warships were welcomed by both the Austrians and the Piedmontese, though a serious French move was never probable.

The Belgian revolt against the Dutch offered Palmerston much more scope, despite divided opinion at home. There were those who feared that any change would have wider repercussions. Equally there were others who welcomed the chance to act with the new liberal monarchy in France. But Palmerston acted essentially as a realistic opportunist. Indeed, he once professed regret that the Low Countries could not remain united, yet failing any better alternative he later seemed ready to consider the creation of a Belgian republic. Given such flexibility it is not surprising that Palmerston emerged with so much credit for the creation of Belgium under a constitutional monarchy, with not unsatisfactory frontiers, and assured of as much protection as a well drafted treaty could provide. When he took office at the end of 1830 the idea of a Belgian partition was among those being canvassed in Europe. For France many things seemed possible – from territorial gains to some form of political influence in whatever Belgian entity that might emerge. With the Polish revolt beginning to distract the eastern powers, a strong British lead seemed necessary if France were not to gain the diplomatic initiative. It was to Palmerston's advantage that the eastern courts could not give strong support to the Dutch monarch, because of the Polish revolt. At the same time he could lean in their direction whenever he needed to restrain the French. In any case political divisions and uncertainties within France herself meant that he was not faced by a single-minded opponent, but by a regime so conscious of its isolation in Europe that it could often be manipulated to meet his needs in Belgium – and all without significant concessions on Britain's part. Palmerston thus drew his main strength from his skilful exploitation of the weaknesses of others.

This is made clear when it is appreciated that although some use was made of the British navy to coerce the Dutch late in 1832, it was due to the intervention of a French army that the Dutch finally surrendered the citadel of Antwerp on 22 December. It is true that before

Palmerston had willingly countenanced the use of French troops in such a mission he had for two years subjected the French to pressure of all kinds, including some strengthening of the fleet, to persuade them that whatever part they played in the Belgian question they could expect no concessions from Britain. There was a crudity at times about Palmerston's approach to foreign affairs, but in this instance it is hard to fault his admixture of diplomacy, bluff and coercion. Although the question was not finally settled until 1839, the Low Countries emerged as attuned to British interests for the next seventy-five years as anyone had reason to expect. Both states proved viable and stable; the balance of power was not injured by the outcome, and was indeed improved by the removal of a source of friction.

From 1832–3 Palmerston appeared to delight in his position as the moral leader of the so-called liberal cause in Europe, but it had by no means been an inevitable development. The initial stance had been basically Canningite. And even after 1832, when his co-operation with France was at its closest, the relationship remained double-edged. The Quadruple Alliance of 1834 was intended to strengthen Britain's hand in the struggle with the eastern powers for influence in Spain and Portugal, but it was also designed to control France and to ensure that she remained the junior partner. Anglo-French relations were at their best when, as in 1834, Britain's relations with Russia were at their lowest, with Palmerston asserting that there existed 'the same principle of repulsion between Russia and us that there was between us and Bounaparte'. Indeed the prime minister in January 1834 feared that rivalries in the Iberian Peninsula and in Germany were in danger of escalating into general war.[10] Not all people, however, saw Palmerston's as the correct or only choice. Aberdeen welcomed the union of the three conservative powers at Münchengrätz 'against the disorganising and revolutionary policy of the present Governments of England and France'.[11] Wellington claimed to John Wilson Croker in 1833 that had he remained in office from 1830 he would have worked above all for the containment of France, the reunion of the Low Countries for the security of northern Europe against France, while by a policy of neutrality in Portugal he would have released naval forces from what he considered their mischievous behaviour in the Tagus for service in the eastern Mediterranean to frustrate the ambitions of Mehemet Ali in Syria.[12] One should not take these claims too literally, but they offer an interesting commentary on Palmerston's conduct. Sir Charles Webster himself commented that if there had been no cleavage between the powers over Portugal and Belgium – a big 'if' – they might have been able to deal with the Near Eastern crisis of 1832–3 in concert.[13]

The harsh suppression of the Polish revolt by Russia, the cruel nature of the Miguelist regime in Portugal (though its successor had many striking failings), and the conduct of Metternich in Germany would have created difficulties among public opinion for any British government that wished to draw closer to the eastern powers. But Palmerston seemed increasingly to relish the collision between conservative and liberal interests, or he at least strove to make a virtue of what he saw as a necessity. Over Spain and Portugal he often sought deeper involvement than most Cabinet colleagues were prepared to tolerate. He also expected too much from intervention. The materials were just not to hand in the Peninsula for the creation of progressive, constitutional monarchical states. In 1838 Melbourne shrewdly asked why constitutional regimes should prove more Anglophile in the long run than any others. Certainly it seems safe to conclude that British interests would have been met by any policy which assured great-power non-intervention in the Peninsula. Britain's minimum requirement was Spanish and Portuguese neutrality in any war in which she might become involved. What Palmerston could argue in 1834 was that matters had by then gone so far that only the dramatic creation of the Quadruple Alliance would meet British needs. In this limited sense he was correct, and in the short run his policy was successful. But he also claimed to see the Alliance as a great moral blow against absolutism throughout Europe, with effects reaching perhaps as far as Constantinople. He even had hopes of adding the kingdom of the Two Sicilies and so weakening Austrian influence in Italy.[14] The eastern powers were impressed – for the time being. Metternich thought Palmerston allied with 'revolution incarnate'. The Alliance brought about the speedy expulsion of Dom Miguel from Portugal, but the struggle in Spain was more prolonged. The Carlists had many strong local roots. The so-called constitutional forces had many deficiencies. Despite some British naval and other assistance the Carlists could only be defeated when an effective Spanish army had been raised against them – in 1839.

Palmerston harboured the illusion that there existed in Spain elements which were sufficiently strong and pro-British to bring about a permanent realignment in that country's foreign policy. He spoke of a truly independent Spain that would be naturally pro-British.

Aberdeen, who replaced Palmerston at the Foreign Office between 1841–6, would have been happy to accept an independent Spain with no such bias. But the question of the marriages of the Spanish Queen and her sister brought out all the complexities in Spanish politics and the possibility of Anglo-French rivalry. Even if Aberdeen had remained in office after 1846 it is far from certain that a crisis would have been averted. The return of Palmerston, however, undoubtedly encouraged the French minister, Guizot, to act quickly lest he be outsmarted in some way. Interestingly enough he also acted out of fear of independent Spanish intrigues.[15] The Spanish Queen was to marry a supposedly impotent Spanish grandee; her sister, an Orleanist prince. Guizot underestimated the strength of the British reaction to this French *coup*: he expected Palmerston to have little support and that the affair would soon blow over. But Palmerston, on his side, failed to impress European politicians with the idea that this was a threat to the European balance of power. For Metternich, indeed, it was rather a matter for congratulation because the Spanish Marriages had split the liberal camp. British pride was hurt, but little else. Nevertheless Palmerston continued to devote much time and energy in tilting at Spanish windmills until his meddling in Madrid reached such extremes that his faithful envoy was summarily sent packing by that most Spanish of military politicians, General Narvaez.

Meanwhile, despite the occasional confrontations and more frequent skirmishes between the liberal and conservative camps, the alignments of the great powers remained essentially fluid. In the main each power was concerned with marginal adjustments of the balance in its favour, and this was particularly true of France. For her, friendship with Britain, even in the 1830s, had only limited advantages since Palmerston was always determined that France should be the junior partner. Not surprisingly many French politicians were anxious to find a more generous ally. But Austria too wanted them in no more than a supporting role – in so far as Metternich was prepared to work with the French. The Anglo-French *entente* therefore limped on through much of the 1830s for want of a viable alternative. As Palmerston remarked in May 1836, 'England alone cannot carry her points on the Continent; she must have allies as instruments to work with. We cannot have the co-operation of our old allies, the three Powers, because their views and opinions are now-a-days the reverse of ours.'[16]

The limitations of British power had been forcibly brought home in

1833 when Palmerston had finally opted to support the Sultan of Turkey against his rebellious vassal, Mehemet Ali of Egypt. At first Palmerston had been uncertain how far British interests were bound up with the survival of the Ottoman Empire. Having belatedly decided to back the Porte, he failed to carry the Cabinet with him. An increase in the navy would have been required since it was already heavily committed in the Belgian and Portuguese affairs. Russia was thus able to step in first as the saviour of the Turks, with the Treaty of Unkiar-Skelessi as a reward. Later in 1833, and again in 1834, Palmerston thought French diplomatic and naval support of value in restraining both Russia and Mehemet Ali. Indeed, despite recurrent difficulties with France, the idea of some decisive Anglo-French manoeuvre against Russia in the Near East continued to appeal to Palmerston down to 1838. So great was his hostility to Russia that the years 1837–8 found him supporting an autocratic ruler in Serbia against Russia who was posing as the defender of local liberties and customs against the central government.[17] Palmerston's thoughts continued to range far and wide, so that in October 1838 he was hopeful of a successful outcome to rivalries with Russia in Persia and Afghanistan which would also add generally to Britain's political influence, with repercussions even in Europe. When the Sultan of Turkey made his desperate and disastrous attempt to expel Egyptian forces from Syria in 1839, Palmerston saw this as his great opportunity to internationalise the Eastern Question and diminish Russian influence.

In fact the Russians were by no means as aggressive and self-confident as he had assumed. The foreign minister, Nesselrode, was particularly anxious to improve relations with Britain, and was very conscious that the Russian position at the Turkish Straits, despite the Treaty of Unkiar-Skelessi, was far from satisfactory. The Tsar's deep hostility towards the Orleanist monarchy made him very receptive to any chance of breaking the Anglo-French *entente*. Thus in a matter of months Palmerston found himself caught up in a diplomatic revolution. He was determined to strengthen the Ottoman Empire, but found the French increasingly disposed to sympathise with Mehemet Ali. The Russians, in contrast, were much closer to his point of view. In this rapidly changing international environment he was able to initiate what was to become the boldest and most impressive undertaking of his whole diplomatic career. At the same time one has only to read the comments of ministerial colleagues to see that his was not the only possible interpretation of the national interest. Lord Holland could see no reason why Britain should not work with France and Mehemet Ali. Territory might be variously distributed in the Middle East without damage to British interests.[18] Other ministers believed that the prospective gains did not warrant the risks Palmerston was prepared to run. Melbourne warned in August 1840 that the last war had given Russia land power in Europe: another might make her a sea power.[19] Palmerston offered a broader view. A strong Egypt would upset the balance of power in the Near East and threaten routes to India which might be of growing importance. He also wished to deprive France of a naval ally in the eastern Mediterranean, and to end the privileged position as protector of the Porte which Russia had secured in 1833. In July 1839 he was musing on the implications of the closure of the Bosphorus and Dardanelles. Although such a closure would protect southern Russia from attack from the sea, it would paralyse 'the left arm of Russia as a naval power' and guarantee 'all the military, naval and commercial interests of Western Europe in the Mediterranean from molestation by the Black Sea Fleet . . .'. He accepted that if only the future of Syria had been at stake there was much to be said on both sides. But Syria was needed to strengthen the Ottoman Empire. A weak Turkey would become a dependency of Russia, while a strong Egypt would aid France. This was an impressive analysis. Indeed Sir Charles Webster later concluded that the Ottoman Empire might have been so much weakened by the rise of Egypt that the fear or actuality of its dissolution could have precipitated a European war. Palmerston helped to avert this catastrophe.[20]

This is probably claiming too much. The Turks and the powers had stumbled through other crises. One of Palmerston's greatest assets in 1840 was the caution of most of the other powers. Yet he deserves full credit for his realisation of the opportunities that existed, and for the courage and skill with which he pursued his aims. Had a stronger Ottoman Empire resulted, the balance in the Near East might well have served British interests. Yet the doubts of his colleagues are also understandable. Those who argued simply as Francophiles can be discounted. The real problem was to divine the intentions of the Russians and the French: above all whether the French were bluffing or not. The commander of the British Mediterranean fleet and the Admiralty viewed with some apprehension the movements of a strong and well-equipped French naval squadron, while strong words were uttered in Paris in support of Mehemet Ali. But Palmerston argued that any French naval advantage could only be temporary, and that most Frenchmen saw this and would not fight. Nor did most Frenchmen look to war as a way of making money as they had in the past. Aberdeen, so often a critic of Palmerston, agreed both that French pretensions in the Near East should be resisted and that France was unlikely to fight.[21]

To deter France, however, was not enough. When Mehemet Ali refused the terms offered him by Britain in partnership with Russia, Austria and Prussia, it was evident that he could be removed from Syria only by force. This had to be done by such British (and other allied) forces as could be mustered, and by the incitement of local rebels against the Egyptians. With winter approaching there was only a limited time available for amphibious operations. The British had also to keep an anxious watch on French naval movements. Palmerston fretted for quick action, but the navy in the eastern Mediterranean faced many problems. That the Egyptians could be defeated so easily was not apparent until it happened. The allies also had some strokes of good luck. With a relatively small naval and military effort the British were thus able to win a position of great diplomatic strength. Mehemet Ali was confined to Egypt. By a new convention concluded in 1841 all foreign warships were excluded from the Straits so long as Turkey was at peace. The Ottoman Empire, of course, could not be revitalised by international diplomacy; it could only be accorded a breathing space. If Britain appeared to be the chief beneficiary, the settlement provided a starting point for better relations between the powers in the Near East, and was marred only by Palmerston's determination to humiliate France. Given his insensitive diplomacy it is not unreasonable to see a link between these events and the Spanish Marriages in 1846. Palmerston did at least decline the suggestions of Russia for a permanent four-power alliance against France. Instead he was urging a forward policy against Russia in central Aisa, confident that the Russians could not turn to France, or, if they did, that any threat to British interests could be offset by a British alignment with the Germanic powers.[22] Here was an interesting, if highly theoretical, projection of the European balance into wider rivalries.

It was probably just as well that Britain and Europe were given a break from the restless ambition of Lord Palmerston by the Peel ministry of 1841–6. Yet Aberdeen was almost as ambitious a foreign minister as his predecessor in that he strove to introduce a wholly new spirit

into British foreign policy. In many ways his approach resembled that
of Castlereagh, but without the congress system, and without
Castlereagh's personal standing in Europe or his superior talents as a
diplomat. Aberdeen believed that there was room for mutual accommodation among the powers if problems were discussed with a predisposition to understand one another's point of view. In April 1845 he
went as far as to claim that 'the present is not a time when any State
can venture obstinately to resist the voice of reason and justice with
impunity'.[23] He perhaps achieved some limited success both with
France and Russia, but only at the level of the somewhat ambiguous
personal understandings with Louis Philippe, Guizot, Nicholas I and
Nesselrode; understandings which were too fragile to withstand the
departure of one of the original contributors, or perhaps even the mere
passage of time. But there was also a deeper calculation in his relations with France. Aberdeen felt the only real danger of war came
from that country, mainly over the future of Spain. He saw Guizot as
the most peaceful of French ministers; hence his at times almost
obsessive efforts to ensure Guizot's survival in office even at the
expense of Britain.[24] It was here that Peel differed from him, arguing
that one could not allow so much to hang upon personalities. Guizot
might fall from office, or Louis Philippe might die, even supposing
that they could be trusted to the extent that Aberdeen claimed. To
Aberdeen's dismay Peel insisted upon some strengthening of British
defences from 1844 as a result of increased tension with France. There
were also debates at this time as to whether the development of steam-
ships would make it possible for the French to launch a surprise attack
across the Channel despite British naval superiority. Technological
change was adding to the tension in Anglo-French relations. By 1846
Aberdeen's *entente* with Guizot appeared to be faltering, even over
Spain.

The Anglo-French rift over the Spanish Marriages appeared to
strengthen the position of the eastern powers. Austria annexed
Cracow, and foreign intervention in the affairs of Switzerland seemed
possible. There the liberal cantons were ranged against the Catholic
Sonderbund. Guizot, however, had no wish to identify himself completely with Metternich and the conservative powers, and he knew
that such an alignment would provoke a major outcry in France. With
his political future at risk Guizot hesitated. Austria was afraid to move
alone, and Britain was thus well placed to give diplomatic support to
the Swiss liberals. While they used their local military superiority to

defeat the *Sonderbund,* Palmerston spun out the deliberations of the
great powers until the end of 1847. British diplomacy, for the reasons
mentioned, proved surprisingly effective in what might have seemed
an unpromising situation.

The French Orleanists claimed that much of the responsibility for
the 1848 revolution in France lay with Palmerston. If they believed this
assertion they were but one group among many which, then and
since, have exaggerated Palmerston's influence upon the course of
events in Europe in 1848–9. Professor Grenville sagely comments that
Palmerston's contribution 'looks best in Blue Books and the columns
of *Hansard'.*[25] In practice his influence varied sharply from place to
place and from time to time: his intentions were often different from
those attributed to him, and some important results – though not
necessarily detrimental to British interests – were contrary to his
hopes. In the first place he must be seen not as the promoter of revolutions but as a politician striving to prevent them. He had welcomed a
reforming Pope in 1846 true to his belief in orderly change as the best
preventive of revolution. Italian affairs, he feared, might provoke the
next European war since, while ambitious French radicals had no
hope of intervention in Germany, rebellion in Italy might afford them
an excuse and lead to war with Austria. The conflict might then
spread to Germany. He concluded: 'at all events, we can have no wish
to see Austria broken down and France aggrandized, and the military
vanity and love of conquest of the French revived. . . .'[26] When Pope
Pius IX appealed for diplomatic support against Austria, Palmerston
seized the pretext to send Lord Minto on a special mission to Italy. He
was to encourage moderate reforms in the papacy, and perhaps
throughout northern Italy, to try to avert revolution. There was some
talk of an Italian commercial league from which British trade might
benefit and which might also contribute to the development of a more
united and independent Peninsula. One detects many naïve hopes in
Palmerston's instructions – not least that Austria could somehow be
appeased. Yet one is also struck by the mission's modesty and caution. In fact it became the victim not the maker of events. The first
revolt of 1848 occurred in Sicily, but it was the fall of the Orleans monarchy in France which set Europe alight.

The Second French Republic made even Palmerston a useful friend
for the most conservative ministers in Europe. Britain was courted on
all sides, including France. An attack on the infant republic by the
conservative powers seemed possible, but Lamartine, the new foreign

minister, argued that 'no coalition was possible on the continent without English assistance and gold'.[27] Britain briefly enjoyed a unique
position on account of her wealth, her political stability, and her
middle-of-the-road political sympathies. She could act as the inter-
mediary, offering reassurance and urging restraint. The March revolutions, however, threw all Europe into the melting pot. There was
renewed danger of war between France and Austria in Italy. British
efforts to prevent a Piedmontese attack on Austria were unavailing,
though the court at Turin fortunately needed little encouragement to
rebuff French overtures. Though defeated at Custozza the Piedmontese preferred peace with Austria to French intervention. Nor was
there any great desire within France for foreign adventures. The political scene at home was confused, but the moderates were steadily
gaining in strength. Palmerston's great fear was independent military
action by France. If this happened Britain would be 'put upon the
shelf and . . . would cut but a sorry figure in Europe'.[28] Political developments in France made this less likely.

Opinions on British policy still vary sharply. An American scholar,
Gordon Craig, describes this as a period when Britain made a major
contribution to the peace of Europe, especially by comparison with
the years after 1856.[29] In contrast, Professor Droz of the Sorbonne has
said of Britain's policies in the late 1840s: 'Everywhere, indeed, by
stirring up national feeling and liberal agitation, she prepared to overthrow the Europe established by the 1815 treaties.' Moreover he
argued that from the defeat of Napoleon, in combination with radical
or conservative forces, 'her object was always to divide and weaken
the Continent'. First on the Atlantic front and then in the Mediterranean, 'she went on advancing her interests throughout the world, in the
face of a Europe which lacked an inner element of stability'.[30] Professor Droz attributes too much purpose and skill, as well as influence,
to British policy, though he reflects views common in Europe from the
period in question. Britain reacted to events rather than created them.
Above all she gained from European divisions, but it was equally in
her interest that those divisions should not spill over into overt conflict. Similarly with respect to Professor Craig's claim one must see
that Britain's contribution to European peace was self-interested, and
was heavily dependent upon many European interests working to
similar ends. This said, it can be argued that British ministers often
made good use of the opportunities that were presented to them. The
British may have done no better than any other power in meeting

Castlereagh's claim that the Concert of Europe required a sense of common duties as well as common interests, but their influence upon the balance of power was often beneficial. Not only was it truly in Britain's interest for a broad equilibrium to exist among the powers in Europe, but from her island position Britain was able to take a more detached view as to what constituted a reasonable equilibrium. This same detachment, helped by the diversity of political sentiment in Britain, also enabled British ministers to see that the balance could not be kept frozen in perpetuity. When change became necessary the idea of an equilibrium among the powers could be used as a rough yardstick against which to measure territorial adjustments. Despite his excesses as a diplomat, Palmerston, in moments of grave crisis, had recourse to policies guided by such considerations, and was second to none in their skilful implementation.

European statesmen frequently had cause to feel between 1815 and 1848 that Britain stood in their path whenever they sought to strengthen the position of their countries. Metternich usually – though wrongly – saw Canning and Palmerston as the friends of revolution. Yet however much Britain turned the balance to her advantage – whether on the Continent or in the wider world – the fact remains that at one time or another every great power sought her as an ally in defence of the balance. It was an unusual period in British foreign policy, and so great a measure of influence could not be sustained at so little cost once European fears of war and revolution began to abate, and as more dynamic and determined political forces began to stir.

8. Metternich's Enemies or the Threat from Below

ALAN SKED

The period 1815–48 appeared to many observers as 'an age of revolution'. In 1817 Serbia revolted against the Turks; in 1820–21 there were revolts and revolutions in Piedmont, Naples, Portugal and Spain; the Greek War of Independence began in 1821 and continued until 1829; 1825 saw the Decembrist revolt in Russia; in 1830 the Belgians revolted against the Dutch and the Poles against the Russians; France also had a revolution in 1830 as had parts of Germany and Italy; in 1832, after a two-year nationwide campaign, the Great Reform Bill was passed in Britain, whose historical geography by now included Cato St, and Peterloo; the revolutionary secret society, 'Young Italy', was founded in 1832 and linked in 1834 to 'Young Europe'. Thereafter the 1830s and early 1840s witnessed a relative relaxation of tension but the winds of change were soon blowing once again. The year 1846 witnessed the repeal of the Corn Laws in Britain and the election of Pius IX to the Holy See in Rome. The year 1847 saw the defeat of the *Sonderbund* in Switzerland and set the stage for the revolutions of 1848.

Perhaps in the light of all these events it is not surprising that men of genuinely European outlook, like Metternich, should have seen not merely common forces at work but even a revolutionary conspiracy. After all there were a number of individuals – like Buonarotti – who declared that they themselves were part of it. Thus when the Chevalier de Menz was sent by Metternich to Italy in 1833 the Chancellor, who prided himself on being 'the Chief Minister of Police in Europe', drew up his instructions in the following terms:[1]

In order the better to acquaint M. de Menz with the degree to which the security police is today linked with politics and, indeed, *(as it were) dominates the latter*, it will not be superfluous to make the following observations. For many years all those who pointed to the existence of a *Comité directeur* working secretly for universal revolution were met everywhere only by incredulity; today, it has been shown that this infernal propaganda exists, that it has its centre in Paris and that it is divided into as many sections as there are nations to *regenerate.* . . . Every thing that refers to this great and dangerous plot cannot, therefore, be observed and surveyed with too much attention.

The recent discovery by the Austrian authorities of Young Italy's secret code had no doubt encouraged the Chancellor's worst forebodings.

But to what extent, in practice, did the 'great and dangerous plot' exist? Can the conspiracy theory of Metternich and those whom he persuaded to believe in it (Alexander of Russia, for example, ascribed the Semenovsky revolt to the sects) be shown to have any basis in fact? A great deal of research has now been done on this subject by historians so that it is possible to answer this question convincingly. The answer is that while it is certainly possible to prove that conspiracies were planned – and sometimes planned in such a way as to mislead moderate liberals (the Decembrist conspirators of 1825, like the Hungarian Jacobins of 1794, were organised into two groups, one with a fairly liberal, the other, which directed the first, with an outright revolutionary programme) – there is no case to be made out that any body ever existed which plotted the overthrow of the entire European social order, certainly no case that any effective one existed.[2] The truth is rather that individual sects or secret societies were usually badly organised and had extremely vague and conflicting aims.

Exist they did, however. The European atmosphere of the Restoration provided an extremely favourable environment for all sorts of political, social and religious secret societies. Romantic, throne-and-alter fanatics conspired to revenge themselves on revolutionaries, while out-of-work officers and dismissed officials from Napoleon's army of civil and military supporters often found it possible to express their feelings and to extol their pasts only under the cover of some secret association or other. Many of these people hoped to regenerate Europe or particular parts of it; some of them were already simply living in the past. The majority of them were to be found in Italy, particularly in the south, where the *Carbonari*, the most famous and most feared of all the sects, had taken root.[3] Estimates of its support indicate that it had a membership of between 400,000 and 600,000 and that it was in a position to threaten the established regime in Naples. In fact it almost certainly played a leading role in the revolution of 1820 there. Yet even the Carbonari was an extremely loosely organised body with no very definite programme, for it contained monarchists and republicans, clerics and anti-clericals, conservatives and revolutionaries. There was a common desire among its members perhaps for some sort of national unity and the expulsion of the Austrians; but it would seem that there were as many valid ways to achieve these aims as there were lodges dedicated to achieving them. Of course, there were secret societies which were better organised. According to Professor Rath,[4] the Federati and the Adelphi posed a greater threat to Austria. But these societies lacked numbers.

Outside Italy, perhaps the sects had influence only in France and the Iberian ports. The *Charbonnerie*, the French equivalent of the Carbonari, is reckoned to have had a membership of 40–80,000 but it had even less success in plotting revolution than its Italian counterpart, subverting only a few French troops in mutinies during the early 1820s.[5] Like the Carbonari too, it included a wide variety of political belief and acted as a kind of umbrella for political groups of different kinds. Every possible variety of opponent to Bourbon rule could be found in it – not merely Bonapartists but also Orleanists and Republicans. The attraction of the sects must therefore have been as much social as political. In an era of counter-revolutionary assertiveness they formed perhaps a sort of alternative society, providing forums where people with different values could meet and criticise the new regimes. In many ways, therefore, they were not very different from the masonic lodges of the *ancien régime*. In fact these lodges still existed and also attracted a wide variety of clientele.

Other countries besides France and the Italian states, of course, had sects and lodges too. The Spanish revolts were often said to have been organised by secret societies and even in Great Britain a number of corresponding societies sporadically revived.[6] It is difficult, however, to take seriously the theory that there was an international conspiracy. With such disunity among the sects in individual countries there would have simply been no point to one. Finally, for all the time and energy invested in the problem, the secret police of restoration Europe were never able to produce the hard evidence with which to back their fears, for the international dimension of the plot was usually supplied merely by reporting the itineraries of exiles. When it came to establishing who was leading the conspiracy, what its programme was and how it was organised, the police could only guess. Sedlnitzky himself confessed to Metternich that he had no idea who was actually behind the threat. It must, in many ways, have been a relief to him when Mazzini *proclaimed* his aims.

Modern writers are prone to adopt a rather more sophisticated attitude to these events. Some, however, are attracted by an interpretation of them which often seems to amount to a new conspiracy theory in disguise. This is the theory that all these revolts and revolutions were caused by the rise of the middle classes or bourgeoisie – terms which invariably but wrongly are used interchangeably.[7] The theory is usually advanced by historians writing on the left, since it already assumes a predisposition to believe that the class basis of society is the main determinant of political change. The argument is then put forward that the middle class was the one which had most to gain from revolution, since, if it could only remove aristocratic influence, it could secure the instruments of power with which to protect its financial interests. After all, the industrial revolution had created a capitalist, exploiting class whose profits were hardly intended for charity. Thus the July monarchy in France is presented as a sort of bankers' political front and the 1832 Reform Act in Britain as a sort of charter for the bourgeoisie. Revolutions elsewhere are interpreted as the rest of Europe catching up. The history of Europe between 1815 and 1848 can then be presented as follows: the French Revolution brought about the fall of the feudal order and the rise of a capitalistic middle class whose interests were threatened by the restoration settlement; unwilling to accept this, it once more overthrew the established order in western Europe in 1830 and challenged the Metternich system itself in 1848. To many people this seems an obvious explanation since the peasants are held to have been too stupid to have had any interest in politics, leaving only the bourgeoisie to confront the aristocrats. The working class unfortunately had still to acquire the numerical strength and class-consciousness required to enable it to play a leading role. Other advocates of essentially the same theory, however, are only too happy to remind us of how fast working-class strength was increasing. Indeed, it sometimes seems as if their class-consciousness was growing with every mile of railway track laid down. All this in turn leads on to the bizarre conclusion that there were revolutions in Europe in 1848 because so much railway-building had been going on while there was no revolution in England because there were too many railways there already.

Such a parody reflects, of course, not so much the views of professional historians as their interpretation by undergraduates.[8] However, it is the sloppy methodology and terminology employed by many professional historians which has misled their student audience. For even the most distinguished writers are occasionally content to resort to historical shorthand terms and Artz, Briggs, Thompson, Droz and others can all be reprimanded in this regard. Other historians – notably Cobban, but also Hexter, Trevor-Roper and Kitson Clark – have all insisted, therefore, on the use of a more precise vocabulary in writing social history.[9] However, despite their work, there are still practitioners around who believe that the shorthand terms will suffice. Miss Lenore O'Boyle, for example, stated her personal preference for them in 1966.[10]

There is no longer any justification, however, for interpreting the period 1815–48 in the traditional sloppy way. Too much research has been done by historians to allow us to see it merely in terms of the rise of the bourgeoisie. It is now known, for example, that in France there was a considerable landowning bourgeoisie even before the French revolution.[11] In fact it already owned as much land there as the Church and aristocracy combined. Moreover, we also now know that the capitalistic middle classes (quite a different thing from 'the bourgeoisie') played almost no part at all in the politics of the revolutionary era. Thus it is difficult to accept that a feudal order was overthrown in France by emerging capitalists in 1789. The period 1815–48 in French history has been revised in a similar way.[12] It was the landed bourgeoisie, already so established in France before 1789 – and which, far from being the same as 'the middle classes' constituted, in fact, an untitled aristocracy – which gained most from the revolution. It thereafter dominated French politics throughout the whole period before 1848. It did this not in competition with the aristocracy but in alliance with it. The idea that the aristocracy was forced out in 1830 is pure nonsense.[13] Legitimists may have withdrawn as part of the 'l'émigration à l'interieur', but legitimacy was a political belief not a social class. The differences between legitimists and Orleanists were political and geographical not social. After 1830 it was exactly the same landed upper class (titled or untitled) which ran France. Moreover, this was true of Paris as well as of the provinces. For far from representing a sort of political centre for the commercial middle classes, Paris and Parisian politics were also dominated by the lan-downing bourgeoisie. In 1842 no less than fifty per cent of electors there described themselves as being 'landowners' or 'without pro-fession'. Only twenty-nine per cent, on the other hand, described themselves as belonging to *professions économiques*.[14] The truth was that the ruling class in France was a mixture of the old and new, the titled and the untitled aristocracy whose social status was determined by the ownership of land. Large sections of the commercial bour-geoisie were probably not yet enfranchised. The right to vote was held by only 1 person in 170, even under Louis Philippe, and the main qualification for it was the amount of land tax paid. Finally, since it was recognised even at the time that French industry was compara-tively backward and unprogressive, there is little reason to expect that French industrialists should have played a politically leading role. If they were incapable of transforming the economy, why should they have succeeded in transforming the state?

In Britain, too, it has been established that no political or social transformation was carried out between 1815 and 1848 by the middle class. Indeed the survival of the economic and political importance of the British landed aristocracy attracted as much comment from con-temporaries as it has from historians since. How then did it come about that Lord Liverpool could support laissez-faire, the Duke of Wellington Catholic Emancipation, Sir Robert Peel the repeal of the Corn Laws and Lord Grey the Great Reform Bill without undermin-ing the aristocracy's political position?[15] First of all it should be remembered that the British aristocracy was powerfully entrenched politically, its influence all-pervasive. Throughout the eighteenth century, as represented in the House of Lords, it had been con-stitutionally and politically closer to the Crown than the House of Commons. Even in the nineteenth century it retained, as part of the legislature, the power of initiative and in its capacity as the highest court of appeal, it exercised judicial functions of the highest order. Peers almost always formed a majority in the Cabinet and through control of pocket boroughs influenced the composition of the lower house. As lords lieutenant in the counties they helped to organise the militia and advised on appointments of justices of the peace. Their social influence was channelled in a variety of different ways; through the extent of their territorial possessions; through their control of local administration; through popular deference to their political leadership; and through their tradition of public service. Finally they never constituted a rigid political caste – the entry of Scottish representative peers, the changing episcopal bench, the influx of eminent soldiers, sailors and statesmen, not to mention the rapid extinction of even recent creations meant that the composition of the Lords was never fixed. From this basis then it was easier to meet the challenge of modern times.

According to Professor Albert Goodwin that challenge was met in the following ways:[16]

> . . . first, through the willingness of the majority of the ruling magistrates and gentry to respond, however reluctantly, to the statesmanlike leadership of their parliamentary and ministerial representatives at times of political and economic crisis; secondly, through the survival, even in the era of parliamentary reform, of much of the electoral structure and political deference characteristic of the eighteenth century; thirdly, through the flexibility of wealth based primarily, but not exclusively on land and the failure of radical proposals for reforms in the system of land tenure; and fourthly, on the absorption by the landed aristocracy of its political rivals from the professional and business world.

The rise of the middle classes even in the country of the most advanced industrialisation was, therefore, not carried out at the expense of the traditional ruling ones.

One could go on to examine the so-called rise of the bourgeoisie in several other countries in Europe to much the same effect. In the German states, for example, the most that was achieved was entry into the bureaucracy for a limited number of the educated middle class. This did not, however, serve to intensify 'the class struggle' since entrants were often absorbed within the ruling class through the device of service nobility.[17] In Lombardy-Venetia, the economically most advanced part of Italy, again there is little evidence that the Austrian government was troubled by a rising middle class. An exhaustive review of the liberal movement there arrived at the following conclusion:[18]

> It would be natural to infer that Italian liberalism reflected a movement by the middle class to gain control of society. The defect of this thesis is that the liberal programme was initiated, expounded

and propagated, not by an aspiring and self-conscious bourgeoisie, with strong economic interests to serve, but by landed proprietors and groups of intellectuals many of whose leaders were of the aristocracy. . . . There is no evidence to colour the view that the liberal publicists were being pushed by a rising capitalistic class or were prompted to act as its mouthpiece.

Likewise it can be demonstrated that in other parts of the Habsburg monarchy opposition to Metternich's policies came primarily from the nobility and gentry – Hungary being a prime example. Even communist historians admit this. A recent account of Hungarian history by the Historical Institute of the Hungarian Academy of Sciences informs us:[19]

It is one of the anomolies of Hungarian social development that the change to bourgeois conditions depended little on the class which should have been responsible for the ideological transformation and for the practical realisation of the actual development, that is to say the bourgeoisie itself. It was the result of grave historical circumstances that when the time came for the actual change to bourgeois conditions, there was no bourgeois force capable of carrying out the task. The bourgeoisie of the royal towns in fact fought on the side of the court, defending feudalism against national independence as represented by the liberal nobility.

Old myths, however, die hard and there are always historians who refuse to accept what would appear to be irrefutable evidence. Lenore O'Boyle, for example, in the article referred to above[20] – it was entitled 'The Middle Class in Western Europe, 1815–48' – poses herself a quite unnecessary problem. She asks[21] 'If business did not choose to rule directly how then did it exert influence? That it did exert influence seems indisputable; there is no other explanation for the restructuring of western European society in this period to suit the convenience of business interests.' She then comments, 'In the nature of the case the indirect assertion of power is hard to see clearly.' Since the invisible is even harder to see than the indirect one can appreciate her problem. However it is amusing to follow the contradictions pursued by her to solve it.

We are told that in France there were three ways in which the businessmen must have exercised their indirect control: through lobbying, through clientage, and through the common acceptance of business values. Since there is not even the slightest shred of evidence to support the 'lobbying' thesis, she wisely drops that line and goes on to examine clientage. In this context (p. 831) she tells us that the lawyers 'were the men who accomplished business's purposes'. However only two pages further on (p. 833) she contradicts herself by asserting that French lawyers were revolutionaries because they lacked sufficient patronage. She adds: 'the striking fact is that there existed in England and the United States, in contrast to the Continent, a large business class that needed and paid well for a wide range of legal services.' She is reduced to suggesting, therefore, that business accomplished a sort of Gramsci-like hegemony because its values had been absorbed by the ruling class. This meant that direct pressure on governments was not necessary[22] – 'There was then really no paradox in the fact that governments whose personnel was never composed mainly or even largely of businessmen followed policies that were essentially more favourable to business than to other interests of society.' This process of absorption, one should add, was made possible because civil servants, according to O'Boyle, are always educated to conserve the values of the economic élite. Thus, here again, we have a contradiction for the economic élite in France comprised a land-owning aristocracy, not a business class. Perhaps the business class did better in Britain where capitalism was much more advanced. Alas Miss O'Boyle informs us that[23] 'England never developed the overwhelmingly middle-class tone of French society.' Her article in the last resort must, therefore, be regarded as an almost classic example of how to force facts to fit in with theories – and even contradictory theories since the three means of indirect assertion she outlines are all of them mutually exclusive – in order to support ideological prejudice.

So much then for 'the rise of the bourgeoisie'. Before leaving the question of class, however, it is instructive to examine the thesis, originally advanced by Louis Chevalier, that the real root of the trouble in Europe's cities in the 1815–48 period was the 'labouring and dangerous classes'.[24] Chevalier's work was done on Paris but it has implications for European history as a whole. Briefly he pointed to the horrific conditions prevailing in France's overcrowded capital and held that the poorest classes of society, who had been forced to seek employment in the city, were driven to despair and revolution by their new environment. Their very humanity revolted at the prostitution, crime, disease, begging and starvation which they found there. This view has been given some backing by the foremost scholar of the 1830 revolution in France, Mr David Pinkney, who has written:[25]

> The connection in 1830 between misery, both economic and moral and rejection by society, on the one hand and revolution on the other, has not been conclusively proved, but there are a number of significant links. Geographically, there is a close correlation between the worst slums where the Parisian savages lived out their miserable lives and the bitterest street fighting in 1830. A similar correlation exists between the areas of high incidence of cholera in 1832, which attacked the poorest quarters and the street fighting in June of that year. . . .

Should we therefore ascribe political revolts in Paris to simple wretchedness and social despair?

There are a number of reasons to suggest that we should not. Charles Tilly, who has investigated urban violence in France points out that the peak years of urban expansion and migration were the late 1850s and 1870s, whereas political disturbance was greatest in 1830–34, 1847–48, 1851 and 1871.[26] The growth of Paris in particular was socially much more explosive after 1851 than before. Moreover disturbances were just as common in slow-growing French cities like Nîmes or Grenoble as in quickly expanding ones like Bordeaux or Lyons. Finally Toulon, Marseilles and St Etienne – all of them rapidly expanding cities – experienced little disturbance at all. Tilly's work has produced another interesting conclusion – it was the older, rather than the newer cities which experienced both political and social revolt. In fact it was the older residents who revolted – not the uprooted and wretched who had to spend their time just keeping themselves alive.

Tilly's evidence is supported by analyses of the lists of dead and wounded of a number of European revolutions. An examination of those killed or wounded in Paris in 1830 and in Milan,[27] Berlin[28] and Vienna[29] in 1848 suggests that the classes most willing to mount the barricades were not the 'dangerous' ones, but skilled workers or craftsmen from traditional trades who were neither uprooted nor poor. These are the same people, in fact, who were described as *sans-culottes* during the original French revolution.

The most extensive studies of 'the crowd in history' have been made by George Rudé whose investigations have covered the major riots in

France and England (with a glance elsewhere) during the period
1789–1848.[30] He concludes from his research that during this period
the 'crowd' which participated in riots was essentially a 'pre-
industrial crowd', distinguishable from those of earlier and post-
industrial times. Its distinguishing features he has classified as
follows:[31]

> . . . first, the prevalence of the rural food riot as the typical form of
> disturbance; second, the resort to direct action and violence to
> property; third, 'spontaneity' and lack of organization; fourth lead-
> ership drawn from outside the crowd; fifth the crowd's mixed com-
> position, with the emphasis on small shopkeepers and craftsmen in
> towns and weavers, miners and labourers (or peasants) in villages;
> and sixth, as a prime motive of rebellion, a 'backward-looking con-
> cern for the restoration of "lost" rights'.

Rudé's analysis is a highly convincing one which compels acceptance as far as it goes. What it does not do is to explain why the 'outside
leadership' was available and why revolts took place (in the towns at
least) when they did. For answers to both these questions there are
other factors which still have to be considered. What Rudé is saying,
in fact, as far as the towns were concerned, is that revolutions or
revolts were usually sparked off by certain specific acts which encountered the spontaneous opposition of all sorts of people – all the typical
sorts of town dweller (except the '*Lumpenproletariat*' whose lives were
too degrading to allow them to worry about politics) – who fought to
restore their rights or perhaps to create new ones under leaders who
themselves were not part of the crowd. Here, therefore, he can only be
referring to the professional or upper classes whose leadership and
opposition to what happened would most likely have been expressed
in more comfortable surroundings than on top of the barricades.
Hence the fact that they are not accounted for in the lists of dead and
wounded.

This again seems highly convincing. In short we are being told that
when Charles X annulled the election results of 1830 and overthrew
the constitution, the crowd spontaneously supported his political opponents; or, to choose another example, after news had arrived in
Vienna in March 1848 of Louis Philippe's fall in France and of
Kossuth's call for internal reforms, the crowd assembled in support of
the Lower Austrian Diet which was known to be deliberating its own

demands for reforms and created the demonstrations which precipitated Metternich's dismissal. Two things, though, emerge from these examples: firstly that the crowd was aware of what was going on – even of what was happening in foreign countries – and secondly that it must have supported certain political ideas. Indeed the conclusion is inescapable that the European revolutions and revolts of the period 1815–48 should not be seen primarily in social terms at all. They were political phenomena produced because people with political awareness and ideas intended to respond in some way or other to the political actions (usually mistakes or acts of political weakness) of the political authorities.

Political awareness in Europe increased dramatically in the period after 1815. The Revolutionary and Napoleonic wars themselves had naturally contributed to the process – the peoples of Europe having been drawn into the political maelstrom in a way never before experienced. Then again the Vienna Settlement had disappointed and outraged many, particularly the students of the German states whose hopes for a united Germany to emerge in some form or another were bitterly disappointed.

Indeed the whole question of student life and universities assumed an unprecedented importance in European politics in the decades after 1815. Metternich, who, as has been seen,[32] went to enormous lengths to destroy the *Burschenschaften*, maintained that German university professors were deliberately educating their students to unify Germany.[33] 'A whole class of future State officials, professors and incipient literary men is here ripened for revolution', he told the Emperor Francis. There was something in this. The future German liberal politician Heinrich von Gagern, who was a student in Jena in 1818, wrote to his father of the student movement there that it aimed 'to spread national consciousness . . . and to work for better constitutions'.[34] Describing one student group, he wrote that it not only drafted constitutions and Church and education statutes, but that it also criticised existing constitutions – [35] 'The state constitutions are examined very closely there and that certainly has the value of making us very well acquainted with them.' Metternich's view of such activities was predictable:[36] 'I deplore', he said, 'that the censorship cannot be instituted for all writings without exception.' After 1819 the *Burschenschaften* were dissolved and the movement petered out. But it emerged again in the 'Germania' movement of 1827–32 which hailed the Polish General Dombrowski in Jena in 1832 and which, at its congress in Stüttgart in the same year, proclaimed its aim as 'inciting a revolution to bring about the liberty and unity of Germany'. Metternich once again resorted to repression but by the 1840s a 'Progressive' movement had emerged which also espoused liberal principles.[37] All these movements were undoubtedly influential in promoting constitutionalism in Germany.

Yet it was not only in Germany that the universities created trouble for the authorities.[38] In Italy the students of the universities of Pavia, Padua and Turin were implicated in the Piedmontese revolution of 1821; the universities of Turin, Modena and Genoa were closed by the government in 1831 on account of their lack of political reliability. The political challenge offered by this new element was reinforced moreover by the creation of new universities – Madrid in 1821 and London from 1828. Metternich predicted that, if the latter were founded, England would experience a revolution. However, the universities only really became politically significant in countries where there was no active political life. One additional factor, finally, may have been of relevance as far as students were concerned – there is some evidence to suggest that the universities at this time were producing more graduates than there were jobs available.[39] Miss O'Boyle, however, would seem to be exaggerating its importance in writing of the existence of an 'intellectual proletariat'.[40]

Another factor which encouraged the growth of public opinion in Europe after 1815 was an increasing awareness of and interest in developments abroad. Influential writers began to publicise the achievements of foreign countries and fashionable circles discussed what might with profit be borrowed from elsewhere. Clearly this process was not entirely new – the Enlightenment had seen the establishment of British ideas in France and the spread of French ideas throughout Europe. But in the period 1815–48 the exchange of ideas was more intense, much less dominated by France and based much more on an examination of particular institutions and, therefore, much less abstract in tone. The interest was no longer in the essential characteristics of man but in what men were doing next door, what kind of countries they lived in and what sort of societies they formed. Thus there is a useful amount of travel literature from the period with observations on the social, economic and political life of a variety of European states. It is difficult to analyse these intellectual cross-currents very satisfactorily but a few generalisations can be made. First there was the discovery of Germany by the

French which, according to Professor Renouvin,[41] led to a 'German-ophilism, whose dominance in French intellectual circles', was 'not of negligeable importance in the study of international relations'. This Germanophilism was the direct result of the publication of works which followed the themes of Madame de Staël's *Allemagne* which since its publication in 1814 had become 'the bible of the Romantics' and which had praised the Germans as an upright, honest, liberal race.[42] Other works – Lerminier's *Au-dela du Rhin* of 1835 for example – upheld this image, although by the 1840s there were writers (Edgar Quinet for example) who were no longer convinced.[43] Perhaps they had heard the warning of Heinrich Heine, delivered to France in 1835:[44] 'You have more to fear from a liberated Germany than from the whole of the Holy Alliance.' Turning to Britain it is true to say that admiration of her both as a parliamentary and an economic power was widespread during this period. Many liberals took her as their model – Cavour and Széchenyi are obvious examples – but even in France during the 1820s and 1830s there was a certain degree of Anglo-mania. This was aided by the literary influence of writers such as Byron and Scott. Indeed Anglophile taste led to the creation in Paris in 1827 of an English theatre which even managed to popularise Shakespeare. One power which never became fashionable, on the other hand, was Russia. As far as Russia was concerned, most European writers – with a few exceptions like Baron von Haxthausen[45] – viewed her as a potential threat to western civilisation. Her suppression of the Polish revolt of 1830, therefore, intensified a Russophobia which was already widespread and which by the 1840s was to approach the hys-terical. Even the devastating critique of Russian conditions published by the Marquis de Custine in his book *La Russie en 1839* was mild com-pared to the Russophobia of the British writer, David Urquhart, whose pamphlets encouraged British public opinion to regard Russia as a potential enemy. Austria also had few supporters outside her frontiers. The Habsburg Empire was seen by 1848 as the 'China of Europe' and had a dreary reputation as a police state. The works of Andrian-Werburg, Schuselka, Sealsfield, Moering, and Beidtel – most of them published originally in Leipzig or Hamburg – gave Europe a low opinion of Austria, as did travellers' accounts also. The publication of Italian works, such as Balbo's *Speranze d'Italia*, did nothing to rescue her reputation. As far as Italy herself, was con-cerned, it is curious to note that, in contrast with the phil-Hellenism which gripped western Europe in the 1820s, the early stages of the

Risorgimento elicited no similar response. Italian exiles were well enough received in London and Paris, but Italy as a *cause* did not exist before 1848. There was, it is true, a great deal of travel literature on Italy, but the peninsula was often seen (in Goethe's phrase) as a 'land of ruins' whose attractions lay in its past. Thus even German liberals who might have been expected to display some sympathy for the Italian cause – for example, Arndt, Mittermaier and Raumer, all of whom were to sit in the Frankfurt Assembly and all of whom wrote books on Italy – were uniformly unimpressed by the prospects for Italian unification. Raumer, in fact, condemned the very idea as 'completely impracticable, unattainable, pernicious'.[46]

A more important factor influencing public opinion was the significant growth in many parts of Europe of the press. Kent Robert Greenfield, for example, has shown how greatly developed the press was in Lombardy by 1848 and has even spoken of a 'Risorgimento of journalism' before 'the third decade of the Restoration'.[47] According to Professor M. S. Anderson,[48] the Press Society, founded in Denmark in 1835 to protest against the censorship in force there, 'soon had branches throughout the country and was an important force in the growth of an effective liberal movement'. There were even occasional press wars: the Galician massacres of 1846, for example, involved Metternich's chancellery in debate with newspapers in France, Germany and elsewhere;[49] in Hungary, his policies in support of the neo-Conservatives were expressed through the *Világ* and opposed by Kossuth's *Pesti Hirlap*.

It was in Britain and France, however, that the press expanded most quickly. By 1836 total sales of London newspapers were not far short of three times what they had been in 1801. *The Times* expanded modestly but others had greater success. In the words of Raymond Williams:[50]

The pauper press [was] quite another matter. After 1815 radical journalists – notably Cobbett and Wooler – reached a large, new audience against every kind of attempt to repress them. Cobbett evaded the Stamp Duty – which in those years was primarily a political tax – by excluding news and publishing only opinion. His *Political Register* sold up to 44,000 at two pence weekly and Wooler's *Black Dwarf* up to 12,000 in the years around 1820, when the circulation of *the Times* was rising to 7,000 and beyond. What is evident is the emergence of a new social basis – essentially a new social class basis – for a new kind of campaigning political journalism.

This new readership was confirmed by the growth both of the number of newspapers published and of their total circulation.[51] 'In 1781 there were 76 newspapers and periodicals published in England and Wales; by 1821 the number had risen to 250. A fair proportion of this increase is accounted for by the growth of the provincial press: the number of English provincial papers rose from about 50 in 1872 to 150 by 1830 and to 230 by 1851.' The figures for general publishing were also significant. In the 1750s there had been only about 100 titles published each year.[52] 'By the 1790s the annual average had risen sharply to about 370 and by the 1820s to over 500 – and to more than 2600 by the 1850s.'

France saw her press expand at a rate even greater than Great Britain's.[53] In 1814 the *Journal des Debats*, the French newspaper with the greatest circulation, had a readership of about 23,000. The total circulation of the main Paris papers in 1830 amounted to only 60,000 copies. However between 1836 and 1845 the equivalent figure went from 73,000 to 148,000. The main reason for this was the establishment of *La Presse* – Girardin's famous instrument for capturing a mass market. *La Presse* was aimed for the first time in European history at an audience which was distinctly popular, it sold cheaply, relied on advertising to boost income, and offered a diet of gossip and serialised novels as well as news and comment.

The growth in influence of the press in Europe was curtailed in these years most obviously by still widespread illiteracy, but also by censorship which even in France was severe at times in the 1820s and 1830s (Britain was the great exception here). On the other hand technical developments meant that the press reached far more people than before and made successes like Girardin's possible. Steam power – used after 1815 – meant that newspapers could print 500 rather than 200 copies per hour. By 1847, 16,000 an hour could be printed – more than three times as many as the total circulation of *The Times* in 1815. The invention of the telegraph and the expansion of railways in the 1830s and 1840s meant that information could also be gathered and disseminated more quickly. The first of the great international news agencies, however, was established (in Paris) as early as 1832.

The importance of the press was quickly recognised. Politicians like Kossuth, Thiers, Cavour and others almost made their career out of it. Others – Canning, Brougham and Palmerston are good examples – placed great reliance on maintaining good relations with editors, Palmerston going to the length of writing anonymous articles praising his own policies and inserting them in friendly newspapers. It was just as well, perhaps, that they took the trouble, for the example of the press in France (where pro-government newspapers found it impossible to attract the readership of opposition ones) showed how irresponsible a press could be.[54] The French government was accused in 1819–20 of complicity in the murder of the duc de Berri; in 1825 it was held to be the prisoner of clerical influence; it was accused of the most profound reaction in 1829; while in Lyons and Paris in 1834 there were newspapers openly advocating its overthrow by insurrection. It was no accident, therefore, that the 1830 revolution should have been launched from the offices of the *National* by Thiers or that the majority of members of the French Provisional Government of 1848 should have been on the editorial staffs of the *National* and the *Réform*.[55]

The rise of public opinion and the growth of the press was a development, therefore, which governments in Europe between 1815 and 1848 feared and suspected. Yet they did so not merely because of the irresponsibility of many newspapers (censorship kept most in check in fact); their principal fear was that the press was propagating new political ideals and philosophies with which they were out of sympathy. These were philosophies of liberalism, nationalism and (towards the end of the period) socialism. Many governments were determined to resist these to the last.

The greatest political challenge to the established order in Europe between 1815 and 1848 was represented by the growth of liberalism. 'Liberals', of course, came in a variety of forms – Guizot was considered to be one, but then so too was his political opponent Thiers and also Odilon Barrot who opposed both of them. In Italy Liberals could support a federation under the Pope or a military state under the King of Piedmont. Irene Collins has, therefore, asked[56] 'what was there in common between the motley groups of students, merchants and soldiers who made the liberal revolution in Spain in 1820 and an experienced French politician like Guizot?' Her answer is:[57] 'Whatever twists and turns were demanded of them by circumstances, they held at heart a simple faith: a belief that progress, leading to perfection could be achieved by means of free institutions.' In practice, in western Europe at least, this meant a demand for parliamentary institutions or an extension of the franchise. As Metternich put it:[58] 'There is . . . scarcely any epoch which does not offer a rallying cry to some particular faction. This cry since 1815 has been "Constitution".'

Continental Liberals tended to look, in part at least, to the British constitution as a model. The French constitutions of 1814 and 1830 were influenced by it as were also the Dutch constitution of 1815 and the Belgian one of 1831. But the Spanish constitution of 1812 and the Belgian one itself were also much admired and held up as examples by Liberals. Yet there were really not very many constitutions to choose from. None existed in Italy (until 1848) and only a very few in Germany. Article Thirteen of the constitution of the German Confederation, it is true, provided for the establishment in each state of constitutions based on diets and in some of the smaller states (Baden, Bavaria, Hesse, Weimar and Württemberg for example) constitutions were actually established in the period 1816–20. But in practice these were of limited influence so long as Austria and Prussia resisted the growth of representative institutions in their own territories. Austria and Prussia, however, had no intention of supporting parliamentary principles. They took the initiative instead of ending the constitutional experiments of 1831–33 in Saxony, Brunswick and Hanover.

If liberalism made little progress in central Europe, its progress in western Europe had its limits also. True, in Britain after 1832, one man in five had the vote, but before 1832 only 440,000 out of 28 million people had been enfranchised. In the Kingdom of the United Netherlands, created in 1815, the electoral system was quite clearly rigged in favour of the Dutch; the Belgian constitution incorporated more liberal institutions but limited the vote to one per cent of the population; while finally, in France the growth of parliamentarism was much criticised. The French experience is held up as a prime example of governments getting into trouble by offending the bourgeoisie. The electorate of only 90,000 under the Restoration and of between only 200,000 and 240,000 under Louis Philippe is held to have been unnecessarily small given the number of educated and politically conscious people in France. According to this argument the monarchies of Louis Philippe and Charles X were doomed to failure since too many potential bourgeois voters were denied their chance to exercise the franchise. This theory, however, does not command immediate acceptance. The Belgian bourgeoisie did not revolt in 1848 despite the narrow limits of the franchise there. Moreover the causes of French revolutions in 1830 and 1848 were rather more complicated than this theory would suggest. The real constitutional crime of Charles X was not his support of a limited franchise but his attempt to stage a constitutional *coup* in 1830 by cancelling the election results and muzzling the press. Otherwise, he might well have survived. He also shared a trait which really blackened the reputation of Louis Philippe – the desire to rule as well as to reign. In fact the principal failing of both monarchs was to identify themselves too closely with particular governments. The case of Louis Philippe, however, was more complicated still. The government with which he was identified did not, unlike Polignac's in 1830, lose the ability to win elections. The constitutional problem during the latter part of the July monarchy was rather that the King's ministers were so comfortably ensconced in power that there seemed no constitutional way of changing them.[59] Moreover, there was no way of knowing whether an extended franchise would have altered this situation – given the lack of organised political parties in France, and the habit of candidates to run as independents, there would always have been room for the King to form a government acceptable to him after the elections. Most of Guizot's opponents were not opposed to constitutional monarchy (even one with a limited franchise); they simply wanted an equal chance to run it.

The second great force at work in the period 1815 to 1848 was the growing one of nationalism. In the decades after 1848 this would prove to have an ever stronger appeal than liberalism; until then, however, the two were still in alliance and most people assumed that they ever would be. The members of Young Italy, Young Poland, Young Switzerland, Young Germany, and Young France[60] 'saw no contradiction between their own demands and those of other nations and envisaged a brotherhood of all, simultaneously liberating themselves'. Mazzini the founder of Young Italy, could also found Young Europe.

Nationalism as a modern political force was born with the French revolution. 'The nation', wrote Siéyès in his most famous pamphlet,[61] 'is prior to everything. It is the source of everything. Its will is always legal. The manner in which a nation exercises its will does not matter; the point is that it does exercise it; any procedure is adequate and its will is always the supreme law.' The Declaration of the Rights of Man of 1789 enunciated the same sentiments less virulently. It read: 'the principle of all sovereignty resides in the nation. Nobody or individual may exercise any authority which does not proceed directly from the nation.' The Terror of 1792–4 was to give one proof of how strongly the claims of French nationalism could be prosecuted. However they were asserted in more obvious ways as well – revolutionary France was given a uniform system of administration and law and was territorially united.

French conquests (and especially Napoleonic rule in Europe) stimulated nationalisms in other lands in turn – Russia, Spain, Germany and Italy are the usual examples given. Yet there is much debate among historians as to what extent *positive* feelings of national consciousness were really created by French rule. Thus Professor Matthew Anderson[62] has cast doubts upon the cases of Russia and Spain, arguing that although nationalism of a kind undoubtedly existed there before 1815 it was 'defensive, religious and highly conservative' and 'had little in common with the forces which were to redraw the frontiers of all central and southern Europe during the following century'. In Spain the French had been resisted mainly because of their treatment of the Catholic Church; in Russia Napoleon had been fought as the foe of the Orthodox Church. None the less, there must have been a certain amount of nationalism around. Napoleon's threats to use 200,000 Poles against the Russians and to dethrone the House of Habsburg in Hungary were not felt to be altogether empty ones.

The Vienna Settlement of 1815, of course, used to be universally condemned for its neglect of nationalism with nearly every historian echoing the sentiments of Joseph de Maistre[63] – 'Never before have nations been treated with such contempt, or kicked about in so infuriating a fashion.' Today the pendulum has swung so far the other way that it has become a commonplace of historiography to regard criticisms of the 1815 Treaties on account of their neglect of national feeling as expressions of naïveté. Yet although it may be true that the statesmen of 1815 could not have been expected to unify Germany or Italy – they had been fighting France for twenty-five years after all for dynastic reasons – there is a danger of underestimating the amount of national feeling which did exist. The Belgians, for example, were clearly unhappy with their union with the Dutch. And in Italy there were numerous contemporary reports of the strength of nationalism there. Indeed the Austrian General Nugent, in a proclamation of December 1813, had actually sought to win Italian support against the French with the promise:[64] 'You have all to become an independent nation.' The Italians were not to be blamed for taking him at his word. Thus Sir Robert Wilson, the British military attaché to the Austrian army, reported:[65]

Independence is the unequivocal demand of the men of letters, the army and the people. . . . The will to be free exists – no Power can suppress the action of that will, supported by the Zeal, the Talents and the Courage of the Italians. The National will may be a creation of Bonaparte's but being created it possesses the *vis vital* and will struggle successfully to maturity. This is not the age when the partial interests of Thrones can be preferred to the justifiable pretensions of the multitude.

Wilson, it is true, was probably referring only to the 'Italians' of Lombardy-Venetia or perhaps to those who had formally been citizens of Napoleon's 'Kingdom of Italy'. Still he was certainly not underestimating their strength of feeling. In Germany on the other hand, the students and few intellectuals excepted, it is probably true that Germans fought from narrower motives than national ones. Dynastic or provincial loyalties may well have been uppermost in their minds and it would be unwise to exclude feelings of simple xenophobia – often a very potent force in producing 'nationalistic' phenomena in Europe. As far as positive nationalism was concerned – that is to say a genuine conviction that the boundaries of the state should coincide with those of the nation – the greatest German publicist of the time (Joseph von Görres) reported of the Germans in 1814 that,[66] 'a great part of the people have not yet been touched by the new life . . . only the smallest group has really understood'.

In northern Italy, as has been noted, there was already considerable national feeling in 1815. Thereafter Austrian rule was to do much to stimulate it. In fact the so-called 'Italian Question' at bottom was really that of how to get rid of the Austrians. For the Austrians with their Germanic system of law, their German-speaking bureaucracy and army and their exclusive vice-regal court steadily lost the support of the north Italian upper classes who were effectively excluded from power. Inevitably, therefore, the latter drifted towards supporting Charles Albert of Sardinia in whose territories a lot of them were landowners and in whose service they could expect to receive jobs.[67] In the rest of Italy, however, the Italian Question was much less potent – at least until the 1840s when the Church under Pius IX also clashed with the Austrians. Until then, however, Italian consciousness had still to be created. From Milan it was easier to communicate with China than with Naples and southern Italy was regarded by northern Italians as almost part of Africa. Local dialects made oral communication almost impossible and the lack of postal links between various parts of Italy meant that Metternich's *'Munizi-palgeist'* retained considerable force. Italian patriots were, therefore, faced with considerable obstacles to overcome before an Italian national consciousness could be created, quite apart from the problems posed (as in Germany) by political divisions and the Metternich system.

These problems were overcome in Italy, as in other parts of Europe, through a number of connected factors. The most important of these were the development of cultural nationalism, the development of a nationalist press, the influence of specific political thinkers and the spread of education in Europe. As a result of these, nationalism was to become the most powerful political philosophy in modern history.

Cultural nationalism was developed in a number of ways – the writing of national histories, the collecting of national folk-songs and the compiling of grammars and dictionaries of various languages being the most important. It was no coincidence that the first half of the nineteenth century saw historians compiling the first great national collections of printed documents (the *Monumenta Germanial Historica* from 1824, the *Documents inedits sur l'histoire de France* from 1833 and the *Rolls Series* from 1836) or that Palacký's great history of Bohemia began publication in 1836. National history became an extremely important instrument for the development not merely of national consciousness but of those national myths without which nationalism would have lacked much force. Likewise the collections of national folk-songs and poems during this epoch (Lonröt for example published the Finnish folk-epic, the *Kalevala*, for the first time in 1835) encouraged national feeling. However the practical resurrection by scholars in parts of Europe of national languages through the creation of national grammars and dictionaries was the most impressive achievement of nationalism during these years:

> In the early and middle decades of the nineteenth century a whole series of Slav languages was rediscovered in this way and equipped by devoted scholars with grammars, orthographies and even the beginnings of a literature. Dobrovsky and Jungmann among the Czechs; Safarik and Kollar among the Slovaks (one of the best examples of a national group whose renaissance was made possible by the resurrection of its language); Gaj among the Slavs of

the Illyrian coast; Kopitar among the Slovenes and Karadjitch among the Serbs were all active in this way.[68]

Even in Italy the creation of a literary language based on the Tuscan dialect of the area around Florence was of great political importance. Manzoni's willingness to write in it, for example, made *I promessi sposi* 'the most influential novel ever written in Italian'.[69] Italian literature, significantly, was (at this time also) instrumental in fostering a national mythology:[70] 'Grossi and Guerazzi found the educated public avid for tales of medieval Italian heroes who once beat the French and the Saracens, and Leopardi's patriotic odes had to be confiscated by the Austrian censorship less they should incite people to revolt. Literature thus helped to reassure Italians that they were not so unfit as some of them imagined for war and politics.' The cumulative influence of all these cultural advances, however, could only spread as knowledge itself disseminated from the universities through high schools and primary schools to the people at large. This meant that nationalism spread with the spread of education and the educational theories of Jahn and Pestalozzi were of some importance here. Even more important, however, was the establishment of systems of national elementary schools. In the period 1815–48 such systems were expanded or begun in Holland, Greece, France, Belgium and Portugal.

The more purely political thrust of nationalism, on the other hand, was created by two other factors: the ideology of certain thinkers plus the development of a nationalist press. The ideas of Herder, Fichte and Schleiermacher were important here, but it was Giuseppe Mazzini who undoubtedly became the most influential prophet of nationalist belief 'Every nation', he wrote,[71] 'has a mission, a special office in the collective work, a special aptitude with which to fulfil it; this is its sign, its baptism, its legitimacy.' Mazzini's theories, however, always contained an element of the irrational – like those of all nationalist thinkers. Thus nationalism could often become an exclusive, arrogant and oppressive creed as its supporters in particular countries saw their national missions and faiths as superior to those of others. This arrogance was often expressed in the articles of the national newspapers established during this period – Kossuth's *Pesti Hirlap* being a good example.

Socialism 'played only a comparatively minor role in the political events of Europe in the early nineteenth century', largely because until Europe had become more industrialised it clearly could not exert much influence.[72] The term itself was only coined in 1831 – by a Frenchman, Pierre Leroux – and reflected the growth of socialist theorising in France. The concept was rooted in the French revolution and one could trace its origins back to various writings of Malby, Morelly and Rousseau and to Babeuf's so-called 'communist' conspiracy of 1796. In fact Buonarotti's account of Babeuf, which was published in 1828 in France, revived a direct interest in his ideas there. Yet by the 1830s and 40s there were a variety of socialist schemes to choose from: the industrial plans of the Saint-Simonians; Fourier's blue-prints for self-governing communities; Proudhon's anarchism; Blanqui's theories of class struggle and dictatorship; Blanc's state-financed 'social workshops'; not to mention Cabet's plan for Icarie – a communist island utopia.

In England too there were socialist ideas around. Robert Owen perhaps invented the term before Leroux. Yet English socialism never acquired the theoretical basis of the French and the earliest 'socialist' writers there,[72] Thomas Hodgskin and William Thompson, were not much in advance of Ricardo in their ideas. Owen's own socialism was not based on ideas of class struggle but on quite the opposite: he founded 'harmony' communities and encouraged 'co-operatives'. In fact he wanted his socialists, as far as possible, to be non-political.

France and England apart, early socialism established a base only really in Germany. The latter was still a predominantly agricultural society dominated by small towns (in 1845 for example seventy-four per cent of the population of Prussia still worked on the land) but, here and there, there were already some centres of industry (Saxony, Lower Rhine [Ruhr, Rhein] Main area) developing. Socialism, however, was imported from France by writers like Wilhelm Weitling and Ludwig von Stein. Indeed the title of Stein's most famous book, published in 1842, was *Socialism and Communism in France Today*. By the 1840s, of course, Marx and Engels had also begun to write. The *Holy Family* appeared in 1844 and the *Communist Manifesto* was written in the winter of 1847–8. Yet 'it is generally agreed that outside the Rhineland (and there only marginally) the *Manifesto* arrived too late to make any significant impression on the German events of 1848'.[74]

The Habsburg monarchy had also seen the beginnings of industrialisation before the revolution of 1848.[75] Outbreaks of machine breaking had occurred in Bohemian factories in 1846 and 1848. But there is little evidence that any socialist movement had as yet developed. Printing workers, it is true, had organised self-help between 1834 and 1846 to protect their members from the economic consequences of illness but this development was exceptional. Only those who had experience of life in Germany or Switzerland would have had the opportunity to come in contact with contemporary socialist ideas. For Sedlnitzky's *Polizeihofstelle* ensured that none were propagated inside Austria itself. In 1844, for example, the two brothers, Charles and Joseph Schestag, spent several months inside the Spielberg for having joined Weitling's 'League of the Just'.

Did the 'utopian socialists' – those who propagated socialist ideals which differed from those of Karl Marx – exercise no influence at all on Europe, therefore, in the period before 1848?[76] The question is a difficult one to answer despite the fact that very few people would respond unhesitatingly in the affirmative. For although it is easy to point out that 'utopian socialism' was millennial – i.e., it assumed that the just society could come about if only this experiment worked or that *coup d'état* succeeded – there is also much evidence that Owenite ideas played an important part in the rise of British trade unionism and that socialists of the Blanqui/Babeuf tradition were active in revolutionary outbreaks in France in the 1830s. Tocqueville, it should be remembered, saw socialism as 'the essential characteristic' of the revolution of February 1848 in France, even if Marx contradicted him. It is difficult, on the other hand, to believe that socialism played any significant role in the Chartist movement in England. Feargus O'Connor, its most influential leader, was 'a radical Tory antisocialist' who described his Land Scheme of 1845 as about as socialist as the Comet. If Bronterre O'Brien (another Chartist leader) made a socialist contribution with his 'Propositions for the National Reform League' and Ernest Jones, yet another, was a Marxist, their influence on British social thought was none the less slight. Chartism simply did not convert the British working class to socialism. In fact Chartism, in the words of G. D. H. Cole[77] 'produced no Socialist theories of its own – only echoes of Owen, of Louis Blanc and of Karl Marx to which the workers, for the most part failed to listen'.

What conclusions, therefore, can one draw about the revolutionary movements of the years 1815–48? Probably the safest is that there was no general factor which could explain them all. Specific revolts were often the specific results of political mistakes on the part of specific rulers, albeit at a time when an increased awareness of what was happening in the world, plus the emergence of new ideas, meant that people of many, almost all, classes were much more ready to respond.

Bibliographical Notes

The Place of Publication is London unless otherwise stated.

I. THE CONGRESS OF VIENNA, 1814–15
AND ITS ANTECEDENTS

Although incomplete, there is a vast documentation of the events leading to the Congress of Vienna and of the Congress itself. Among the important collections are Georg F. von Martens, *Nouveau recueil des traités . . . depuis 1808*, 16 vols (Göttingen, 1817–42); Comte d'Angeberg, *Le Congres de Vienne et les traités de 1815*, 2 vols Paris, 1864) Edward Hertslet, *A Map of Europe by Treaty . . . Since 1814*, 4 vols (1875–91) C. K. Webster, *British Diplomacy 1813–1815* (1921). There is an abundance of memoirs and collections of correspondence (both of which categories, besides giving the idiom and atmosphere of the period, are often the authority for important facts). Among these are the memoirs of Prince Metternich, Prince Talleyrand, K. A. von Hardenberg, Caulaincourt (indispensable for events leading to the Treaty of Fontainbleau), Prince Czartoryski, Rosenkrantz, and the correspondence of Castlereagh, Stein, Nesselrode, and Wellington. Secondary authorities, with ample bibliographies, are numerous. The organisation of the Congress and Castlereagh's role are brilliantly described by C. K. Webster, *The Congress of Vienna* (1919) and *The Foreign Policy of Castlereagh, 1812–1815* (1931). Although this second work by no means sets out to belittle the importance of Metternich, Talleyrand, Hardenberg and the Russian diplomats, by concentrating on the English documentation and by emphasising Castlereagh's role which had hitherto been largely ignored by continental historians, it gives an account which today needs to be supplemented from other sources. On Metternich, H. Ritter von Srbik's detailed study, *Metternich: der Staatsmann und der Mensch* 2 vols (Munich, 1925) is most illuminating and so too is the brilliant monograph by Enno E. Kraehe, *Metternich's German Policy* vol. 1 (Princeton, 1963) which unfortunately has not yet been followed up by a promised volume dealing with the period 1814 to 1820. On Talleyrand, there are Georges Lacour-Gayet, *Talleyrand, 1754–1838*, 4 vols (Paris, 1928–34) and Guglielmo Ferrero, *The Reconstruction of Europe: Talleyrand and the Congress of Vienna*, trans. T. R. Jaeckel (New York, 1941). One of the most satisfactory works on the Tsar Alexander is P. K. Grimsted, *The Foreign Ministers of Alexander I* Berkeley, 1969) which is based on Russian sources. Of special interest to readers of this volume is Edward Vose Gulick, *Europe's Classical Balance of Power* (Ithaca; New York, 1955) which contains an excellent bibliographical essay. In the second part of this book the author (who contributed ch. XXIV on 'The Final Coalition and the Congress of Vienna' to vol. IX of *The New Cambridge Modern History* (Cambridge, 1965)) discusses the origins of the final coalition against Napoleon and the negotiations at Vienna in terms of the European balance of power.

4. RUSSIA AND THE EASTERN QUESTION, 1821–41

Inevitably a high proportion of the most important writing on this subject is available only in Russian. The most comprehensive general works on the reigns of Alexander I and Nicholas I, both old but still important, are N. K. Shil'der, *Imperator Aleksandr Pervyi: Ego zhizn i tsarstvovanie* (The Emperor Alexander I: his life and reign), 4 vols (St Petersburg, 1897–8) and T. Schiemann, *Geschichte Russlands unter Nikolaus I*, 4 vols (Georg Reimer, Berlin, 1904–19). S. S. Tatischchev, *Vneshnaya politika Imperatora Nikolaya Pervogo* [the foreign policy of the Emperor Nicholas I] (Skorokhodov; St Petersburg, 1887) is a substantial work which is still of value. Of modern Soviet works on the 1820s, O. Shparo, *Osvobozhdenie Gretsii i Rossiya (1821–29)* [Russia and the Liberation of Greece, 1821–1829] (Mysl'; Moscow, 1965) is marked by a strong prejudice against the west-European states, particularly Great Britain; I. S. Dostyan, *Rossiya i balkanskii vopros: iz istorii russko-balkanskikh politicheskikh svyazei v pervoi treti XIX v* [Russia and the Balkan question: from the history of political relations between Russia and the Balkans in the first third of the nineteenth century] (Nauka; Moscow, 1972) is a more satisfactory book which contains a good deal of interesting information. A. V. Fadeev, *Rossiya i vostochnyi krizis 20–x godov XIX veka* [Russia and the eastern crisis of the 1820s] (Izdatel'stvo Akademii Nauk SSSR; Moscow, 1958) is also very useful and probably the best treatment of the period from the Russian standpoint. In western languages there are the recent book by Eberhard Schütz, *Die europäische Allianzpolitik Alexanders I. und der griechische Unabhängigkeitskampf, 1820–1830* (Otto Harrassowtiz; Wiesbaden, 1975) which stresses heavily the influence on the Tsar of wider European considerations and does not in fact carry the story beyond 1825; and the still excellent and compact English account in C. W. Crawley, *The Question of Greek Independence, 1821–1833* (Cambridge University Press; Cambridge, 1930). British policy during the critical years 1826–7 is treated in detail in H. W. V. Temperley, *The Foreign Policy of Canning*, 2nd edn (Cass, 1966). On the work of the special committee of 1829 there is a still important article by R. J. Kerner, 'Russia's new policy in the Near East after the peace of Adrianople', *Cambridge Historical Journal*, v (1937). G. H. Bolsover, 'Nicholas I and the Partition of Turkey', *Slavonic and East European Review*, XXVII (1948–9) is a useful article based largely on materials from the Austrian archives; while P. E. Mosely, *Russian Policy and the Opening of the Eastern Question in 1838 and 1839* (Harvard University Press; Cambridge, Mass., 1934) is a short and pointed study which is almost unique among works in western languages in being based on research in Russian archives. V. A. Georgiev, *Vneshnyaya politika Rossii na blizhnem vostoke v kontse 30–nachale 40–x godov XIX v.* [the foreign policy of Russia in the Near East at the end of the 1830s and beginning of the 1840s] (Izdatel'stvo Moskovskogo Universiteta;

Moscow, 1975) is a detailed study based upon much archive material, though marked, like most Soviet writing on this period, by too great a readiness to see Russia as the victim of her own leaders and the hostility of the other great powers. British policy in its interrelations with that of Russia is covered in detail by Sir C. K. Webster, *The Foreign Policy of Palmerston, 1830–1841;* 2 vols (Bell; 1951) and H. W. V. Temperley, *England and the Near East: The Crimea* (reprint, Cass; 1964), Book II.

5. THE METTERNICH SYSTEM, 1815–48

For a general discussion of Metternich students are referred to the collection of articles and extracts assembled by Enno E. Kraehe in *The Metternich Controversy* (Holt, Rinehart and Winston; N.Y., 1971). For his internal policies the following are indispensable: Aurthur G. Haas, *Metternich, Reorganisation and Nationality, 1813–1818; A Story of Foresight and Frustration in the Rebuilding of the Austrian Empire* (University of Tennessee Press; Knoxville, 1964); Alan Sked, 'Metternich and the Federalist Myth' in Alan Sked and Chris Cook (eds), *Crisis and Controversy: Essays in Honour of A. J. P. Taylor* (Macmillan; 1976); Egon Radvany, *Metternich's Projects for Reform in Austria* (Martinus Nijhoff; The Hague, 1971); and Donald E. Emerson: *Metternich and the Political Police, Security and Subversion in the Hapsburg Monarchy (1815–1830)* (Martinus Nijhoff; The Hague, 1968). For Hungary there is simply nothing in English to compare with E. Andics, *Metternich und die Frage Ungarns* (Akademiai Kiado; Budapest, 1973). On Italy see Alan Sked, 'An Imperial Crisis: Austrian Policy towards Northern Italy, 1847–49' (unpublished doctoral dissertation; Oxford, 1974). Alan Reinerman, 'Metternich and Reform: The Case of the Papal State, 1814–1861', *Journal of Modern History*, vol. 42, no. 4 (December 1970) pp. 524–48; Paul Schroeder, 'Austria as an obstacle to Italian Unification and Freedom, 1814–1861', *Austrian History News Letter*, vol. 3 (1962), pp. 1–32. Metternich's foreign policy is treated in Paul Schroeder, *Metternich's Diplomacy at its Zenith: Austria and the Congresses of Troppau, Laibach and Verona* (University of Texas Press; Austin, 1962) and Paul Schroeder, 'Metternich Studies since 1925', *Journal of Modern History*, vol. XXXIII, no. 3, pp. 237–60. The latest biography of Metternich (which also covers his foreign policy) is by Alan Palmer, *Metternich* (Weidenfeld and Nicolson; 1972). Finally the reader is referred to a useful collection of documents edited by Mack Walker entitled *Metternich's Europe, 1813–1848* (Harper Torchbooks; New York, 1968); and to G. de Bertier de Sauvigny, *Metternich and his Times* (Darton, Longman and Todd; 1962).

For works in foreign languages the reader is referred to Schroeder's article on 'Metternich Studies', and the bibliography in Radvany's *Metternich's Projects*.

7. BRITAIN AND THE EUROPEAN BALANCE, 1815–48

R. W. Seton-Watson, *Britain in Europe, 1789–1914* (Cambridge University

Press; 1937) is still a useful, detailed introduction, but it has been valuably supplemented by K. Bourne, *The Foreign Policy of Victorian England, 1830–1902* (Clarendon Press; Oxford, 1970) which provides many key documents. Paul Hayes, *Modern British Foreign Policy: the Nineteenth Century, 1814–80* (Adam and Charles Black; 1975) is rather uneven. The most important works for the period 1815–41 remain those of Sir Charles Webster, *The Foreign Policy of Castlereagh, 1815–22* (G. Bell; 1925) *The Foreign Policy of Palmerston, 1830–41* (G. Bell; 1951), and H. W. V. Temperley, *The Foreign Policy of Canning, 1822–27* (G. Bell; 1925). For the 1840s Roger Bullen, *Palmerston, Guizot and the Collapse of the Entente Cordiale* (Athlone Press; 1974) is especially useful and ranges more widely than the title suggests. For Palmerston's career in general between 1830 and 1848 the best guide is Donald Southgate, *The Most English Minister* . . . (Macmillan; 1966). Aberdeen's career as foreign secretary is covered by Lucille Iremonger, *Lord Aberdeen* (Collins, 1978), although attention should be paid to N. Gash, *Sir Robert Peel: the Life of Sir Robert Peel After 1830* (Longman; 1972). Britain also figures prominently in Lawrence C. Jennings, *France and Europe in 1848* (Clarendon Press; Oxford, 1973). The commercial dimension of British foreign policy is explored by D. C. M. Platt, *Finance, Trade and Politics in British Foreign Policy, 1815–1914* (Oxford University Press; 1968) and the naval by C. J. Bartlett, *Great Britain and Sea Power, 1815–1853* (Clarendon Press; Oxford, 1963). Insights into contemporary criticism of British foreign policy are provided by A. J. P. Taylor, *The Trouble Makers: Dissent over Foreign Policy 1792–1939* (Hamish Hamilton; 1957).

8. METTERNICH'S ENEMIES OR THE THREAT FROM BELOW

Students of the period 1815–48 are recommended to read the following works to acquaint themselves with the latest literature on the period:
M. S. Anderson, *The Ascendancy of Europe, Aspects of European History, 1815–1914* (Longman; 1972) and George Rudé, *Debate on Europe, 1815–1850* (Harper Torchbooks; New York, 1972). Professor Anderson's book is by far the best comparative history of nineteenth-century Europe at present in print, while Professor Rudé's is an excellent guide to the literature for students of the first half of the century. I have relied on both for my article – or Professor Anderson in particular for the development of nationalism and on Professor Rudé for the history of socialism and social movements.

Notes and References

INTRODUCTION *Alan Sked*

1. This is not to imply that in the case of either France, Poland or the United Netherlands, rulers were bound by treaty to grant constitutions.

2. See Donald E. Emerson, *Metternich and the Political Police, Security and Subversion in the Hapsburg Monarchy (1815–1830)* (Martinus Nijhoff; The Hague, 1968) p. 119.

3. Quoted in Mack Walker (ed.), *Metternich's Europe, 1813–1848* Harper Torchbooks; New York, 1968) p. 80.

4. Ibid, pp. 37–9 For the text of the Holy Alliance.

5. J. H. Pirenne, *La Sainte-Alliance*, 2 vols (Neuchâtel, 1946–49).

6. See Walker, p. 41.

7. For the text see Michael Hurst (ed.), *Key Treaties for the Great Powers, 1814–1914*, vol. 1 (1814–1870) (David and Charles; 1972) pp. 121–4

8. For text see Walker, pp. 127–9.

9. For text see Kenneth Bourne, *The Foreign Policy of Victorian England 1830–1902* (Clarendon Press; Oxford, 1970) pp. 198–207.

10. Quoted by G. de Bertier de Sauvigny in *Metternich and his Times* (Darton, Longman and Todd; 1962) p. 247.

11. Ibid, p. 251.

12. Ibid.

13. Viktor Bibl, *Metternich, Der Dämon Osterreichs* (Johannes Gunther Verlag; Vienna, 1936) p. 200.

14. G. A. C. Sandeman, *Metternich* (Methuen; 1911) pp. 239–40.

15. Jacques Droz, *Europe Between Revolutions, 1815–48* (Fontana; 1967) pp. 243–4.

16. Bibl, p. 204.
17. Ibid.
18. Quoted in Walker, pp. 74–5.
19. Bourne, p. 31.
20. Droz, pp. 243–4.
21. Lucille Iremonger, *Lord Aberdeen* (Collins; 1978) p. 147.
22. Ibid.

1. THE CONGRESS OF VIENNA, 1814–15, AND ITS ANTECEDENTS   *Douglas Dakin*

1. For details of the organisation of the Vienna Congress, see C. K. Webster, *The Congress of Vienna, 1814–1815* (1919).

2. See E. V. Gulik, *Europe's Classical Balance of Power* (1955) pp. 1–91 *et passim*.

3. Text in C. K. Webster, *British Diplomacy 1813–1815* (1921) [hereafter cited as *BD*].

4. For a thorough study of Metternich's diplomacy in this period, see E. E. Kraehe, *Metternich's German Policy*, vol. I, *The Contest with Napoleon, 1799–1814* (1963).

5. Text in G. F. von Martens, *Nouveau recueil des traités* ... *depuis 1806,* (1817–1842) vol. III, pp. 234–8.

6. Kraehe, p. 156.

7. *BD*, pp. 1–4.

8. The text of the so-called Wurschen proposals is given in W. Oncken, *Oesterreich und Preussen im Befreiungskriege* ..., vol. II (1879) p. 318.

9 The text is given in G. F. Martens, *Recueil des traités* ..., vol. III, pp. 105ff.

10. Metternich's accounts will be found in his *Memoirs* (English edn, 1880–2) vol. I, pp. 185–92 and vol. II, p. 540.

11. This view is strongly put by Kraehe (pp. 180ff) who discusses in some detail the views of other historians.

12. The text, including the secret clauses, is given in G. F. Martens, vol. III, pp. 117–26.

13. Text in G. F. von Martens, vol. I, pp. 610ff.

14. See *BD*, pp. 111–12, 114–18.

15. *BD*, pp. 19–29.

16. See Kraehe, pp. 225ff.

17. See ibid, pp. 255–6.

18. See ibid.

19. *BD*, p. 120.

20. Treaty of 11 January 1814.

21. See Kraehe, pp. 281–2.

22. See *BD*, pp. 133ff.

23. See Kraehe, p. 288.

24. The standard work on this congress is A. Fournier, *Der Congress von Chatillon 1814* (1900).

25. See Kraehe, p. 297.

26. *BD*, pp. 152–3.

27. Text in *British and Foreign State Papers*, I, pt I, pp. 121–9.

28. For the events of the ten days of April 1814, the *Mémoirs* of Caulaincourt is an essential source.

29. See *BD*, pp. 175–7.

30. English text in E. Hertslet, *The Map of Europe by Treaty* (with maps), vol. I (1875) pp. 1–28.

31. On the negotiations in London, see C. K. Webster, *The Foreign Policy of Castlereagh* (1931), vol. I, pp. 288–323.

32. See ibid, p. 322.

33. See ibid, pp. 362ff; *BD*, pp. 201–2.

34. See Webster, *Castlereagh*, pp. 345ff; *BD*, pp. 201ff.

35. Text in *BD*, pp. 213–15.

36. See *BD*, pp. 222ff.

37. See Webster, *Castlereagh*, p. 362; *BD*, pp. 258.

38. These are to be found in the *Mémoires du Prince Talleyrand*, 5 vols (Paris, 1891–2) vol. II, pp. 214–54.

39. G. Pallain (ed.), *Correspondance inédite de Talleyrand et du roi Louis XXVIII* (1881).

40. Text in *British Foreign and State Papers*, vol. II, pp. 1001–5.

41. For a full account of the negotiations concerning Murat, see Webster, *Castlereagh*, pp. 253ff and pp. 313ff.

42. The texts of the 1814–15 territorial treaties and other instruments, including the Vienna Congress Treaty of 9 June 1815, will be found in Hertslet.

43. Text in Hertslet, pp. 342–69.

44. Ibid, pp. 372–5.

45. See ch. 2 below.

46. *BD*, pp. 306–7.

47. See Gulik, pp. 259 and 261.

48. See *BD*, pp. 395–403.

49. See ibid, pp. 404–9.

50. See Bibliographical note.

2. ALLIED DIPLOMACY IN PEACETIME: THE FAILURE OF THE CONGRESS 'SYSTEM', 1815–23 *Roy Bridge*

1. *BD*, p. 281.
2. H. Contamine, *Diplomatie et diplomates sous la restauration, 1814–30*, p. 60.
3. Ibid, p. 54 ['The representative of France who knows the Crimea best'].
4. Ibid, p. 68.
5. C. K. Webster, *The Foreign Policy of Castlereagh*, vol. II, p. 55.
6. B. de Sauvigny, *Metternich et la France après le congrès de Vienne*, vol. I, pp. 189–90.
7. Ibid, p. 191.
8. Ibid.
9. Ibid, pp. 194–5.
10. Webster, *Castlereagh*, vol. II, p. 147.
11. Ibid, p. 146.
12. Metternich, *Mémoires*, vol. III, p. 267.
13. De Sauvigny, I, p. 207.
14. Ibid, p. 208 ['One should kiss his feet'].
15. K. Hammer, *Die französische Diplomatie der Restauration und Deutschland, 1814–30*, pp. 83ff.
16. Contamine, p. 81.
17. De Sauvigny, *Metternich et la France après le congrès de Vienne*, vol. II, p. 307.
18. Webster, *Castlereagh*, vol. II, pp. 237–40.
19. De Sauvigny, vol. II, p. 322.
20. Ibid.
21. Ibid.
22. Ibid, p. 321.
23. Ibid, pp. 331–2.
24. Ibid, p. 353.
25. Ibid, pp. 365, 378 ['wise constitution'].
26. Ibid, p. 380.
27. Hammer, p. 105.
28. De Sauvigny, vol. II, p. 389.
29. Metternich, *Mémoires*, vol. III, p. 492.
30. De Sauvigny, vol. II, p. 475.
31. Ibid, pp. 437–9.
32. Ibid, pp. 447.
33. Ibid, p. 423.
34. Ibid, p. 468.
35. Contamine, p. 82.
36. De Sauvigny, p. 486.
37. Ibid, p. 514.
38. Webster, *Castlereagh*, vol. II, pp. 322–3.
39. De Sauvigny, vol. II, p. 429.
40. Webster, *Castlereagh*, vol. II, p. 360.

41. Contamine, p. 83.
42. Ibid.
43. De Sauvigny, vol. II, p. 514.
44. I. Nichols, *The European Pentarchy and the Congress of Vienna, 1882*, p. 9.
45. Hammer, p. 113.
46. Ibid.
47. C. M. Woodhouse, *Capodistrias*, p. 291.
48. Ibid.
49. Metternich, *Mémoires*, vol. III, p. 557.
50. Nichols, p. 50.
51. Ibid, p. 254.
52. Ibid, p. 265.
53. Nichols, p. 26.
54. Ibid, p. 20.
55. Ibid, p. 91.
56. De Sauvigny, vol. II, p. 625.
57. Nichols, p. 45.
58. Ibid, p. 73.
59. Ibid, p. 89.
60. Ibid, p. 123.
61. Ibid, p. 104.
62. Ibid, p. 116.
63. Hammer, p. 115.
64. Nichols, p. 188.
65. Ibid, p. 209.
66. Ibid, p. 315.
67. Ibid, p. 315.
68. De Sauvigny, vol. II, p. 722.
69. Nichols, p. 315.

3. THE GREAT POWERS AND THE IBERIAN
PENINSULA, 1815–48 *Roger Bullen*

1. From 1815 to 1818 the four victorious allies, Austria, Great Britain, Prussia and Russia maintained an army of occupation in France. The French claimed that this constituted permanent intervention in their internal affairs. The allies saw their occupation in a different light; it was the punishment inflicted upon France for the crime of deserting the Bourbons and allowing Napoleon to renew the war in the west in 1815. The allies did not admit that between 1815 and 1818 they intervened in France.

2. G. de Bertier de Sauvigny, *Metternich and his Times* (1962) p. 73.

3. J. Hall, *England and the Orleans Monarchy* (1962) p. 15.

4. This was why British and French ships could not blockade the Carlist ports in the north of Spain in the 1830s. The Law officers of the Crown reported to Palmerston that they could not join the Spanish blockade without a declaration of war. See Roger Bullen 'France and the Problem of Intervention

in Spain 1834–1836', *HJ*, **xx**, ii (1977) pp. 363–93.

5. C. K. Webster *The Foreign Policy of Castlereagh 1815–1822* (1925) p. 146.

6. De Sauvigny, p. 74.

7. For a brief and helpful discussion of this see A. W. Ward *The Period of Congresses 1815–1822* (1919) pp. 37–45.

8. N. Riasanovsky, *Nicholas I and Official Nationality in Russia 1825–1855* (Berkeley, 1967) pp. 245–6.

9. For Palmerston's remarks on this see K. Bourne, *The Foreign Policy of Victorian England 1830–1902* (1970) Documents 13 and 15, pp. 223–4, 226–8.

10. See Carsten Holbaad, *The Concert of Europe* (1970) pp. 127–31.

11. See Roger Bullen, 'Party Politics and Foreign Policy: Whigs and Tories and Iberian Affairs 1830–6', *Bulletin of Institute of Historical Research*, vol. LI, no. 123 (May 1978) pp. 37–59.

12. N. Riasanovsky, p. 246.

13. See Bourne, p. 246.

14. See W. Bruce Lincoln, *Nicholas I, Emperor and Autocrat of All the Russians* (1978) p. 198.

15. See Roger Bullen, *Palmerston, Guizot and the Collapse of the Entente Cordiale* (London, 1974) p. 247 [hereafter Bullen, *Palmerston and Guizot*].

16. For the Spanish background see Raymond Carr, *Spain 1808–1939* (Oxford, 1966) pp. 120–9 and for Portugal see H. V. Livermore, *A New History of Portugal* (Cambridge, 1969) pp. 258–68.

17. Bourne, p. 210.

18. Patricia Grimsted, *The Foreign Ministers of Alexander I* (Berkeley, 1969) p. 251.

19. For Castlereagh's State Paper of May 1820 see Bourne, pp. 198–207.

20. Holbraad, p. 34.

21. Paul Schroeder, *Metternich's Diplomacy at its Zenith 1820–1823* (Austin, Texas, 1962) p. 87.

22. C. M. Woodhouse, *Capodistria, the Founder of Greek Independence* (Oxford, 1973) p. 273.

23. Grimsted, p. 283.

24. De Sauvigny, *La restauration* (Paris, 1955) pp. 253–4.

25. Ibid, pp. 255–6.

26. H. V. Temperley, *The Foreign Policy of Canning 1822–1827* (2nd edn, 1966) p. 75.

27. See Carr, p. 141.

28. Bourne, p. 210.

29. Temperley, pp. 83–6.

30. Ibid, pp. 121–4.

31. Ibid, pp. 114–18.

32. Livermore, pp. 258–64.

33. Temperley, pp. 201–5.

34. Ibid, pp. 201–5.

35. Ibid, p. 370.

36. Ibid, pp. 374–87.

37. W. Bruce Lincoln, 196–7.

38. Bullen, *Palmerston Guizot*, p. 13.

39. Ibid, p. 1719.

40. For this policy see Roger Bullen, 'England, Spain and the Portuguese Question in 1833', *European Studies Review*, vol. IV, no. I (1974) pp. 1–22.

41. Bullen, *HJ* pp. 363–93.

42. Bourne, pp. 226–8.

43. See Michael Hurst, *Key Treaties for the Great Powers 1814–1914* 2 vols (Newton Abbot, 1972) pp. 235–7.

44. Bullen, *HJ* pp. 363–93.

45. Ibid.

46. Ibid.

47. Ibid.

48. J. H. S. Allison, *Thiers and the French Monarchy* (1926) pp. 233–8.

49. Bullen, *HJ*, pp. 363–3.

50. Bullen, *Palmerston, Guizot*, chs II, IV, V and VI.

51. Ibid, pp. 226–7.

52. Ibid, p. 240.

53. Ibid, p. 254.

54. Ibid, p. 239.

55. Ibid, p. 240.

56. Bourne, p. 224.

4. RUSSIA AND THE EASTERN QUESTION, 1821–41   Matthew Anderson

1. Alexander, like many of his contemporaries, believed that revolutionary movements throughout Europe were centrally controlled by a directing body in Paris.

2. I. S. Dostyan, *Rossiya i balkanskii vopros: iz istorii russko-balkanskikh politichskikh svyazei v pervoi treti XIX v.* (Moscow, 1972) pp. 201ff.; O. B. Shparo, *Osvobozdenie Gretsii i Rossiya* (Moscow, 1965) pp. 92–3, 116–23.

3. A very good example is A. V. Fadeev, *Rossiya i vostochnyi krizis 20–x godov XIX veka* (Moscow, 1958) ch. I.

4. S. S. Tatishchev, *Vneshnaya politika Imperatora Nikolaya Pervogo* (St Petersburg, 1887) p. 360.

5. Nesselrode to Pozzo di Borgo (Russian ambassador in London), 1 November 1838, BL Add. MSS 36469.

6. S. Goriainov, *Le Bosphore et les Dardanelles* (Paris, 1910) p. 84.

7. B. Nolde, *Vneshnaya politika. Istorischeskie ocherki* (Petrograd, 1915) p. 81.

See the criticisms of a semi-official historian of the old regime in S. S. Tatishchev, *Iz proshlogo russkoi diplomatii* (St Petersburg, 1880) pp. 64–7; and of the most recent Soviet writer on the subject, V. A. Georgiev, *Vneshnaya politika Rossii na blizhnem vostoke v kontse 30 – nachale 40–kh godov* (Moscow, 1975) pp. 103–8.

9. *Vneshnaya politika Imperatora Nikolaya Pervogo*, pp. 545–6.

10. Georgiev, *Vneshnaya politika Rossii*, p. 187.

5. THE METTERNICH SYSTEM, 1815–48   *Alan Sked*

1. E. Radvany *Metternich's Projects for Reform in Austria* (Martinus Nijhoff; The Hague, 1971) p. 15.

2. Ibid, p. 136 (Radvany gives a slightly different translation).

3. Ibid, p. 67, ft. 36.

4. Ibid, p. 15.

5. Ibid, p. 14.

6. Ibid, p. 136.

7. A. Sked, 'An Imperial Crisis: Austrian Policy towards Northern Italy, 1847–49' p. 66, ft. 2.

8. Radvany, p. 110.

9. Ibid.

10. Radvany, p. 110.

11. Antonio Schmidt-Brentano, *Die Armee in Osterreich Militär: Staat und Gesellschaft, 1848–1867* (Herald Boldt Verlag; Boppard am Rhein, 1975) p. 106.

12. C. A. Haillot, *Statistique militaire et récherches sur l'organisation des armées étrangères* (Paris, 1846) vol. I, p. 12.

13. Viktor Bibl, *Metternich der Dämon Osterreichs* (Johannes Gunther Verlag; Leipzig and Vienna, 1936,) p. 208.

14. Ibid.

15. Bibl, p. 230.

16. Sked, p. 114.

17. J. H. Blumenthal, 'Vom Wiener Kongress zum Ersten Weltkrieg', in *Unser Heer 300 Jahre österreichisches Soldatentum im Krieg and Frieden* (Vienna, Munich, Zurich, 1963 p. 216.

18. Sked, p. 180, ft. 1.

19. Ibid, p. 56.

20. Ibid.

21. Sked, p. 58.

22. Ibid, p. 54.

23. Ibid, p. 59.

24. Ibid, pp. 78–9.

25. Ibid, p. 82.

26. Ibid, p. 100.

27. Ibid, p. 103.

28. Ibid, p. 108.

29. Ibid, p. 109.

30. Sked, 'Metternich and the Federalist Myth', *Crisis and Controversy* (1976) p. 11.

31. E. Andics *Metternich und die Frage Ungarns* (1973), p. 81.

32. Ibid, p. 41.

33. Ibid, p. 116.

34. Sked, 'An Imperial Crisis', p. 101.

35. E. L. Woodward, *Three Studies in European Conservatism* (Constable and Co.; 1929, p. 86.

36. Ibid.

37. Ibid, p. 87.

6. FRANCE AND EUROPE, 1815-48: THE PROBLEM
OF DEFEAT AND RECOVERY   *Roger Bullen*

1. 'The Prussians intoxicated by their success wished to inflict every possible burden and humiliation on the conquered.' C. K. Webster, *The Foreign
Policy of Castlereagh 1812–1815* (1931) p. 462.

2. The French resisted the allied demands for territory throughout the
early stages of the negotiations. Talleyrand, who was the French representative at Vienna, insisted that the French could never be reconciled to the loss of
'the sacred soil of France'. Both Castlereagh and Wellington pointed out that
the French had never respected the territorial integrity of other states. C. K.
Webster, *British Diplomacy 1813–1815* (London, 1921) pp. 379–81. The collapse
of the Talleyrand-Fouché government in France and the appointment of a
new ministry led by Richelieu resolved the crisis over the territorial demands
of the allies. Bertier de Sauvigny, *La Restauration* (Paris, 1955) pp. 166–71.

3. For the text of the treaty see Michael Hurst, *Key Treaties for the Great
Powers 1814–1914*, 2 vols (Newton Abbot, 1972) vol. I, pp. 128–34.

4. In his *Les Grands notables en France*, 2 vols (Paris, 1964), A. J. Tudesq writes
'il faut toutefois reconnâitre que la critique de ces traités est une formule de
style, un lieu commun de l'éloquence politique . . . .' ['it must always be recognised that criticism of these treaties is a matter of form, a commonplace of
political eloquence'] vol. II, p. 785.

5. In 1817 the number of occupying troops was reduced from 150,000 to
120,000.

6. On this see de Sauvigny, *La restauration*, pp. 205–8.

7. In a speech in the Chamber of Deputies in August 1831 Thiers said 'Puis
qu'il n'était pas sage de réunir la Belgique à la France, de déchirer les traités
de 1815, de confondre la question politique territoriale avec la question de
principe . . . .', ['Since it was not wise to reunite Belgium with France to tear
up the treaties of 1815, to confuse the political territorial question with the
question of principle . . .'] *Chambre de députés*, 9 August 1831.

8. *Le National*, 12 August 1831.

9. De Sauvigny, *La restauration*, p. 175.

10. Henri Contamine, *Diplomatie et diplomats sous la restauration 1814–1830*
(Paris, 1970) pp. 76–8.

11. For example the *Journal des Débats* declared on 1 August 1831 'Nous
n'appelons pas la France a recommencer en Europe le rôle de Napoléon.'
['We do not call on France to resume Napoleon's role in Europe.']

12. See for example *Note sur la situation générale* by Chateaubriand (N.D.)
AMAE, M et D, la Russie 41.

13. See Tudesq, *Les grands notables en France*, vol. II, pp. 794–7.

14. Contamine, *Diplomatie et diplomats sous la restauration 1814–1830*, 95–98.
Bois-le-Comte was the director of political affairs during the last years of the
Restoration and Desages throughout the July monarchy. On the role of the
officials see the *Mémoire* by Bois-le-Comte in *Papiers Bois Le Comte*, AMAE
Fonds France, 2152.

15. Perhaps the most obvious example was Drouyn de Lhuys.

16. See A. J. Tudesq, *Les grands notables en France*, vol. II for a long discussion of liberal ideas on foreign policy.

17. The real war to come, declared *Le National* 8 August 1831, is the war of the people of Europe against the kings of Europe.

18. See R. J. Bullen, *Palmerston, Guizot and the Collapse of the Entente Cordiale* 1974, pp. 162–70.

19. See L. C. Jennings, *France and Europe in* 1848 (Oxford, 1973).

20. For a brief discussion of this see de Sauvigny, *La restauration*, pp. 256–9.

21. See R. J. Bullen, 'France and the Problem of Intervention in Spain 1834–1836', *HJ* xx, ii (1977), pp. 363–93.

22. On the relations between the governments and the press see Irene Collins, *The Government and the Newspaper Press in France 1814–1881* (Oxford, 1959) Ch VII and VIII.

23. AMAE, M et D., la Russie 41, *Mémoire sur les dispositions actuelles du Cabinet Imperial*, December 1823.

24. 8 December 1840.

25. C. Vidal, *Louis Philippe, Metternich et la crise italienne de 1831–1832* (Paris, 1931), p. 158.

26. 21 July 1841.

27. De Sauvigny, *La restauration*, pp. 376–85.

28. Desages to Rayneval [?] May 1838, AMAE, *Papiers Desages*, l'Espagne, vol. II.

29. Quoted in Douglas Porch, *Army and Revolution France 1815–1848* (1974).

30. Villèle, *Mémoires et correspondance* 4 vols, (Paris, 1904,) vol. IV, pp. 281.

31. A. J. P. Taylor, *The Struggle for the Mastery in Europe 1848–1918* (Oxford, 1954), p. 3-

32. *Note sur l'état des forces navales de la France* (Paris, 1844).

33. *Etats des relations politiques et commerciales de la France au moins de Juillet 1830*, by Bois-le-Comte; AMAE, M et D, Fonds France 725. In 1819 Capodistria informed a French diplomat that for France to be a useful ally to Russia she must rebuild her fleet 'sans bruit mais sans cesse'. Mémoire de M, Beclu sur sa mission à Varsovie AMAE; CP la Russie 16.

34. In 1841 Barante, the French minister at St Petersburg, informed Guizot that Nesselrode was anti-French because he had formed his 'opinion politique et ses habitudes à l'époque des congrés de Vienne, d'Aix la Chapelle et de Vérone', Barante to Guizot, 13 January 1841; Claude de Barante, *Souvenirs de Baron de Barante*, 8 vols (Paris, 1890–1901) vol. VI, pp. 563–6.

35. Many Russians, wrote La Ferronays, regard France as 'un pays perdu, démoralisé, et la cause de la désorganisation de la société européene' ['a lost, demoralised land and the cause of the disorganisation of European society'], La Ferronays to Pasquier, 1 September 1820, AMAE CP la Russie 161.

36. *Le National*, 8 August 1831.

37. Villiers to Palmerston, 3 November 1835; Broadlands Papers; BP CG/ CL/216.

38. See Douglas Johnson, *Guizot–Aspects of French History 1787–1874* (1963), p. 265.

39. L'alliance russe peut seule nous seconder dans le projet de nous rélèver

de nos derniers désastres et de faire des acquisitions . . .' ['The Russian alliance alone can help us recover from our recent disasters and make gains . . .'], Bois-le-Comte, *Etats des relations politique*, M et D, Fonds France, 725.

40. Ibid.

41. Barante to Broglie, 12 January 1836, Barante, *Souvenirs*, vol. v, 239–51.

42. P. K. Grimsted, *The Foreign Ministers of Alexander I* (Berkeley, 1969), 226–68.

43. For a discussion of the Near-Eastern aspects of the plan see V. J. Puryear, *France and the Levant* (Hamdon; Connecticut, 1968) 76–9. The Plan itself and other documents connected with it may be found in AMAE CP la Russie 178. Polignac began his letter to Mortemart, the French ambassador at St Petersburg, by stating 'Dans aucun cas la France ne pourrait souffrir que l'Angleterre, la Prusse ou l'Autriche s'agrandissent si elle même n'augmentait sa puissance territoriale sans cela elle regardirait comme entièrement rompu l'équilibre politique déjà tellement affaibli a son désavantage au Congrès de Vienne . . .' ['In no case could France allow England, Prussia or Austria self-aggrandisement without increasing her own territorial strength. Without this she would regard the political balance, already so weakened to her disadvantage at the Congress of Vienna, as completely broken . . .'], Polignac to Mortemart, 4 September 1829.

44. Broglie to Barante, 16 October 1835; Barante, *Souvenirs*, vol v, 197–209.

45. See R. J. Bullen, 'France and the Problem of Intervention in Spain 1834–1836', *HJ* xx, ii (1977) 363–93.

46. See R. J. Bullen, 'Party Politics and Foreign Policy – Whigs, Tories and the Iberian Peninsula 1830–1836', Bulletin, *Institute of Historical Research*, LI, no.123 (May 1976) 37–59.

47. AMAE, *Papiers Bois-le-Comte*, vol. I, *Mémoires*, Fonds France 2152.

48. Thiers to Barante, 15 April 1836; Barante, *Souvenirs* v, 339–42.

49. 'Du point on je suis, il me semble qu'aucun des trois grandes puissance, et l'Autriche pas plus que les autres, n'est disposés à changer, à modifier la situation politique. Chacune d'elles serait plutôt occupée à nous séparer de l'Angleterre, qu'à se rapprocher à nous.' ['As I see it, it would seem that none of the three great powers, and Austria no more than the others, is disposed to change or to modify the political situation. Each of them would prefer to separate us from England, than to move towards us.'] Barante to Thiers, 20 April 1836, ibid, 344–55.

50. Emile Ollivier, *L'Empire libéral*, 14 vols (Paris, various dates) III (Paris, 1898), 96–118.

51. For an account of the Spanish crisis see de Sauvigny, *La Restauration*, 256–9 and the same author's *Metternich et la France aprés le Congrès de Vienne*, 2 vols (Paris, 1968, 1970) vol. II *Les Grands Congrès 1820–1824*, chs XIX and XX.

52. For the Italian revolution of 1830 and Austro-French conflict in Italy see C. Vidal, *Louis Philippe, Metternich et la crise italienne de 1831–1832*. Ch. X.

53. H. T. Deschamps, *La Belgique devant la France de Juillet* (Paris, 1956) 58.

54. Douglas Johnson, *Guizot*, 296–9.

55. R. J. Bullen, 'France and the Problem of Intervention in Spain 1834–1836' *HJ*, 20, 2, (1977) 363–93.

56. L. C. Jennings, *France and Europe in 1848* (Oxford, 1973) ch IV and V.

57. *Mémoire lu et approuvé au Conseil du Roi*, September 1829, AMAE, CP, la Russie 178.

58. Alistair Horne, *A Savage War of Peace*, (1977) 29.

59. Alexis de Tocquville, *Oeuvres complètes* vol. III, *Ecrits et discours politique*, ed. J. J. Chevalier et A. Jardin (Paris, 1962) 57.

60. For a full discussion of Guizot's foreign policy see Douglas Johnson *Guizot* and R. J. Bullen Palmerston, *Guizot and the Collapse of the Entente Cordiale*.

61. See R. J. Bullen 'Guizot and the Sonderbund Crisis', *EHR, vol.* LXXXVI July 1971, no. CCCXL, 497–526.

7. BRITAIN AND THE EUROPEAN BALANCE,
1815–48 *Christopher Bartlett*

1. Gavin B. Henderson, *Crimean War Diplomacy and other Historical Essays* (Jackson; Glasgow, 1947) p. 206.

2. See for instance the comments of the distinguished nineteenth-century statistician, G. R. Porter, *The Progress of the Nation* (Methuen; 1912) pp. 500–1.

3. D. C. M. Platt, *Finance, Trade and Politics in British Foreign Policy, 1815–1914* (Oxford University Press; 1968) pp. 181–5. 366–7; Lucy Brown, *The Board of Trade and the Free Trade Movement* Clarendon Press; Oxford, 1958) vol. I. pp. 95–6.

4. Sir Charles Webster, *The Foreign Policy of Palmerston, 1830–41* (G. Bell; 1951) vol. I, pp. 157–8.

5. Cited by Roger Parkinson, *Clausewitz* (Wayland Publications; 1970) p. 287.

6. H. W. V. Temperley, *The Foreign Policy of Canning, 1822–27* (G. Bell; 1925) p. 467.

7. Wendy Hinde, *George Canning* (Collins; 1973) pp. 422–4.

8. Roger Bullen, *Palmerston, Guizot and the Collapse of the Entente Cordiale* (Athlone Press; 1974) pp. 6–7.

9. Jasper Ridley, *Lord Palmerston* (Constable; 1970) p. 139.

10. H. C. F. Bell, *Lord Palmerston* (Frank Cass; 1966) vol. I, pp. 146.

11. *The Correspondence of Lord Aberdeen and Princess Lieven, 1832–54*, E. Jones Parry (ed.), (Camden Soc., 3rd ser., vol. LX) sec. I, p. 12.

12. John Brooke and Julia Grandy (eds) *The Prime Ministers' Papers Series: Wellington, Political Correspondence*, vol. I, *1833 – November 1834*, (HMSO; 1975) pp. 315ff.

13. Webster, *Palmerston*, vol. I, p. 291.

14. Christopher Howard, *Britain and the Casus Belli, 1822–1902* (Athlone Press; 1974) pp. 53–5.

15. Bullen, ch. 4, especially pp. 103–7.

16. Webster, *Palmerston*, vol. II, p. 414.

17. Webster, *Palmerston*, vol. II, p. 859.

18. Abraham D. Kriegel (ed.) *The Holland House Diaries, 1831–40*, (Routledge and Kegan Paul; 1977) p. xliii.

19. Webster, *Palmerston*, vol. II, p. 859.

20. Webster, *Palmerston*, vol. II, pp. 621–2.

21. *Aberdeen–Lieven Correspondence*, vol. I, pp. 150–1.

22. Webster, *Palmerston*, vol. II, pp. 751, 773–5.

23. *Aberdeen–Lieven Correspondence*, vol. I, pp. 240–1.

24. *Aberdeen–Lieven Correspondence*, vol. I, pp. 160–1, 174ff., 211, 231.

25. J. A. S. Grenville, *Europe Reshaped, 1848–78* (Harvester Press; Hassocks, Sussex, 1976) p. 85.

26. Bell, vol. I, pp. 412–13.

27. Lawrence C. Jennings, *France and Europe in 1848* (Clarendon Press; Oxford, 1973) p. 6.

28. Bell, vol. I, pp. 433.

29. J. P. T. Bury (ed.), *The New Cambridge Modern History, 1830–70*, vol. X, (Cambridge University Press; 1971) pp. 267, 269–70.

30. Jacques Droz, *Europe between Revolutions, 1815–48* (Fontana/Collins; 1967) pp. 243–4; also 215ff.

8 METTERNICH'S ENEMIES OR THE THREAT FROM BELOW   Alan Sked

1. Count F. A. Gualterio, *Gli Ultimi Rivolgimenti Italiani, Memorie Storiche con Documenti Inediti*, 4 vols (Florence, 1852) 2, 286–7.

2. See J. M. Roberts, *The Mythology of the Secret Societies* (Secker and Warburg; 1972).

3. See, J. R. Rath, 'The Carbonari: Their Origins, Initiation, Rites and Aims', *AHR* ixix (1963–64).

4. Ibid, p. 370.

5. See P. Savigear, 'Carbonarism and the French Army', 1815–1824, *History*, LIV (1969).

6. For Britain, see M. I. Thomis and P. Holt, *Threats of Revolution in Britain 1789–1848* (Macmillan; 1977).

7. With the exception perhaps of Lenore O'Boyle (see below) most historians, of course, do not consciously subscribe to a conspiracy theory. However, as a university teacher I can testify to the number of students who are easily misled by the sloppy language used by professional scholars. This justifies the complaints which are discussed by G. Rudé, *Debate on Europe* (1972) pp. 134–9.

8. Ibid.

9. Ibid.

10. See Lenore O'Boyle 'The Middle Class in Western Europe, 1815–48', *AHR*, ixxi (1966) pp. 826–45.

11. For the controversy over the role of the bourgeoisie in the French Revolution and the international debate begun by Cobban see Eberhard Schmitt, *Einführung in die Geschichte der Französischen Revolution* (Beck'sche Elementarbücher; Munich, 1976).

12. See A. Cobban, 'The Middle Class in France, 1815–48', in A. Cobban, *France Since the Revolution* (Jonathan Cape; 1970) pp. 7–21.

13. See D. H. Pinkney, 'The Myth of the French Revolution of 1830' in D. H. Pinkney and T. Ropp (eds), '*A Festschrift for Frederick B. Artz*', (Durham N.C., 1964).

14. Cobban, p. 19.

15. For the following analysis see Albert Goodwin, 'The landed aristocracy as a governing class in XIX century Britain' in *Rapports du Comité International des Sciences Historiques* (XII Congrès International des Sciences Historiques, Vienne, 29 Août – 5 Septembre 1965), vol. 1 (Grands Thèmes, Verlag Ferdinand Berger; Horn/Vienna, 1965) ed. H. L. Mikoletzky, pp. 368–74.

16. Ibid, p. 370.

17. See John Snell, *The Democratic Movement in Germany, 1789–1914* (North Carolina Press; Chapel Hill, 1976) p. 25.

18. Kent Roberts Greenfield, *Economics and Liberalism in the Risorgimento. A Study of Nationalism in Lombardy 1818–48* (rev. edn, Baltimore, 1965) pp. xvii and xii.

19. E. Pamlényi (ed.), *A History of Hungary* (Collet's; 1975) p. 239.

20. O'Boyle.

21. Ibid, p. 830.

22. Ibid, p. 833.

23. Ibid, p. 840.

24. For this discussion, see Rudé, pp. 78–87.

25. Quoted by Rudé, pp. 81–2.

26. Ibid, p. 83.

27. See Pio Pecchiarni 'Caduti e fereti nelle Cinque Giornate di Milano: ceti e professioni cui appartenaro' in *Atti e Memorie del XXVII Congresso Nazionale* (Milan, 19–20–21 Marzo 1948) pp. 533–37.

28. See R. Hoppe and J. Kuczynski, 'Eine Berufsbzw. auch Klassen – und Schichten – analyse Märzgefallen 1848' in Berlin in *Jahrbuch für Wirtschaftsgeschichte*, 1964, Pt. IV, p. 204 opp. 206–7.

29. The 1848 document collection at the Weidner Library, Harvard, contains a few lists of those killed and wounded in Vienna in 1848.

30. Rudé, p. 197.

31. Ibid.

32. See ch. 5, p. 117.

33. Mack Walker (ed.) *Metternich's Europe, 1813–48* (Harper Torchbook; New York, 1968) p. 85.

34. Ibid, p. 44.

35. Ibid, p. 46.

36. Ibid, p. 67.

37. For a brief history of the German student movement in the period 1815–48 see Karl Griewank, *Deutsche Studenten und Universitäten in der Revolution von 1848* (Jena, 1949) pp. 8–18.

38. See Anderson, *The Ascendancy of Europe, Aspects of European History, 1815–1914* (Longman; 1972) p. 86.

39. See Lenore O'Boyle, 'The Problem of an Excess of Educated Men in Western Europe, 1800–1850', *Journal of Modern History*, vol. 42, No. 4 (Dec. 1970) pp. 471–95.

40. Ibid, p. 494.

41. Pierre Revouvin, *Histoire des Relations Internationales, Le XIX Siècle, Premiere Partie, De 1815 à 1871*, pp. 19–20.

42. Ibid.

43. Ibid.

44. Ibid.

45. Anderson, p. 15.

46. See Theodor Schieder, 'Das Italienbild der deutschen Einheitsbewegung', pp. 141–162, 145 in *Studien zur Deutsch–Italienischen Geistesgeschichte* (Bohlau Verlag; Cologne-Graz, 1959).

47. Anderson, p. 87.

48. Ibid.

49. See 'Die gute Presse Ostreichs und ihr Verhalten bei dem galizischen Ereiguissen' in *Unsre Gegenwart und Zukunft*, vol. 3 (Leipzig, 1846), pp. 67–107.

50. Raymond Williams, 'The Press and Popular Culture: An Historical Perspective', in G. Boyce, J. Curran and P. Wingate (eds), *Newspaper History from the 17th Century to the Present Day* (Macmillan; 1978) pp. 46–7.

51. Ivon Asquith, 'The Structure, Ownership and Control of the Press, 1780–1855' in Boyce, Curran and Wingate, p. 99.

52. Williams, p. 42.

53. Anderson, pp. 89–90.

54. Ibid.

55. See Francois Fejtö (ed.), *The Opening of an Era 1848* (Allan Wingate; 1948) p. 25.

56. Irene Collins, *Liberalism in Nineteenth-Century Europe* (The Historical Association, London, 1957) p. 4.

57. Ibid.

58. Walker, p. 120.

59. This point is emphasised by Douglas Johnson in Roger Mettam and Douglas Johnson, *French History and Society, The Wars of Religion to the Fifth Republic* (Methuen; 1974) p. 98.

60. E. J. Hobsbaum, *The Age of Revolution* (Abacus; 1977) p. 164.

61. Quoted by A. Cobban in *Aspects of the French Revolution* (Paladin; 1968) pp. 23–4.

62. Anderson, p. 145.

63. Fejtö, p. 2.

64. Donald E. Emerson, *Metternich and the Political Police, Security and Subversion in the Hapsburg Monarchy (1815–1830)* (Martinus Nijhoff; The Hague, 1968) p. 57.

65. Ibid, p. 58.

66. Anderson, p. 144.

67. See Alan Sked, *The Survival of the Habsburg Empire, Radetzky, the Imperial Army and the Class War 1848* (Longman; 1979) Part III.

68. Anderson, p. 151.

69. Denis Mack Smith, *Italy*, new rev. edn (University of Michigan Press; Ann Arbor, 1969) p. 10.

70. Ibid.

71. Anderson, p. 147.

72. Rudé, pp. 113–14.

73. Ibid, p. 115.
74. Ibid, p. 116.
75. See Hans Hautmann and Rudolf Kropf, *Die Osterreichische Arbeiterbewegung vom Vormärz bis 1945* (Europaverlag; 1974) pp. 29–30.
76. See Rudé, pp. 113–20.
77. Quoted by Rudé, p. 120.

Notes on Contributors

ALAN SKED is Lecturer in International History at the London School of Economics. His published works include *The Survival of the Habsburg Empire: Radetzky, the Imperial Army and the Class War 1848* and *Crisis and Controversy: Essays in Honour of A. J. P. Taylor* which he edited with Dr C. P. Cook.

MATTHEW ANDERSON is Professor of International History in the University of London. His published works include *Europe in the Eighteenth Century, The Ascendancy of Europe, Aspects of European History, 1815–1914* and *The Eastern Question*.

CHRISTOPHER BARTLETT is Professor of International History in the University of Dundee. His published works include *Great Britain and Sea Power 1815–1853* and *A History of Post-War Britain, 1945–1974*.

DOUGLAS DAKIN is Professor of Modern History in the University of London. His published works include *British and American Philhellenes during the War of Greek Independence, 1821–1833* and *The Greek Struggle for Independence, 1821–33*.

ROY BRIDGE is Reader in International History in the University of Leeds. His published works include *From Sadowa to Sarajevo* and *Great Britain and Austria–Hungary; 1906–14: A Diplomatic History*.

ROGER BULLEN is Lecturer in International History at the London School of Economics. His published works include *Palmerston, Guizot and the Collapse of the Entente Cordiale*.

Index